Lens to the Natural World

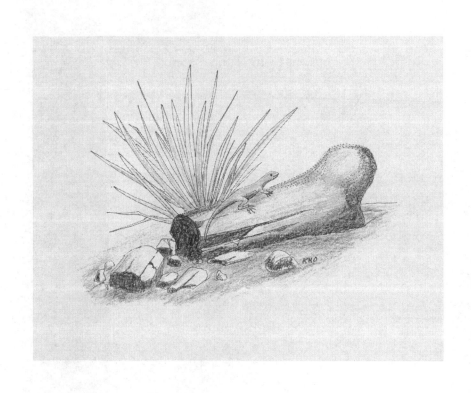

Lens to the Natural World

Reflections on Dinosaurs, Galaxies, and God

KENNETH H. OLSON

WIPF & STOCK · Eugene, Oregon

LENS TO THE NATURAL WORLD
Reflections on Dinosaurs, Galaxies, and God

Wipf & Stock
An Imprint of Wipf and Stock Publishers
199 W. 8th Ave., Suite 3
Eugene, OR 97401

www.wipfandstock.com

ISBN 13: 978-1-61097-454-7

Manufactured in the U.S.A.

For Rochelle, Marcene, Heather, and Garrett

Contents

Foreword

THIS IS A BOOK about nature and how it is regarded. *Lens to the Natural World* is well titled, since the theme of perception runs throughout.

I am a vertebrate paleontologist specializing in dinosaurs: their evolution, anatomy, growth, and behavior. Rocks and fossils from the dim past provide windows through which we can reconstruct the history of our planet. Dinosaur fossils are also an inspiration to many young people, who may later go on to work in some branch of science.

We live in unsettled times and not just in political and economic senses. If it is true that what is honored in a culture will be cultivated there, then it is not too much to say that science does not have the honor and respect in as many segments of society as it once did and that, of late, support for it has lagged. The reasons are many. Some think of science mostly in terms of technology; they frame it largely in terms of such advances as found in new cars and computers, of faster telecommunications, better medical techniques, and so forth. There is much benefit to all of us in all those realms, but focusing on that sort of thing is a limited view.

Science is also about the quest for knowledge simply for its own sake. It is, first of all, about curiosity. It is about finding where the paths of inquiry may lead beyond pragmatic or immediate benefit. The practical application may or may not come, but the scientific questions are worthwhile nonetheless. "Why? Because I was just wondering." All scientific endeavor of the highest order has that as its primary motivation.

There is also something of an anti-intellectual trend in our culture: the idea that every opinion is of equal worth, that "no one can tell me what to do or think" and that experts are suspect. However, in the words of Martin Luther King Jr., "Nothing is more dangerous than sincere ignorance."

Science, like anything else, can be abused, and not all that is labeled as such belongs in that realm. It must be said quite openly that this is the case with so-called creation science promulgated by *some* expressions of religion.

Nearly thirty years ago, in his book *In the Beginning . . .*, paleontologist Chris McGowan called attention to the pressure being applied by certain groups to have their literal biblical interpretation of creation given "equal time" to that of evolutionary concepts in the public schools. His words apply now more than ever: "The problem is, though, that what the creationists are offering is *not* science. They are selling good old-fashioned fundamentalist religion, all spruced up with scientific terminology and ideas to look like science." And, if you do not agree with them, you are against God, something that surprises hundreds of millions of religious people who think otherwise. As McGowan says, "What is clear from reading their literature and attending their debates is that they do not represent mainstream Christianity, and that they are as unorthodox in their theology as they are in their science."

In great contrast, *Lens to the Natural World* provides a perspective of faith that is enriched by scientific exploration, celebrates wonder, and opens the door to questions on many levels.

There are now hundreds of popular books about dinosaurs. There are numerous ten-foot shelves of theology, with many of such works written by geniuses in the field. There is, however, a near vacuum in terms of books dealing with the implications of science for religion and for the rest of the humanities in a manner that is both faithful to central truths and, at the same time, directed to a wide audience. This work succeeds admirably in that complex endeavor.

Ken began his higher education in wildlife biology, before going on to philosophy and then theology. When he first told me of this writing project (probably while delivering a plaster jacket containing the latest dinosaur specimen he had discovered), he indicated that it would be "a work of science and religion and philosophy and literature." So it is. The many literary allusions from a lifetime of reading enrich and enliven the text and speak to the imagination as well as the intellect. Read on. Enjoy.

Jack Horner

Preface

IT IS SAID THAT the English biologist J. B. S. Haldane was once asked what the diversity of life tells us of the Creator and is alleged to have replied, "God must have an inordinate fondness for beetles!" (Approximately one-fifth of all the world's species of living things were classified as such.) The dinosaurs, also, were of many and various kinds. In size, they ranged from very small to the largest land animals ever to have existed, and new discoveries have shown that many had surprising adaptations to the world around them. In color and form, some of them must have been truly spectacular. Their diversity stretched over more than 150 million years of earth's history, enough to give credence to the idea that God must have loved dinosaurs.

This collection of essays is about them and about a whole range of other prehistoric creatures, the settings they inhabited, and about the science of paleontology, which seeks to reconstruct their Lost Worlds from the evidence of fossils in the rocks. In addition, it also concerns the world we know today, which also is filled with countless forms of marvelous beings. Thus, these pages have to do, overall, with our context in the natural world, from our terrestrial home in earth's biosphere to the entire universe of glittering galaxies strewn through deep space on a scale beyond comprehension. Still further, they have to do with our attitudes toward all of it. What is Nature, anyway? The answer is not nearly as simple as is the question.

These reflections take seriously the fact that science has relocated our own species in an immensity of both space and time. One is surely led to ask about our place in it all, and questions emerge having to do with science and religion, with their relationship to one another and, in particular, with creation and evolution.

In a terse line with both profound truth and wide application, Longfellow wrote, "There are no birds in last year's nests." Indeed, we must live in the present and look to the future. However, we also learn from the past, which, as geology shows, is long beyond all words. Will the Tree of Life have abundant nests year after year for untold generations to come?

We are not above nature, as we have so often imagined. Not only are we in the midst of it, we are part of it, intimately connected to the smallest protozoan, as well as to those vast systems of stars, the dust of which is in our blood and bones. This means that we, too, *are* Nature and that we must, in a much wider sense than ever before, all be naturalists and love and care for the earth.

Acknowledgments

Pᴿᴵᴹᴬᴿʸ ɢʀᴀᴛɪᴛᴜᴅᴇ ɢᴏᴇs ᴛᴏ my wife Rochelle for enabling this work in countless ways. She was the first to say that I should put these reflections into print and provided the necessary organizational and computer expertise for this endeavor. Our daughters Marci and Heather and our son Garrett never tired of the subject; on the contrary, they have been anxious to accompany me on expeditions to explore the prehistoric world.

Gratitude is also extended to many others, who, over the years, have encouraged me to write and publish, including:

Paleontologist Dr. Jack Horner of The Museum of the Rockies on the campus of Montana State University, Bozeman, not only for his interest in this project but also for his affirmation relating to my collecting specimens of dinosaurs and other fossils for the Museum over the course of some thirty years.

Staff and volunteers at The Museum of the Rockies, whose enthusiasm for my presentations dealing with science and religion as well as paleontology helped me to see the need for a book such as this.

The same is true for students and faculty of Concordia College, Moorhead, MN, where I am especially grateful to Dr. Arland Jacobson.

Numerous individuals in Lutheran (ELCA) congregations I have served, in particular those of Zion Lutheran Church, Lewistown, MT, who expressed interest in a resource of this kind.

Finally, appreciation is extended to the publisher, Wipf & Stock, for bringing this project to fruition.

Grateful acknowledgement is made for permission to quote from the following sources:

"New Year Letter," copyright 1941 & renewed 1969 by W. H. Auden, "Shorts II," copyright © 1976 by Edward Mendelson, William Merideth and Monroe K. Spears, Executors of the Estate of W. H. Auden., from *Collected Poems of W. H. Auden* by W. H. Auden. Used by Permission of Random House, Inc.

"New Year Letter" and "Shorts II" by W. H. Auden, currently collected in *Collected Poems* by W. H. Auden (Vintage, 1991). Copyright © 1939, 1941, 1991 by W. H. Auden, used in the United Kingdom with permission of the Wylie Agency LLC on behalf of Faber & Faber.

Also, concerning usage of the Auden quotations cited above: Copyright © 1940 by W. H. Auden, renewed. Reprinted by permission of Curtis Brown, Ltd.

The lines from "when god decided to invent." Copyright 1944, © 1972, 1991 by the Trustees for the E. E. Cummings Trust, The lines from "i thank You God for most this amazing." Copyright 1950, © 1978, 1991 by the Trustees for the E. E. Cummings Trust. Copyright © 1979 by George James Firmage, from *Complete Poems: 1904-1962* by E. E. Cummings, edited by George J. Firmage. Used by permission of Liveright Publishing Corporation.

Alfred Publishing Co., Inc. for an excerpt of the lyrics to *It Ain't Necessarily So* (from *"Porgy and Bess"*), words and music by George Gershwin, Du Bose and Dorothy Heyward, and Ira Gershwin © 1935 (Renewed) George Gershwin Music, Ira Gershwin Music, and Du Bose and Dorothy Heyward Memorial Fund. All rights Administered by WB Music Corp. All Rights Reserved. Used by permission.

Creators Syndicate for use of the captions to two cartoons of *The Far Side©* by Gary Larson: "Creationism Explained" (Release date: 3-27-85) and "The picture's pretty bleak, gentlemen . . . The world's climates are changing, the mammals are taking over, and we all have a brain about the size of a walnut." (Release date 11-7-85) Used by permission.

LSU Press for an excerpt from the poem "Monet Refuses the Operation" by Lisel Mueller in *Second Language* © 1986 by Lisel Mueller and published by Louisiana State University Press, Baton Rouge. Used by permission.

Excerpt from "Glass House Canticle" from *The Complete Poems of Carl Sandburg*, Revised and Expanded Edition, copyright © 1970,

1969 by Lilian Steichen Sandburg, Trustee, reprinted by permission of Houghton Mifflin Harcourt Publishing Company.

The National Film Board of Canada for an excerpt of the narration to film *Universe* © 2009 by the National Film Board of Canada. Used by permission.

The Union of Concerned Scientists for two excerpts of the narration to the video *Keeping the Earth: Religious and Scientific Perspectives on the Environment* © 1996 by The Union of Concerned Scientists. Used by permission.

PART I

Our Context in Nature

1

Into the Badlands

Isn't it astonishing that all these secrets have been preserved for so many years just so that we could discover them?

Orville Wright

THE PRAIRIES OF THE West stretch and roll for hundreds of miles. However, in places, the land abruptly falls away. With each rain, channels that are usually dry widen and deepen by eroding the debris of former ages; they all lead, by one way or another, to the Missouri River Breaks. Boulders of the Rocky Mountains disintegrate and mix with the sands and silts of the High Plains in a long but inexorable passage to the Gulf. In the process, strata comprising the skeleton of the earth itself are laid bare, and sunlight falls once again where it has not for millions of years. Such are the Badlands.

These regions in several states were named by the earliest French voyageurs *mauvaises terres*, the evil lands. To those who lurched toward the setting sun in the wagon trains of the westward migrations, these crumbling terrains were definitely bad for travel, and routes were sought to circumvent them. Beginning in the 1870s, however, crews from eastern universities with their fledgling discipline of paleontology (literally, "the study of ancient being") were drawn specifically to those scarred landscapes in Wyoming, Colorado, Kansas, Utah, Montana, and the Dakotas.

In 1877, railroaders discovered huge dinosaur bones weathering out at Como Bluff, Wyoming. Ten miles away, fossil bones were on the surface in such profusion that a sheepherder had used vertebrae to build the foundation and part of the walls of his cabin. The dinosaur rush to such regions was on, and excavations at Como Bluff and at so-called Bone Cabin Quarry began to reveal the largest of the dinosaurs: the giants of the Jurassic Period. Collecting on behalf of Yale University, the English clergyman Arthur Lakes documented his fieldwork in a series of watercolors. One painting showed himself and another man clad in parkas and digging in a trench to excavate the great bones, this in the midst of winter with snow banks all around. This laconic inscription was used: "Pleasures of Science." Thus, the first workers in the field had begun to visualize for the public the hitherto unimagined Lost World of the dinosaurs in the American West.

Today, the desolate Badlands are the Goodlands for paleontology, the science that seeks to reconstruct the prehistoric world from the mineralized bones and other fossils that erode out of such strata.

The sandstone cap-rock on which I am standing provides a view of the banded sedimentary layers extending in every direction. I gaze at the gray, brown, tan, and rust-colored tones, which change with the angled light from morning to mid-day to afternoon. Sitting down on the ledge, I ease off my backpack to pause for a long drink of water and a short lunch consisting of a jelly sandwich. I also blow the dust off the lenses of my binoculars, this in order to better watch a band of showers moving slowly a few miles south. It is rain that has carved these hills.

I swing my legs over the rim and begin to work my way down the slope, leaning into it and steadying myself in the sliding talus with the pick that always accompanies me on such explorations. The wind is blowing, and it takes a moment to identify the location of the sound that halts me in my tracks, tense and alert—that unique, vibrating buzz of a rattlesnake. Its gravel-hued coils lie beneath a sagebrush just two feet away. The forked tongue darts out and in, tasting the air, and the black slits in the unblinking eyes follow my slightest movement. I am the intruder. So, I slowly step away from the sinuous creature, which, today, occupies a hidden and very obscure presence in the western grasslands.

It is, however, a reminder that the Class to which it belongs once ruled the entire earth in what has thus been called the Age of Reptiles. In the air, light-winged pterodactyls soared on the thermal currents with little effort. In the oceans, the waves were plied by huge marine reptiles, some of them as much as forty feet in length. During one segment of time, known as the Cretaceous Period, the waters occupied a shallow basin that went through the heart of North America from the Gulf of Mexico to the Arctic and stretched a thousand miles wide from the rising Rocky Mountains to what is now Minnesota. The boundaries of this sea came and went in transgressive and regressive phases, and, therefore, the sediments it left behind alternate with those laid down on land by rivers, lakes, and swamps. In those latter formations are found the dinosaurs of the Western Interior.

For thousands of years, native peoples had seen the bones weathering out of cliffs and ravines, and their traditions include mythologies pertaining to them, as well as certain observations that anticipated the findings of modern science.

On the return trip of the Lewis and Clark expedition, Clark came upon what he thought was the bone of a large fish embedded in rock. This was along the Yellowstone River, east of present-day Billings, Montana and near a spot known as Pompey's Pillar. He recorded the event in his journal of July 25, 1806:

> Dureing the time the men were getting the two big horns which I had killed to the river I employed my self in getting pieces of the rib of a fish which was Semented within the face of the rock this rib is about 3 inches in Secumpherence About the middle it is 3 feet in length tho a part of the end appears to have been Broken off . . . I have several pieces of this rib.

The specimen is now lost, so it is impossible to confirm its identity. However, given its size and the area in which it was found, there is little doubt the expedition produced the first dinosaur specimen found by a non-native person in the American West.

The first scientific description of a dinosaur fossil was made in 1824 by English clergyman and dean at Oxford, William Buckland. (He was an eccentric, who kept a pet hyena at home, as well as a bear that he often dressed in academic robes to attend university functions.) Buckland's specimen was a jawbone of a meat-eater that he named *Megalosaurus*, "large lizard." Since then, more than a thousand different species of dinosaurs have been studied and named. For more than 150 million years they thrived, multiplied, and diversified as they passed through the sieve of changing environments. And, then, they were gone.

The last of their kind are entombed in the rocks over which I walk in eastern Montana. Layers several hundred feet thick, dating from 65–68 million years ago, comprise the so-called Hell Creek formation. It contains strange "duckbilled" dinosaurs that migrated in herds made up of hundreds and even thousands. Other herd animals included one of the spectacular ceratopsians or "horned-faced" dinosaurs, *Triceratops*. The skulls of these elephant-sized creatures, in addition to sporting long horns, had bony shields that projected back over the neck. Tank-like armored ankylosaurs lumbered through the bushes. A variety of smaller saurians filled other roles in the ecosystem, including ostrich-like runners that likely fed upon insects and lizards and perhaps rat-sized small mammals. Raptors pursued their prey with sickle-like claws, and, most dramatically, like a huge bipedal caricature of a human being, strode the seven-ton carnivore, *Tyrannosaurus rex*.

The bones of all of them have been found here. In addition, there were turtles, lizards, and thick-scaled garfish. Crocodiles and alligators bespeak a subtropical climate much like that of Florida or Louisiana today. Unknown then was the winter frost that, today, in the northern part of the continent, cracks and splits the dinosaur bone. Then, there were swamp cypress trees in Montana, and impressions of the fronds of palm trees can occasionally be found when slabs of rock are overturned; abundant fossil pine-cones indicate the presence of towering redwoods. One thinks of lines in Joseph Conrad's novel, *Heart of Darkness*: "Going up that river was like traveling back to the earliest beginnings of the world, when vegetation rioted and the big trees were king." In all, a picture is presented of a landscape having lush vegetation and coursed by numerous rivers and streams—a landscape so very much unlike the Badlands of today.

And yet, in the mind's eye, it's all there. In the words of naturalist Loren Eiseley, "How often, if we learn to look, is a spider's wheel a universe, or a swarm of summer midges a galaxy, or a canyon a backward glance into time. Beneath our feet is the scratched pebble that denotes an ice age, or above us the summer cloud that changes form in one afternoon as an animal might do in ten million windy years."

You can sometimes walk for hours without spotting a trace of anything. Most of what is found consists of bits and pieces of bone that have weathered out long ago; these have deteriorated from the extremes of cold and heat, snow and rain. They do serve, however, as indicators for the most productive zone, the right horizon wherein conditions were right for fossilization. I follow the contour lines of such exposures where these fragments occur. Sooner, or more likely later, I may well find something better, such as one or more complete bones, or—the chances are remote, but best of all—a skull. The trick is to find them at the right time, when erosion has just begun to expose the relic; then, there's the chance to dig back, reveal, and excavate this treasure of the earth.

This finding represents the intersection of two lines, the chances of which are infinitesimally small. The first one is the path of the dinosaur bone itself, the sculptured form that served function in a dynamic creature and which, at death, is laid down in waterborne sediments. Over the ages, water percolates through the layers and deposits minerals in minute spaces in the bone, hardening and, in some cases, turning it into a stony replica of the original. Millions of years pass, during which thousands of feet of sediment accumulate over it containing other diverse creatures such as the rhinoceros, small horse, giant pig, camel, and saber-toothed cat. Then, the erosion cycle begins, in a process that is still transforming the Great Plains in our day. Down the long reaches of time, the rocks are slowly worn away, until at last, the fossil bone is at the surface once more.

This particular line must now intersect with a second one that represents the appearance on earth of a unique species, this at a time when mental and cultural development enables recognition of the fossil for what it is. A representative individual arrives at the right time and place, makes the discovery as the bone is exposed, collecting it "in the nick of time," just before it, otherwise, would be rendered to oblivion by the forces of nature.

As such, the process has always struck me as resembling a picture we have all seen: that of an Alaskan brown bear standing in the rapids of a river as, in one tiny instant, its jaws snatch a migrating salmon from a leap upstream.

That intersection can occur in many places by accident, as dinosaur bones might be encountered when excavating for the basement of a house or in the ditch of a road, turned up by heavy equipment. But it happens most often to fossil hunters, who have come, for just this purpose, to the Badlands.

It's as close as we are likely to get to time-travel. Simply finding a fossil has a way of linking a person to events and beings of a bygone age.

Something then crosses over from eras inconceivably remote to occupy the shattered femur at the toe of your boot or the golden, glistening, and finely serrated tooth in your hand. A connection is created with those vanished eons by a physical fragment: a fossil. Then, one sees the landscape—and perhaps the whole world—in a new way.

Keith Parsons writes in *Drawing Out Leviathan*:

> So *Tyrannosaurus rex* remains, burning bright in the forests of the Cretaceous night, safely extinct in the depths of time, long, long before our theories could frame its fearful symmetry. Knowledge begins with wonder, and that is the great value of dinosaurs for us, the primal wonder inspired by knowing that such beings once actually walked on the planet . . . We would like to know everything about them, but are frustrated by the myriad of centuries separating us. When we think about the dinosaurs, therefore, imagination must always supplement fact. With creatures as wonderful as dinosaurs, this is the way it should be.

The dinosaurs still exist: in our imaginations and in that stark but sublime desolation we call the Badlands.

2

Stories in Stone

Fossils

And this our life, exempt from public haunt,
Finds tongues in trees, books in the running brooks,
Sermons in stone, and good in everything.

Shakespeare

Fossils may be defined as any material trace or evidence of prehistoric life, and they are of numerous sorts.

Most abundant are the shells of marine invertebrates, such as clams, oysters, and snails, wherein the shell is very little altered from what it was in life. A fossil may consist of a piece of mineralized bone, the flattened skeleton of a fish, a single tooth, or the carbonized imprint of leaf from a long-vanished forest. Insects, complete to the smallest detail, are locked in amber, once the flowing sap of pine trees in which they became entrapped. Tracks left by dinosaurs or other creatures on some damp beach have hardened into a stony matrix and represent, in a sense, the fossilized behavior of the animals that made them. (It is said that many years ago, a prospector notified a university about dinosaur tracks that he had found. He sent a photo of one on a thick slab of rock, which he had dug up and weighed. "Think of the size of the great dinosaur that made this wonderful track," he wrote. "Think of how big he must have been in life when just one of his footprints weighs 562 pounds!")

In any case, many of these objects can be rather easily recognized, and one can say, "Here is a fossil; it is something of a creature from the distant past."

Photographic editor Frances Schultz has written: "The past survives only on average. A tiny fraction of all dinosaurs fossilized; a tiny percentage of all photographs survive. This is as it should be, or we would be knee-deep in bones and Kodak moments." Nevertheless, fossils are found in some abundance, even amid the stone, steel, and concrete canyons of New York City. In a stroll around Manhattan, you can see fossils from other continents, as well as from several regions of the United States. Limestone, largely made up of small marine creatures, was a widely used building material in the last century, and such stone from Indiana sheathes the Waldorf Astoria and the Empire State Building. Some of the highly polished stone on building facades is limestone that, over the long reaches of time, was metamorphosed by heat and pressure into marble. The lobby of the Tishman Building on Fifth Avenue is finished in what the building trade calls "French rouge antique," a red limestone that was laid down in the bottom of the ancestral Mediterranean Sea some 360 million years ago. In the walls can be seen various fossils of shelled creatures of the time, many of them coiled and chambered structures built by ancient relatives of the living squid and octopus. At Saks Fifth Avenue, the yellow-colored rock framing the doorways consists of slices through a fossilized reef built by corals. At Tiffany's, the glittering diamonds in the display window are also encased by fossils, this time of crinoids or sea lilies, ancient relatives of the starfish and feather stars. In the Roosevelt Rotunda at the American Museum of Natural History are 100-million-year-old clams in a decorative limestone from Portugal. In Rockefeller Center, the huge lobby of the RCA building is covered with a near-black stone mottled with white snail shells and other fossils that were laid down in a tropical sea 475 million years ago. Those dark slabs came from quarries on Isle La Motte in Lake Champlain in Vermont, and such stone was also used in the Metropolitan Museum of Art.

In our bedroom is an antique washstand from England. A close look with a ten-power magnifying glass reveals that the polished gray marble top is studded with the intricate structures of ancient corals.

However, recognition of this sort did not come easily to our ancestors. It is true that some of the Greeks of ancient times had a general sense for the nature of these things. Philosophers and historians of the day, such as Aristotle and Herodotus, noticed that marine forms could be discovered far inland and drew the proper conclusion that the sea had once occupied those locations. Ovid of Ancient Rome wrote, "Nothing lasts long under the same form. I have seen myself what was once firm land become the sea; I have seen earth made from the waters, and seashells lie far away from the oceans."

Such knowledge was largely forgotten in succeeding centuries. During the Middle Ages, a popular view was that fossils "grew" in the rocks, much as crystals do. People spoke of the *vis plastica* or "plastic force" that fashioned various shapes, many resembling living animals. Unknown seeds were thought to germinate within the rocks to create the objects, or they were explained as having been triggered by "emanations" from the stars. An alternative explanation attributed fossils to the biblical deluge of Noah.

The term "fossil" was coined by Agricola in the sixteenth century. At that time, it simply meant any curious object that was dug up and could refer to odd-shaped rocks and to cultural objects such as arrowheads.

Gradually, a more accurate understanding spread, this in consequence of the growing inclination to distrust mere authority in matters of natural history and, instead, to favor first-hand experience and observation. Petrus Serverinus, a sixteenth-century Danish alchemist, advised: "Go, my sons, burn your books and buy stout shoes, climb the mountains, search the valleys, the deserts, the seashores, and the deep recesses of the earth . . . observe and experiment without ceasing, for in this way and no other will you arrive at a knowledge of the true nature of things." Passages in Leonardo da Vinci's *Notebooks* indicate he realized that shells found in the mountains were from ocean sediments that have been elevated to such heights over long spans of time. Nearly two more centuries were to pass before such insights would have a much wider audience.

Fossils inform of creatures and environments of the remote past. In addition, some are beautiful. Upon being shown a trilobite, most people are fascinated by the symmetry of its segmented body and by its many-faceted eyes set in stone. The rainbow hues of light refracting in the layers of an ancient cephalopod's smooth shell entrance every eye, and the thin, lace-like lines that separate its hollow chambers are simply exquisite.

The Information Age, with its preoccupation with numbers, computers, and quantitative analysis, leads some to shy away from aesthetic pleasure as a part of science. Yet, a real part it is. Princeton researcher

Glenn Jepsen wrote this passage some five decades ago: "As the successive layers of matrix are cleaved away to expose a petrified bone of a carnivorous dinosaur, a paleontologist may thrill to see it as a beautifully formed organization of elements that have served many functions in earlier eons."

In the first volume of the recent biography of Darwin by Janet Browne, *Charles Darwin: Voyaging*, the author relates that as a young man Darwin was, in his own words, "an idle sporting man." His father was more emphatic: "You care for nothing but shooting, dogs, and rat-catching, and you will be a disgrace to yourself and all your family." However, by the time he was sailing around the South American continent on the *HMS Beagle* in 1833, he had been captivated by the stories in stone he was learning to read. "I wish any of you could enter into my feelings of excessive pleasure, which Geology gives, as soon as one *partly understands* the nature of a country," he exclaimed in a letter to his family. "There is nothing like geology: the pleasure of the first days partridge shooting or first days hunting cannot be compared to finding a fine group of fossil bones, which tell their story of former times with almost a living tongue."

George Gaylord Simpson, one of the twentieth-century's foremost paleontologists, shared this enthusiasm: "To those who follow it, the pursuit of fossils is more exciting and rewarding than the pursuit of living fish, flesh, or fowl. It has all the elements of skill, endurance, suspense, and surprise; and the resulting trophy may be a creature never before seen by man."

Clues to previous worlds, the intriguing form and image of the fossil itself, and the adventure of the pursuit: those are reasons enough for some to engage in this endeavor. However, there is at least one more reason—and this is an intimate one—for every person to have an appreciation for the subject: it has to do with the fact that the earth recycles everything. In fact, this aspect of the story begins even before the existence of the earth itself. Astronomers and physicists have expanded the tale to include the idea that the iron in our blood and the calcium in our bones were formed in the interior of stars, the only place where temperatures are reached that are high enough to create the heavy elements of the periodic table. Then, such elements were scattered into space by the unimaginable force of a supernova explosion, the debris of which was swept up into the orbit of the next generation of newly-formed stars, enriching their planets with the building blocks of life and eventually producing creatures compounded of dust and the light of a star.

Each time an animal dies, its decomposed constituents are sent back into the cycle, "dust to dust, earth to earth, ashes to ashes." So it has always been. And that means, among other things, that we *are* part dinosaur.

Suppose we had a piece of toast for breakfast this morning. The chances are good that the wheat from which the flour was made was grown in the middle western states. The plants now cultivated and harvested there are constituted by minerals in the soil, soil that once made up sediments of ancient deltas and floodplains that were laid down in the age of dinosaurs. Only the tiniest fraction of those great beasts were ever preserved in any part by the process of becoming a fossil; almost all of their elements were returned to the earth, being available, thus, for nature's processes to recycle them into other forms of life. Given the inconceivable number of atoms and molecules that make up a living being such as ourselves, it is a near-certainty that some of those very same particles that once walked around in a dinosaur millions of years ago are now walking around in us! John Muir said, "When we try to pick out anything by itself, we find it hitched to everything else in the universe." We do indeed.

It is, after all, a *universe*. The very term connotes oneness and a wholeness that includes absolutely everything, as in an old verse attributed to Augustus Wright Bamberger, "There's part of the sun in the apple / There's part of the moon in the rose / There's part of the flaming Pleiades / in every leaf that grows." Ancient peoples sensed this interrelatedness and expressed it with myths and rituals of many kinds. The Roman emperor and Stoic philosopher Marcus Aurelius wrote, "All parts of the universe are interwoven, and the bond is sacred. Nothing is unconnected with some other thing." He said even more than he knew, because that connection, we now understand, extends even back through all the immense journey of life over several billion years and has links to the farthest reaches of the cosmos.

The nineteenth-century English poet, Frances Thompson, summed it up with the simple and beautiful thought that you cannot pluck a flower without troubling a star. It's the story told by the fossil that lies on my desk as I write these words.

3

Deep Time

"Time is to Nature endless and as nothing."

James Hutton (1775)

AGATHA CHRISTIE, OF MYSTERY novel fame, was married to an archaeologist. She liked to say that was a very good deal, because the
older she got, the more interest her husband showed in her.

Time is one of the basic constituents of the universe; any and every
experience has this elusive dimension. Within our brains are complex
biologic clocks that react to light and dark and time our sleeping and
waking. The world over, there are intervals of growth and dormancy that
occur time and time again. The garden flower regularly opens with the
dawn, and the calendar can be counted on to transform the aspen leaves
to golden hues. Immense flocks of birds migrate over the earth, taking
instinctive cue from the sun, seasons, and time.

How difficult it is to express the nature of time. We are immersed in
it, caught in its flow, yet we really have no definition of it that does anything more than scratch the surface. "What, then, is time?" Augustine
wrote at the close of the fourth century. "If no one ask of me, I know; if I
wish to explain to him who asks, I know not."

As time passes, the world around us changes, and so do we. Our
memories take us back to an event that happened ten or twenty years
ago, and it seems but an instant since then. Yet we look in the mirror and
know, without doubt, that something has happened, that there has been

a meantime between then and now. Events replace one another in swift succession, and the process goes on without pause. We look at an old picture, brown, faded, and cracked. The image is of people who appear much like our own selves; they are at a reunion or celebration . . . and they are no longer part of our world. Time has passed.

No other instrument or machine is so everywhere-present as the ones that mark its passage; a watch is on nearly every wrist. We measure days by the rotation of the earth. We mark longer periods with the year, the time it takes the earth to make one orbit in its revolution around the sun. (I recall one person who expressed some surprise upon learning that the earth went around the sun in 365¼ days, who said, "Isn't that a coincidence! It takes exactly one year!") The other planets, of course, have different "years." It takes Neptune 164 of our earth's years to make a single one of its own.

Accurate measurements of time were a long time in coming. Inscribed on many sundials are the words, "I count only the sunny hours," a saying meant to accent optimism but also indicating the sundial's limitations. The Romans made timepieces from candles and from vessels that dripped a certain quantity of water. Hourglasses gave us the metaphor "the sands of time" as well as the phrase, "time is running out." There is something pensive and thought provoking about grains of sand trickling down in an hourglass. While time itself is invisible and ineffable, it helps to get a feel for it, to think that time is something like that. More recently, many grandfather clocks carried the Latin phrase *tempus fugit* inscribed on the dial: "time flies."

Clocks, as we know them, were developed during the Middle Ages in the monasteries of Europe to call the monks to prayer. The very word "clock" is from a Dutch word for bell, and, until the fifteenth century, most clocks had no face or dial because the function was to "sound" the hours.

A seventeenth-century Frenchman contrived an ingenious one using another sense altogether. He designed a clock face so that in pitch darkness he could reach for the hour hand, which then guided him to a hole in which a particular spice had been placed; there was a different spice for every hour-position on the clock. Having memorized which was which, he could say, "Let's see: cinnamon—it must be 2 a.m." Thus, in spite of not being able to see the clock, he could taste the time.

Recently, humanity has become increasingly expert at dividing time into smaller and smaller segments. There are now clocks that use vibrating cesium atoms to measure time to an accuracy of one part in a million million. Such an instrument would lose only one second in thirty thousand years—a single tick between the last Neanderthals of Europe and what will likely be the first colonists on Mars.

The Greek language has two words for time. The first is *chronos*, i.e., chronological time. It is time marked on our clocks and calendars in terms of seconds and minutes, hours, months, years. It is time that flows evenly along and it can be divided into segments, each of which is the same duration and all alike: it is *quantitative* time.

However, time, as we experience it, is also *qualitative*, indicating that not all time is of equal import or significance. The day you spent working on your tax report and the day you had "the time of your life" were likely not one and the same. To indicate time charged with significance, the word employed is *kairos*. There is no one English word for it, but it might be translated as "the time of opportunity" or "the *right* time." It is the time, which, for good or ill, is either seized or lost; in either case, it will never come again.

Suppose two people work high above on a flying trapeze without a net below. The one person swings, then lets go of the bar and flies through the air, meeting the other in perfect timing and, in a split second, is caught and is safe. There are no second chances for that connection. Or recall when the first astronauts would ride the huge Saturn V booster rockets that would put their capsules in orbit around the earth, enabling them to go on to the moon. At the moment of blast-off, if something went wrong and the alarm sounded, they had three and one-half seconds to push the button that would eject them clear of the impending explosion—that and no more. There would still be plenty of time, in the sense of *chronos*, but not for that "life or death" decision; that little slice of time would be crucial time: *kairos*.

It is indeed true that not all time is weighted the same. In the Old Testament book of Ecclesiastes, chapter 3 is a section that is often read at funerals, weddings, and many other occasions, because it speaks of the right time for various events and emotions. "For everything there is a season, and a time for every matter under heaven: a time to be born, and a time to die; a time to plant, and a time to pluck up what is planted; a time to kill, and a time to heal; a time to break down, and a time to build up; a time to weep, and a time to laugh; a time to mourn and a time to dance . . . a time to seek, and a time to lose; a time to keep and a time to cast away; a time to rend, and a time to sew; a time to keep silence, and a time to speak; a time to love, and a time to hate; a time for war, and a time for peace." (Eccl 3:1–4, 6–8. Revised Standard Version)

There have been at least three quite different perspectives by human beings toward the passage of time, three different ways of orienting oneself in relationship to it.

In the first place, it may be that truly ancient peoples lived in a kind of *timeless* realm. As the snows came and went, wandering peoples drifted with the seasons. There was no calendar and the only record left behind may have been flint tools from a campsite. Perhaps myths developed about the "the old ones" or "the dream time," but almost everything was lost in the course of passing millennia. People lived largely in the present. Only in a few places can one find anything resembling that today. Peter Mathiessen stayed with many of the tribal peoples of East Africa prior to recounting his travels in his book, *The Tree Where Man Was Born*. He described the Hadza hunter-gatherers, thus: "For people who must live from day to day, past and future have small relevance, and their grasp of it is fleeting; they live in the moment, a precious gift that we have lost."

Secondly, there is the *cyclical* conception of time, the idea that it is moving in vast circles. The ancient Maya had an accurate calendar some 1400 years ago, with much of their ceremonial and social life revolving around the mystery of time's passage and their attempt to predict the huge cycles of their imagination. The Hindus, still today, see the universe as moving in vast arcs of hundreds of millions of years. In that system of belief, an individual goes through one incarnation after another, so time is likened to a wheel. The ancient Greeks and Romans believed the universe itself was eternal; they had a circular or, at least, a "spiral" conception of time. Their saying, "History repeats itself," is old, indeed, and expresses the idea that there were whirlpools in the stream, where things came to be, then passed on, perhaps only to come again.

Such a concept of time, while it may seem remote and abstract, might have great practical significance in one's daily life, should one adopt it, for it is, ultimately, a pessimistic view: history is going nowhere and humanity is tramping about on a kind of eternal treadmill. Historian

Will Durant has written of what he calls the "indispersible gloom which broods over so much of Greek literature."

Ecclesiastes is one of the most heavily Greek-influenced books of the Bible, and it has this tone. The book is included in Scripture, some say, to illustrate the consequences of such a point a view. Thus, in addition to those beautiful verses about there being "a time for every matter under heaven," there are passages like these: "What does man gain by all the toil at which he toils under the sun? A generation goes and a generation comes, but the earth remains forever . . . What has been is what will be, and what has been done is what will be done; and there is nothing new under the sun . . . all is vanity." (Eccl 1:4, 9, 12:8b)

The third conception of time is *linear*, i.e., there is an arrow, a direction to time's passage: time is going somewhere. In this perspective, the universe, everything we know, has not always been. It had a beginning. Time moves "forward" and each moment in the present and the future is different from the past, unique. The universe, thus, is evolving.

This is the dominant time frame found in the Bible. There, time is the medium of the divine drama, wherein God is moving creation from a beginning toward the goal of fulfillment or consummation. Many have noticed that such a view is compatible with that of modern physics and astronomy, which speak of the universe beginning in a single instant: the primordial explosion that has come to be known by the trivial name of the Big Bang, then developing onward and outward from there over the course of nearly 14 billion years. Robert Jastrow, the founder and past director of NASA's Goddard Institute for Space Studies, wrote of the scientist searching for answers who follows his data back to that initial event, but who is stymied by the fact that every bit of the evidence needed for studying the cause of it has been obliterated in the explosion. All the fingerprints have been erased, and the first cause is forever beyond reach: "The scientist's pursuit of the past ends in the moment of creation . . . He has scaled the mountains of ignorance; he is about to conquer the highest peak; as he pulls himself over the final rock, he is greeted by a band of theologians who have been sitting there for centuries."

An old saying is to the effect that if one marries the science of the time, one will soon be a widow/widower, a caution that must be kept in mind. However, there are more than a few who maintain that science itself owes a huge debt to this fundamental Christian perspective that time is linear. The idea is that science, which traces causes and effects and evolutionary sequence, could only develop if you had, as you did in Western Europe, some such idea of the linear, progressive, or developmental character of time that infused the entire culture.

One aspect of time is that which is *past*. In a sense, we never experience anything but the past. The sounds you are now hearing come from a thousandth of a second back in time for every foot traveled to reach you. And what is true of sound is true of light, but on a "faster" scale. When we look up toward the sun, we see it as it existed eight minutes ago, for it takes that long for light, traveling at 186,000 miles per second, to traverse the 93 million miles of space to earth.

All winter long the great galaxy M31 in Andromeda hangs in the night sky. This near twin of the Milky Way is the farthest thing that any human being has ever seen with the naked eye. If you know right where to look, you can see the hazy, glowing patch of light that our large telescopes reveal to be a spiral of perhaps 200 billion stars. It is 2.3 million light years away! That is to say, its light that reaches us tonight began its journey to us that far back in time, and what we see is a ghostly image formed that far in the distant past. Thus, deep space takes us into deep time, as well.

The attempt to transcend our limitations in time is a persistent theme in literature. H. G. Wells wrote a short story in which he imagines the possibility of science tapping into the "memory" of the human race itself: "A day may come when these recovered memories may grow as vivid as if we in our own persons had been there and shared the thrill and fear of those primordial days; a day may come when the great beasts of the past will leap to life again in our imaginations, when we shall walk again in vanished scenes, stretch painted limbs we thought were dust, and feel again the sunshine of a million years ago."

In 1955, Albert Einstein learned of the death of his best friend, Michele Besso and wrote a brief letter to the family (as it turned out, just a few months before his own death): "He has departed from this strange world a little ahead of me. That means nothing. For us believing physicists, the distinction between past, present and future is only a stubborn illusion."

Virtually everyone knows of one of Einstein's ideas, that time may pass differently, depending upon the speed at which an object is moving, i.e., that time is relative to motion. At 99 percent of the speed of light, a month in a spaceship might be a year on earth. An imaginary space traveler might return to earth in what she thought was five years, only to find her friends and family had aged fifty or be all dead and gone. A movie that captured the public imagination decades ago, *2001: A Space Odyssey*, had such a theme, and there have been numerous others since. There has been much silly stuff written about time travel; however, the universe may be strange beyond our imaginings.

There are additional ideas concerning the unevenness of time's passage. In England's Chester Cathedral is an inscription on the face of a clock, part of which reads: "When, as a child, I laughed and wept, time crept. When, as a youth, I dreamed and talked, time walked. When I became a full-grown man, time ran. And later, as I older grew, time flew." All of us have known something of that. As kids, we waited for our parents to finish shopping and it "seemed like an eternity." We have heard the elderly talk about how, for them, "time has flown."

The Swedish paleontologist Björn Kurtén suggests that whether time seems to pass slowly or quickly is not, in fact, just seeming; rather, it depends upon our *pace* of living. Thus, he says, a child's wound heals more rapidly, tied to bodily processes. He points out that a child makes decisions quickly, while the old take their time thinking it over; we may say this is due to experience and the wisdom of age, but it might reflect a different *tempo* of life, so that both are ruminating on the subject to about the same degree.

Kurtén suggests that time, for human beings, has something of a "logarithmic" character, the distance from year one to ten being as long as the distance from ten to one hundred. Thus, during one-half of our subjective lifetimes, we are children, illustrating why these are the teachable years.

Perhaps, says Kurtén, how time is experienced is relative to size, as well. Smaller animals live at a frantic pace. Although a generation for a shrew may be only a few weeks, it may "live" just as much as an elephant of seventy years, only at a much faster rate; the hearts of the two animals make about the same number of beats in a lifetime. A single day to a hummingbird with its frenetic metabolism would be as long and as full of experience as several months for a ponderous, huge animal with its slow heartbeat. So, experientially, do the mayfly and the Galapagos tortoise both "get the same?" Interesting, isn't it?

We do continually transcend time by way of memory and imagination. Someone has said that a highbrow or intellectual is a person who looks at a sausage and thinks of Picasso. In a similar vein to that rather clever remark, a paleontologist looks at the ordinary crust of the earth with its rocky layers, which are as common and mundane as sausage is to breakfast, and sees therein the record of life on earth. All that separates the various beings in the passage of a billion years is time, and what is that? Henry David Thoreau wrote, "Time is but the stream I go a-fishing in. I drink at it; but while I drink I see the sandy bottom and detect how shallow it is. Its thin current slides away, but eternity remains. I would drink deeper, fish in the sky whose bottom is pebbly with stars." He saw beyond mere measurement and chronology to time's mystery.

The nature of time baffles all of us. A joke in paleontological circles concerns people on tour through a natural history museum in the southwestern United States. The guide told them, "These dinosaur skeletons, some of the earliest ones, are 200 million *and three* years old!" Everyone was amazed. "How can you be so precise?" they asked. He replied, "Well, when I got the job, they *told* me they were 200 million years old—and that was three years ago."

It is nearly impossible to hold in the mind numbers of this magnitude and to see ourselves in relation to them. Of course, some make no attempt, something like the sailor who was asked the distance to the sun; he said, "It's far enough away so that it will not interfere with anything I want to do in the Navy." Locating our context in both space and time is central to our humanity but is far from easy. A sign outside an astronomy lab reads, "Caution: The study of astronomy may be hazardous to your sense of self-importance!" Concepts of deep time, like those of deep space, can be threatening for many people.

It is intimidating to consider that so much of earth's history has gone on before we arrived. After all, we are accustomed to thinking and acting as if everything revolved around us. It used to be said of Frederick the Great that he loved music, but that this was not so much music as it was the flute, and not so much the flute as *his* flute. The story of the Garden of Eden is about the egocentricity of human nature. The Greek myth of Icarus, in pride flying too close to the sun, is concerned with it also. Bertrand Russell once said, "Every man would like to be God, if it were possible; some few find it difficult to admit the impossibility."

One of the main principles of geology, the science of the earth, is that the forces of nature operate (with the exception of the occasional catastrophe) in a uniform manner, i.e., that the forces operating today are the same as the ones that have done so throughout earth's history. Therefore, the landscape we see about us is mostly the result of the accumulated effects of small increments of change over time. A bit of rock falls off a cliff. The tiny amount of acid in rainwater eats away at the rock. Raindrops act as miniature bombs that blast small craters in soil, loosening bits to be carried away by every little rivulet to join creeks and rivers, carrying more and more and finally emptying into the oceans. And the key is the immensity of time.

James Hutton is often called the father of geology. In 1775, he presented a paper before the Royal Society in Edinburgh in which he laid out the following scenario: The everlasting hills would one day be gone, their elements being redistributed bit by tiny bit into other strata. Eventually, such deposits might be uplifted by forces deep within the earth to create hills and mountains once again. Looking into the earth's crust, Hutton concluded that the present is the key to the past; the same processes at work now have been ceaselessly at work over long ages. "I find no vestige of a beginning and no prospect of an end," he said. The time scale involved in the mechanisms of the earth is so vast as to be beyond all our imaginings.

Stand on the rim of the Grand Canyon and look down into that deep chasm and you are gazing at formations laid down as much as a billion years ago. John Wesley Powell, in 1869 the first one to float the Colorado River down the length of the Canyon, saw therein the angled roots of mountains that have been completely eroded away and then overlain by thousands of feet of horizontal strata. He came to see that mountains cannot long remain mountains but that they are ephemeral topographic forms, saying, "Geologically, all existing mountains are recent; the ancient mountains are gone." The mile-deep strata in the Canyon with its shells in the limestone from ancient seas, basalt from volcanic flows ages ago, and the roots of those once mighty ranges all displace us from the center stage of earth's history.

That is part of the explanation, I think, for all the contorted efforts of the so-called creationist movement to shoehorn all of geologic time into a mere 6,000–10,000 years. Deep time—460,000 *times* the larger number—hugely reduces the proportion of the play for our own scene to be enacted, and *hubris* cannot accept that consequence.

However, much *has* been going on without us. The philosopher Immanuel Kant wrote, as far back as 1775 (clearly groping for words with which to give expression to the scope of the vast processes of nature beginning to be explored in his time), "Millions and whole mountain ranges of millions of centuries will pass, within which forever new worlds will be formed." The poets, also, expressed what science found, as did Walt Whitman: "Long and long has the grass been growing. Long and long has the rain been falling. Long and long has the globe been rolling 'round."

How can we begin to comprehend how the earth uses time? Radiometric dating of meteors, the oldest known rocks, gives an estimate of the age of the solar system at 4.6 billion years. By way of illustration, if a year is represented by a postcard, the age of the earth would be a string of such cards placed from New York City to New Orleans, *on edge.* Or, one could represent the 4.6 billion years with a line fifteen miles long. In that scheme, the last six thousand years from ancient Mesopotamia to the present, which brackets what we usually call "civilization," would be represented by just the last single inch. In vertical scale, if the history of the earth were represented by a cliff a mile high, then all of historic time occupies just the uppermost tenth of an inch, and a single lifetime occupies less than the thickness of the finest hair.

Comparisons can be made with a one-year calendar. There are many variations on this theme, in which the earth's beginning some 4.6 billion years ago becomes January 1. Life in the sea begins about the first day of spring, March 21. It takes until Thanksgiving for aquatic creatures to begin to pioneer the land. The dinosaurs do not come on stage until December 13. They endure for more than 150 million years and, on this scale, disappear the day after Christmas. It is not until the late evening of December 31, on New Year's Eve, that our human ancestors, the first hominids, appear in Africa. Near the very end of the last minute of the year, the Roman Empire rises and falls and, at a mere 3.5 seconds to midnight, Columbus lands in the New World.

With that type of long, long lens through which to view time, we can begin to understand how the earth has changed over the ages. Thus, the Atlantic Ocean has not always existed. Rather, the continental plates including Europe and North America have been separating and still are moving apart at the rate of approximately an inch a year—approximately the growth rate of our fingernails—but over 200 million years, the Atlantic Ocean has been formed.

We tend to think of the landscape as fixed, yet it is changing constantly. Near the farm where I grew up in the Midwest, there was a car-sized granite boulder alongside the road. Several fine fractures existed in the rock, trapping small pockets of windblown soil, and in one of them, on the spine of the huge rock, a small sapling took root. Year after year, our family noticed the tree send its roots deeper and deeper into the crevices. Rain and melting snow drained into the cracks to freeze and become icy wedges and chisels to chip away at the granite. Now the sapling is fully a tree and its irresistible growth is prying the massive rock into smaller and smaller pieces, beginning a process by which the boulder will eventually be reduced to the soil around it.

Erosion over a wide area of a landscape is too gradual to be noticed, but every rain carries immense volumes of silt and sand to the sea. In some places, the erosion is more graphic. The excavating power of the Colorado River in the Grand Canyon has been almost beyond description. Several dams have slowed the flow, but accurate records exist from the time before the dams were built, and they show an average load of silt of some 500,000 tons was being moved every day. However, in full flood, the river carried per day an estimated 55 million tons of silt, gravel, cobblestones, and boulders past the gauging station. Comparisons fail for such colossal earth moving, but consider this: To transport such a load in one twenty-four hour day with five-ton dump trucks would require a parade of more than 11 million of them. They would pass a given point at the rate of 125 per second! Thus, in the course of some 5 million years, the immense canyon was carved.

At Niagara Falls, the ledge over which the river flows is being cut back three or four feet per year, a process that means that the gorge is advancing upstream toward Lake Erie and in 25,000 years will reach it and empty the lake. Then, the other Great Lakes, one by one, will also be drained, becoming again the mere river valleys they were in an earlier epoch.

If a single picture could be taken every 100 or 500 years and put into a film to speed up the movement of what is happening, we would see the hills change shape like so many clouds. Time's passage means change, oceans encroaching on the land, continents moving—transformation.

The Rocky Mountains did not always exist. In many regions, they are composed of layers that were once sediments accumulating on the floor of shallow seas from 350 million to 1 billion years ago. Those silts and limes hardened into rock and were then pushed upward at the rate of only an inch or so a year. Over 70 million years, the inches would add up to miles, but the mountains are now being eroded at least as fast as they rise. Again, these are the *young* mountains. All the truly ancient mountains are gone; whole ranges have been eroded away several times, a raindrop and a particle at a time . . . because the earth has an abundance of time with which to work.

"A thousand ages in Thy sight are like an evening gone," sings an old hymn that echoes the Psalms. God has plenty of time. The physicist Freeman Dyson later occupied the position once held by Einstein at Princeton's Institute for Advanced Study. In his book *Infinite in All Directions*, Dyson wrote, "Mind is patient. Mind has waited for 3 billion years on this planet before composing its first string quartet."

4

If These Bones Could Speak

The hand of the Lord was upon me, and he brought me out by the Spirit of the Lord and set me down in the midst of the valley; it was full of bones . . . and lo, they were very dry . . . So I prophesied as I was commanded, . . . there was a noise, and behold, a rattling; and the bones came together, bone to its bone . . . and breath came into them, and they lived, and stood upon their feet, an exceedingly great host.

Ezekiel

WE COULD NOT KNOW the extent of it at first, but the valley was indeed full of bones. More than twenty years ago, my fifth grade son, Garrett, and I were hunting dinosaurs on the prairies of the Great Plains, something we did for two weeks every summer vacation. Always in July, our trips coincided with the hottest weather when temperatures usually climbed to more than 100 degrees in the shade. (That's something of a euphemism; there was never any shade.) We usually slept in tents, and the sudden, violent, mid-night thunderstorms generated by the heat often sent us running to the pickup cab, our path lit by near-constant lightning flashes, certain that without such refuge we would be blown away. It is all part of what one does to find fossils; however, it is pretty mild when compared to the challenges that confronted the earliest dinosaur seekers, those who explored the badlands with horses and wagons and were often days from the nearest settlements.

We camped not far from a two hundred-foot cliff overlooking a small river that had cut its winding, convoluted way down through the banded sedimentary rocks from the period of time that holds the last of the dinosaurs. The river now occupies a narrow bed that is sometimes reduced to a trickle, but it was not always such a diminutive stream, for it lies within a much larger, much more ancient channel, one of the countless channels for melt-waters from the last continental glacier. Twelve thousand years ago and some distance to the north, the front of the retreating ice would have been nearly a mile thick and waters a mile wide would have swirled and churned in the broad valley just beneath us.

Now, a herd of black cattle grazes down there in the distance; somewhat apart are several bison that a rancher has added to his operation, a practice that is becoming increasingly common in the West. A few cottonwoods dot the flood plain, most of them huge and dying, since new trees are dependant for propagation upon high water, which no longer comes due to the flow being retained and controlled by irrigation dams. A golden eagle rides the thermals above, making lazy spirals in the blue sky. Coyotes howl at first and last light; otherwise, the loudest sound is that of a bumblebee moving between coneflowers, intent upon its business, oblivious to ours.

Ours has to do with still another riverbed, over five thousand times more ancient, the cross-section of which has been exposed by erosion about a third of the way down the cliff. We had found miscellaneous fragments of bone at the bottom. When that happens, one follows the pieces upward, hoping to find the source. Perched on the side of the sixty-degree slope, hacking footholds and probing with picks and knives, the horizon that had been producing the eroded bone was revealed, and it exceeded anything we could have imagined. Wherever we probed at this zone of twelve inches in thickness, there was rust-colored bone—leg bones, ribs, foot bones, ossified tendon, vertebrae, and pieces of skull! The skeletal elements were log-jammed together at a density of about thirty bones per square meter. None of the bones were in place, hooked together as a skeleton; instead, they had been moved in high water and packed together in random fashion, i.e., they were *disarticulated*. I was interviewed by a newspaper concerning the site, and, when the article was published, it stated that the bones were *inarticulate*, which would mean they couldn't speak. However, in their own way, they spoke volumes.

Thus, in addition to working ten hours a day at the excavation, the beginning or the end of a typical day often found one simply in contemplation of the mysterious world of the dinosaurs, more of which was beginning to be revealed with each shovelful of dirt. Regarding such moments, the world-famous paleontologist Robert Bakker writes in his 1986 book, *The Dinosaur Heresies*, "Reverie is normal in Wyoming at sunrise. I suppose a no-nonsense laboratory scientist, clad in his white lab coat and steely-eyed objectivity, might think I was wasting my time communing with the spirit of the fossil beast. But scientists need long walks and quiet times at the quarry to let the whole pattern of fossil history sink into our consciousness."

We would return year after year to this same spot, each time cutting in several feet to excavate a platform where we could work to expose and map the extent of the dinosaur material. Then came the process of removing the smaller bones, digging around the larger ones and applying plaster jackets so they could be safely removed, hauling them by rope and stretcher up the steep incline. The huge extent of the bone-bed on the cliff face was now apparent: it was more than four hundred yards wide. After several summers of such exploration by just the two of us, a crew of college students and adults was assembled to work for two or three weeks each summer. A small front-end loader was employed to remove some of the overburden in a process that resembled terracing a road on the side of a mountain. Over the course of a dozen years, more than 6,000 dinosaur bones were removed from the site, and it is likely that acres more still remain in that side-hill.

All the bones are from a single species of dinosaur, the large hadrosaur, or so-called "duckbilled" plant-eater named *Edmontosaurus*. In addition, we found a number of shed tyrannosaur teeth, suggesting the scene had been a windfall for the carnivores. Bones of other species are absent, indicating that this does not represent a gradual accumulation at the site over time but is the result of a single event. Collections like this, composed of individuals of different sizes, from quite small to nearly forty feet long, provide evidence that such creatures must have traveled in large herds, perhaps in migration. In the Far North, entire herds of caribou may drown in the attempt to cross a wide river in flood stage, and it may be that something similar happened here with a mass kill of dinosaurs. After the carcasses began to decompose, another high-water event must have separated and jumbled the skeletal elements and moved them downstream, there to become packed together and covered by sediment. Locked in the darkness, they remained until another river would begin to expose them to the light of day nearly 70 million earth orbits later and in an utterly different world.

Part of the message of the bones is delivered where they are found, in place. It is a truism in paleontology that as much as half the important data from a specimen can be obtained from its context in the field, paying attention to the conditions under which it was deposited in its original environment. The specimen is then fully excavated and moved to a museum or university lab, where it is cleaned, hardened, missing parts restored, i.e., "prepped" or prepared for study or display.

"Dem bones, dem bones, dem dry bones." So goes the old spiritual that talks about "the hip bone connected to the leg bone, the leg bone connected to the knee bone," and on and on. The song's inspiration is, of course, that prophetic passage from Ezekiel chapter 37. The passage has inspired more than song.

Edwin H. Colbert was one of the leading paleontologists of the previous generation; for more than three decades, he was curator of dinosaurs at the American Museum of Natural History in New York City. He once spoke to his research staff with a huge sauropod or "brontosaur" pelvic bone in front of him, saying: "Bones are truly fascinating things, marvels of structure and form . . . Everything about a bone has meaning: it is a structure shaped for strength or for a particular function . . . it is an integral element of a dynamic, mobile creature, the complexity of which makes our vaunted mechanical vehicles seem simple and crudely limited."

One thinks here of the words of Walt Whitman, "The narrowest hinge of my hand puts to scorn all machinery." Colbert continued:

> The astute paleontologist sees in his fossils more than petrified bones . . . In his mind's eye he can clothe the bones with muscles and other soft parts of living animals, and he can cover the ancient animals with skin or scales or hair and picture them as they once appeared in their native environment . . . One might think that he is akin to Ezekiel, who said: "So I prophesied . . . and the bones came together, bone to its bone. And I beheld, and lo, there were sinews upon them, and flesh came up and skin covered them above . . . and breath came into them, and they lived." These are the undisputed remains of animals that lived great ages

ago, and it is about them that we must speak. May our words
never be dry.

Not every dinosaur specimen arrives at a museum or research facil-
ity, in fact, far from it. Today, fewer and fewer do, because of the dramatic
increase in commercial collecting over the past two decades. Private collectors, as well as companies established for this purpose, sell specimens.
A few go to museums that buy fossils (most museums do not, at least not
those of dinosaurs), but many of them go to private individuals, and many
go overseas without scientists ever seeing them. The situation was exac-
erbated when, in 1997, the largest and most complete *Tyrannosaurus rex*,
nicknamed "Sue," was auctioned off for more than 8 million dollars. A
number of *T. rex* specimens have been found since, but the incident surely
contributed to the commercialization of fossils, especially dinosaurs, and
the granting of permission to search for scientific purposes on private land
has sharply declined since. I have been extremely fortunate to work with
several landowners who have a fine concern for science in general and for
the educational value of such objects.

It is a complex situation. On the one hand, some fossils are common, including many invertebrates. Entire mountain ranges are made
of limestone, which means they are literally composed of uncountable
trillions of organisms that flourished in ancient seas. Some vertebrate
animals have left abundant fossils, also. Sharks, for instance, shed and
replace their teeth continually; a single one may shed thousands in a
lifetime. The same was true in prehistory, making for huge numbers of
fossil shark teeth.

On the other hand, some types, such as many dinosaur fossils, are
rare; indeed, some are one of a kind. These represent priceless clues to
the history of life on earth and should belong to posterity, instead of becoming mere commodities that go to the highest bidder. It is sometimes
to "make ends meet" that such items are sold, but not always. Some of
the poorest people I know are farmers and ranchers but so are some of
the richest. Where one stands on this issue seems to have little to do
with wealth or the lack thereof. In response to the question, "How much
is enough?" many will always answer, "Just a little more." Some will say,
"A person has to live, doesn't he?" Yes, but the oft-unasked question is
"What *for*?"

Thoreau wrote about a neighbor who lived on Flint's pond, "who regarded even the wild ducks that settled in it as trespassers," an individual

who "would have drained it and sold it for the mud at its bottom." It was "his farm where everything had its price, who would carry the landscape, who would carry his *God*, to market, if he could get anything for him . . . on whose farm nothing grows free, whose fields bear no crops, whose meadows no flowers, whose trees no fruits, but dollars."

To illustrate the rarity and the scientific value of some specimens, consider the horned dinosaur *Torosaurus*. The first descriptions of the creature accented the fact that huge bony frill or shield extending from the back of the skull over the neck is much larger than that of its more common cousin, *Triceratops*, of which perhaps two hundred skulls have been found. In addition, the frill of *Torosaurus* has two large holes in it. The rarity of this beast can be seen by the fact that only three skulls had been found in more than one hundred years. The first two were located in 1891 by an expedition to Wyoming from Yale University. Those were approximately 50 percent complete but enough to give it a name. Nothing more showed up until 1944 when an incomplete juvenile skull was found in South Dakota by the Philadelphia Academy of Sciences. Then, in Montana in 1996, I excavated a huge *Torosaurus* skull and delivered it to the world-class Museum of the Rockies at Montana State University in Bozeman, which now houses the largest collection of American dinosaur specimens in the world. It is there that I have practiced my serious avocation as a research associate in paleontology. At nine feet long, it was the largest dinosaur skull in the world.

Rare as they are, I thought I would never see another one in the ground. Then, in 1999, I was visiting a rancher and seeking permission to explore his land, something he readily gave. As I was about to leave, he took me into his garage to show me a piece of bone he had picked up twenty-five years earlier. It was apparent to me that it was a fragment of the skull of a ceratopsian or horned dinosaur, so I was anxious to see how much more could be found. The site was located, and over the next few weeks I made seven trips there to begin exposing what would turn out to be specimen number five of *Torosaurus*, the most complete and best preserved one yet. The next summer, several of us from the Museum of the Rockies were involved in the remainder of the excavation at the base of a twenty-five foot cliff. Jackhammers, picks, and shovels were used to cut a pickup-sized cave in the sandstone wall and the skull was jacketed in two pieces that together weighed an estimated four thousand pounds. Another winter passed, but in the summer of 2001 the Army National

Guard was available for a training exercise in which two Black Hawk helicopters would lift what could be moved in no other way. On July 21, at the crack of dawn, when the air is most still, the great skull nine feet long and over six feet wide rose into the air. (One of the pilots said later, "I don't know why we had to get up at three-thirty in the morning to come and get something that's been in the ground for 68 million years!")

The event was filmed by several media outlets and carried "live" by NBC television's *Today Show*, and CNN picked it up and sent it around the world. It was an event illustrating both the popularity of dinosaurs and the large number of people and the amount of resources necessary to rightly handle a specimen of this importance.

The world-renowned dinosaur specialist Jack Horner, who oversaw the excavation, was asked, "So, is this the kind of moment paleontologists live for?" "Well, it certainly is," he replied. "The next great moment will be when we can get it to the Museum where *everyone* can see it."

And that's the point. Such things belong to the ages. The two giant skulls are now central exhibits in a new dinosaur hall, where their bones will speak to the public of the diversity of life through time. Over generations, millions of people will be able to see them and most will surely stand in awe before these, two of the largest skulls of any land animal ever.

Torosaurus has been known by that name for more than a century, but an unexpected perspective was recently provided by a scientific paper published in 2010 by Horner and one of his graduate students, in which they conclude that the few existing skulls of *Torosaurus* may actually be the final growth stage of very aged individuals of *Triceratops*. In a situation not uncommon in paleontology, a number of others disagree, illustrating the sort of debates that often take place in science. However, and in line with "a rose by any other name would smell as sweet," these specimens—whatever their designation—are still of wonderful creatures from the primeval world of the dinosaurs and, as such, will continue to stir the imagination.

The word "museum" comes from the root verb "to muse," i.e., to think, to reflect, consider, or to wonder. This is a purpose far deeper than mere entertainment, which usually consists of *a*-musement, i.e., to *not* think, to neither consider nor wonder. Among the latter is much television programming, wherein the average scene is three and a half seconds. One is reminded of George Bernard Shaw's visit to New York

City when he was being driven down Broadway. About the profusion of neon lights and advertising, he said that it must be beautiful, if you cannot read.

Natural history museums exist to expand our understanding; we cannot wisely guide our course in relationship to the life-systems on which we depend without sound knowledge of how they operate. Practical considerations aside, they also have the purpose of eliciting our admiration for the dynamics of planet earth and the complexity of life. Without that, it is as though we stand in a gallery that has the great works of art all facing the wall. A simple appreciation of our place in nature is essential to our humanity.

There is, however, a subtle danger to which institutions are prone as they attempt to describe the natural world. Many nature and science museums are not as much about nature as they are about technology. Even when the subject is that of various animals, the fact that robotics and synthetic sounds often dominate will lead to the subconscious focus not on the creature but on the human inventor. Nature is divided into bite-sized segments that are isolated from their contexts and hyped by electronics. The displays are often, therefore, less about the world and more about our domination of it. It is a mentality with a long pedigree, as Cicero boasted, "We are absolute masters of what the earth produces. We enjoy the mountains and the plains . . . We sow the seed and plant the trees. We fertilize the earth . . . We stop, direct, and turn the rivers. In short, by our hands we endeavor by our various operations in this world to make it, as it were, another nature."

Consider the zoo in almost any large urban center, even the most spacious and ecologically minded, and, in the words of Scott Russell Sanders:

> You will find nature parceled out into showy fragments, a nature demeaned and dominated by our constructions. Thickets of bamboo and simulated watering holes cannot disguise the elementary fact that a zoo is a prison. The animals are captives, hauled to this space for our edification or entertainment. No matter how ferocious they may look, they are wholly dependent on our care. A bear squatting on its haunches, a tiger lounging with half-lidded eyes, a bald eagle hunched on a limb are like refugees who tell us less about their homeland, their native way of being, than about our power . . . Snared in our inventions,

> wearing our labels, the plants and animals stand mute. In such
> places, the loudest voice we hear is our own.

Planetariums simulate not only the naked-eye vision of the sky but sights from deep space that, otherwise, would be closed to all but a few. As such, they more nearly facilitate the muse. Some things, of course, should not need such help. A few decades ago, when, for the first time, a lunar eclipse was shown on television, most people watched it on the silver screen, this when they could have stepped outside and seen the real thing.

A dinosaur bone, however, needs neither magnification nor exaggeration. It is what it is, whether in isolation or in an articulated skeleton: a tangible artifact from a creature that lived in an inconceivably remote period on planet earth.

Museums often use casts made from molds of the bones. These are near-identical reproductions and have several advantages, including that they can be shipped across the world for study or posed in mounts when the actual bone would be too heavy or fragile or when such exhibits would be too costly. But the authentic bone itself has a mystique that is unrivaled. Even the first-graders have learned to ask about a dinosaur specimen, "Is it *real*?" If not, at least some of the interest departs. If it *is* real, the eyes grow wide with excitement and wonder. The fact that museums can display such objects of fascination, often close-up, contributes to the popularity of the whole subject of dinosaurs. Some have called dinosaurs "nature's special effects," with the added attraction that they were real.

It is quite an understatement to say, concerning the role of dinosaurs in today's culture, that they are popular. It was in 1842 that England's Sir Richard Owen coined the name *dinosaur* to describe a new order of reptiles, this after the Greek words *deinos* for "terrible" or "frightfully great" and *sauros,* for "lizard." *Deinos* might be equally well translated "*awful*," this in the original sense of awe-full, and "Awesome!" is a phrase heard often in dinosaur halls these days.

The fascination with things prehistoric has meant that paleontologists who study dinosaurs no longer work in obscurity but have become celebrities. Blockbuster movies like Steven Spielberg's *Jurassic Park* (mostly about Cretaceous instead of Jurassic dinosaurs) fuel the imaginations of millions. Jack Horner was advisor to that film, as well as the sequels, and his persona served as the model for the main character played by Sam Neill. (Perhaps the reader will remember an early scene in *Jurassic Park III*, in which the paleontologist drives up to the dig site in a Museum of the Rockies pickup.)

In 1996, Arizona State University at Tempe hosted a month-long extravaganza concerning dinosaurs and other prehistoric beasts. The thousands who attended viewed entire skeletons on display, as well as a many other fossils. (Since then, there have been numerous other such *Dinofest* events at other sites around the country.) Included was a four-day symposium that featured dozens of researchers. The paleontologist Peter Ward describes the atmosphere of the event: "All the big name dinosaur guys were there, and the two biggest of all, Jack Horner and Bob Bakker, could easily be found simply by looking for the biggest crowd. As each passed through a room or hall, a retinue of attendees, groupies, and curious onlookers followed."

Publicity in this era knew little bounds. Horner appeared on the cover of *US News and World Report* with the banner, "What Dinosaur Detective Jack Horner Does in the Real Jurassic Park," i.e., Montana. In the 1990s, numerous magazines put forth cover articles, such as that by *Newsweek* bearing an image of *T. rex*: "Could Dinosaurs Return? The Science of Cloning." Television documentaries on the subject of dinosaurs are continually in production, and newspapers report on dinosaur digs. Entire industries exist to crank out dinosaur toys and, of course, T-shirts are nearly ubiquitous.

Horner's discoveries of dinosaur eggs (some containing embryos) and babies in nesting sites at the front range of the Rocky Mountains in Montana had made news the world over. They were the first complete such eggs ever found in North America. It was not only a discovery, however. It led to an image of entire nesting colonies of giants. In describing their environment, Horner provided a new picture of huge reptiles caring for their young, and he named the dinosaur involved *Miasaura*, meaning "Good Mother Lizard." Baby dinosaurs became hugely interesting to millions. (Among the very best works to show how paleontology actually works are his *Digging Dinosaurs: the Search that Unraveled the Mystery of the Baby Dinosaurs* and his *Dinosaur Lives: Unearthing the Evolutionary Saga*. A fascinating new look at the iconic *Tyrannosaurus rex* is found in Horner's *The Complete T. rex*. Written specifically for amateurs to aid in properly treating and identifying dinosaur fossils is his *Dinosaurs under the Big Sky*.)

In 2010, Horner was interviewed about dinosaurs on CBS television's *60 Minutes*. In addition to authoring numerous articles in scientific journals, he has appeared in a host of documentaries and been the subject of many magazine and newspaper articles. Thus, a case could be made for saying he is one of the most famous or recognizable living scientists of any sort in the world today. Yes, the subject of dinosaurs is fascinating.

Reasons why dinosaurs are so popular are many, and not all may be fully open to analysis. They surely do speak to the mind's ability to conjure up scenes long past and populate them with creatures we could never see in any other way. Charles H. Sternberg, born in 1850, was one of the greatest of all fossil hunters, collecting prize specimens of dinosaurs, marine reptiles, and prehistoric mammals for several of the world's premier museums. He wrote, "It is thus that I love creatures of other ages . . . They are never dead to me; my imagination breathes life into 'the valley of dry bones,' and not only do the living forms of the animals stand before me, but the countries which they inhabited rise for me through the mists of the ages."

For children, the fascination may have something to do with the "monster" image of many of them, this combined with the fact that, being extinct, they are now safe to confront. For any and all, the puzzle of extinction also exerts an attraction; how could a group so successful for so long disappear?

For adults, interest in dinosaurs surely has much to do with new information about them that has emerged in the last twenty years. Approximately every six or eight weeks, a new dinosaur species is described and named; there are now more than a thousand. No longer is their image that of the painfully obsolescent, slow, cold-blooded, stupid, green tail-draggers in the swamp that were simply too outmoded to survive. That image is humorously portrayed in *The Far Side* cartoon by Gary Larson that shows a *Stegosaurus* standing at the podium during a dinosaur convention. Speaking gravely to his "dino" audience, he says, "The picture's pretty bleak, gentlemen . . . The world's climates are changing, the mammals are taking over, and we all have a brain about the size of a walnut!" In fact, dinosaurs dominated the world scene for at least 150 million years, indicating they were masters of survival. Active and dynamic creatures they were, and many of them, particularly the meat-eating "theropods," are likely to have been warm-blooded.

In 1964, John Ostrom and his crew from Yale University were working in the badlands of Montana when they struck paleontological gold. In the resulting scientific paper, he wrote, "Among the important discoveries made was that of the spectacular little carnivorous dinosaur described here—an animal so unusual in its adaptations that it undoubtedly will be the subject of great interest and debate for many years among students of organic evolution." It was *Deinonychus*—the name means "terrible claw"—a creature similar to Velociraptor, those fierce, if rather enlarged, killers portrayed in the kitchen-scene in *Jurassic Park*. Ostrom was right: the specimen ignited a wide-ranging debate on several aspects of dinosaur relationships, including that of their relationship to birds.

In addition to laying eggs and having three-toed feet, some dinosaurs had hollow bird-like bones. There is evidence that they had air-sacs, which, as in birds, extended from the lungs into much of the rest of the body and into some of the bones of the skeleton. Some even had clavicles (to become wishbones). Fossils of small dinosaurs found in China clearly show feathers, which may have been brightly colored. These are just a few of numerous characteristics shared with birds.

In fact, most paleontologists now regard the system of animal classification developed by Linnaeus, which served well for more than two hundred years, to be in need of revision, and they go so far as to say that recent discoveries strongly support the idea that birds *are* dinosaurs. If this is true, then we can say that at least some of the dinosaurs are still with us. In biologic nomenclature, *Aves* is the Class occupied by birds. Not only the scientific literature but now almost every new dinosaur book talks about "avian" dinosaurs (i.e. birds) and "non-avian" (traditional) dinosaurs. As an example, the popular book, *Discovering Dinosaurs in the American Museum of Natural History*, has a chapter entitled, "Why Did Non-Avian Dinosaurs Become Extinct?" Another chapter includes a photo of the world's smallest bird perched on a penny (and about the same size). Below is this caption: "The smallest dinosaur is the bee hummingbird, *Mellisuga helenae,* found only on Cuba."

Robert Bakker, as long ago as 1975, published a lengthy *Scientific American* article titled "Dinosaur Renaissance," in which he detailed several aspects of the anatomy of a number of prehistoric creatures and concluded with the statement, "The dinosaurs are not extinct. The colorful and successful diversity of the living birds is a continuing expression of basic dinosaur biology."

Therefore, when V-shaped flocks of Canadian geese are seen coursing through the skies in the month of March, some of us are prone to think, "The dinosaurs are migrating. Spring cannot be far behind."

The bird-dinosaur connection became vivid for me over the course of a recent springtime that found me making an 800-foot ascent in the foothills of a nearby mountain range. It is a climb upward through time. There, each step may span thousands of years of strata, in this case of marine shale and limestone that was laid down in the Jurassic Period some 150 million years ago. Oyster shells are exposed in the rocks and have weathered out in profusion. This was also the time, elsewhere, of *Archaeopterix,* the primitive bird with a bony tail, teeth set in sockets in its jaws, and claws on its wings. Now, millions of years after those ancient oceans left behind their telltale fossils, my path leads near a large ponderosa pine tree where a pair of golden eagles has built a huge nest. My heart is beating faster from carrying the needed equipment up the steep slope but also in anticipation of seeing the wild creature that, to me, holds a fascination above all others.

I enter the small portable blind, which had been staked down almost two months before and camouflaged with pine branches in order not to disturb the birds. In a few minutes, my equipment is in place: tripod, camera, and an extreme telephoto lens that magnifies approximately twenty-four times and enables detailed images of what would otherwise be indiscernible. Soon, an eagle chick in a white, downy covering perches on the edge of the nest. The chick has a large head and stubby wings and looks like—a dinosaur. (Many researchers now imagine the young of even the large meat-eating dinosaurs, such as *T. rex,* to have had downy feathers for insulation.)

Several weeks later, the bird has grown to be nearly as large as an adult eagle. The parents have fed it well. (On one occasion, I photograph it feeding upon half the carcass of a whitetail deer fawn that had been carried into the tree.) A small airplane passes overhead, and the young eagle's eyes follow it with intense interest, as if thinking, "You can *do* that?"

Now, with a full set of feathers, the dark brown raptor often faces the wind and flaps its wings, even rising a bit from that platform of sticks in the sky. Then comes the day when it works its way out onto the far end of the branches that support the nest. There, it flaps a bit more, then stands motionless, gazing far outward and beyond. Not quite ready yet to catapult into empty space, an awkward turn-around is executed, and it moves back to the safety of the only world it has ever known. That scene, repeated several times, was reminiscent of a youngster edging out on the diving board at the local swimming pool: hesitating, wondering whether to take that first plunge, wanting it, yet fearing it. The next day, when I came back, the young eagle was nowhere to be seen. The thin air would now be its home for much of its life. The dinosaur had flown. Paleontologists say birds are dinosaurs, and I believe it.

Among the pieces of information contributing to a renewed interest in the prehistoric world are some that we never thought could be obtained, such as the presence of a so-called "medullary" bone layer found in a *Tyrannosaurus rex* femur that confirms the beast's gender. Such bone, rich in calcium, is deposited in the skeletons of female birds (more connection) during the egg-laying cycle. So, it seems this *rex,* (first named "Bob" after Bob Harmon of the Museum of the Rockies, who found it) is really a female. The discovery was described by Mary Schweitzer, Horner, and others, in the journal *Science* in 2005. In that same year, they detailed still another remarkable find having to do with the same specimen. Following an acid-bath process to dissolve away hard, fossilized bone, some soft tissue remained behind: elastic, vessel-like material with cell-like structures within. This was a first-of-its-kind revelation, and the preservation astonished dinosaur researchers around the world. More work was done on the specimen in 2007, using mass spectrometry to find proteins, and they were found to be most closely linked to—you guessed it—birds. New techniques are leading to new discoveries.

Some phenomena are less subtle and the bones speak quite graphically, which is the case with a unique *Triceratops* dinosaur pelvis I excavated some years ago. It shows fifty-eight bite-marks made by the teeth of *Tyrannosaurus rex.* The specimen consists of one of the hip-bones plus the ten fused vertebrae in between the hips called the sacrum. The left hip-bone has had some 15 percent of it bitten off, and the other one is gone completely. Bite-marks of every size and description abound. In a sense, it is fossilized feeding activity of *Tyrannosaurus.* Based on this fossil, paleontologist Greg Erickson and I described such behavior in *The Journal of Vertebrate Paleontology* in 1996. The specimen has also been featured in a number of television documentaries, books, and magazines, and Erickson referred to it in a cover article in *Scientific*

American that sought to depict the lifestyle of this, one of the very largest of dinosaurian carnivores.

One bite-mark shows that a tooth entered at an angle, dragged backwards, making a long groove, then splintered off bone. Numerous other marks are of various depths. A *Tyrannosaurus* tooth can fit in many of the holes, leaving no doubt about the source. Sometimes, such teeth are compared to steak knives, but that is misleading; the teeth are not narrow, for slicing. Instead, they are round/oval in cross-section, and shaped something like bananas (and the same size!). They are robust and strong, designed for puncturing and tearing off huge hunks of meat and for breaking bone. Erickson further studied the specimen by having a hydraulic press constructed with metal "teeth" and, with it, duplicated such marks in modern bone. It seems that *T. rex* had a bite-force of at least 3,300 pounds, which is the largest of any known animal and is the equivalent of having the weight of a good-sized passenger car bearing down upon the teeth.

The information that can be gleaned about the behavior and physiology of an extinct creature, even across tens of millions of years, is quite amazing. The bones of the fearfully great reptiles can now speak in ways never previously imagined, something that is at least part of the explanation for why dinosaurs are striding so large across our culture today.

5

To Be a Naturalist

On Seeing

As long as I live, I'll hear waterfalls and birds and winds sing. I'll interpret the rocks, learn the language of flood, storm and the avalanche. I'll acquaint myself with the glaciers and wild gardens, and get as near as I can to the heart of the world.

John Muir

WHAT DOES IT MEAN to be a *naturalist*? Consider this definition: A naturalist is one who studies nature with the intent of greater understanding; who seeks to help or enhance, not harm, the world's natural processes, and who loves the natural world. So understood, the term can—and I would suggest, *should*—apply not merely to those who are professional naturalists but in a broad sense, also, to any and every human being.

The science that interests me most is paleontology, and I am drawn also to geology, ecology, and astronomy. In these endeavors, it must be said that I am an *amateur*. It was not always so, but it is now unusual for an individual to know more than a little about science and also about those things that were known before science came on the scene, because knowledge about our world has so largely become the province of specialists. The scientific approach has produced many results, unlocking aspects of the operations of nature that would never have opened to any other key; modern medicine is an obvious example, and there are

41

numerous others. However, in some arenas, it may not be excessive to say that specialization has been carried to such a length that the situation resembles people down in little grooves, making progress straight ahead, perhaps going a long way in that direction, but the grooves are so deep that they cannot see out of them to all the other grooves. There is the cliché that we "know more and more about less and less." Not only does the chemist not know what the physicist is doing but the organic chemist can barely talk to the colloid chemist and be understood, or so I'm told, unless they are talking about football and not about their main business.

The result is that we have all these bits and pieces, with few people concerned with connections or with anything like a larger picture, something called a worldview. We have become experts at taking things apart, and this down to smaller and smaller scale, but we are far less adept at putting the pieces back together to produce an integrated frame of reference for the whole. How many courses in business or technology exist for each course in the humanities? Much attention is paid to making a living but much less to making a life. The consequence of having many specialists and almost no generalists is a culture that lacks coherence, one with little in terms of shared outlooks and values and wherein millions struggle with questions of meaning and purpose. Is it possible that amateurs with a broad exposure would have anything to offer here?

The term amateur surely does often signify someone who knows only a little about a subject, who, for example, in the sciences, doesn't know a proton from a crouton. However, that need not be the case. It can refer, simply, to one who does something else to make a living. In the England of the 1800s, there was little education in the sciences; instead, the great institutions focused upon instructing young gentlemen in the classics: language, literature, and the like. However, natural history was pursued as an avocation by the majority of the English clergy, and there was hardly a study that did not have a cabinet containing a collection of local fossils. One chronicler of the history of science, Eiseley, writes, "It was the amateur who laid the foundations of the science today. The whole philosophy of modern biology was established by such a 'dabbler' as Charles Darwin, who never at any time held a professional position in the field." Of the amateur: "his was the sunrise of science, and it was a sunrise it becomes us ill to forget."

Darwin had some formal education in biology at Cambridge, but no degree in the subject. He was an amateur naturalist. After graduation, he was in line to enter a course of preparation for the clergy when, instead, he shipped out on the *Beagle*, being allowed to go along as the ship's "naturalist." William "Strata" Smith was a self-educated surveyor who, in 1801, produced the first geological map, this of the entire country of England! At the time, he was scorned by those in powerful positions, but he is now recognized as one of the founders of modern geology. The Austrian monk and amateur botanist Gregor Mendel worked out the basics of genetic inheritance with peas in his monastery garden. Jane Goodall headed for Gombe in central Africa without a college education, and her later work with chimpanzees would capture the attention of millions. Physics and mathematics were the avocations of the young Albert Einstein, who wrote his most important papers while he worked as a mere clerk in a Swiss patent office. "Never lose a holy curiosity," he said, and he didn't.

Examples could be multiplied, but consider the case of Joseph Wood Krutch. He was a renowned drama critic, who, for his very serious avocation, studied and wrote a great deal about the plant life of the desert southwest. About such interest, he said:

> This is an age of specialists, and I am by nature and as well by habit an amateur. This is a dangerous thing to confess, because specialists are likely to turn up their noses. "What you really mean is," they say, "a dilettante—a sort of dabbler of the arts and sciences. You may have a smattering of this or that, but you can't be a real authority on anything at all," and I am afraid they are at least partly right. But not long ago, my publisher asked me for a sentence or two to put on a book jacket which would explain what he called my "claim to fame." And the best I could come up with was this: I think I know more about plant life than any other drama critic and more about the theater than any botanist!

Isn't it rather grand that he could say that? In addition to highlighting the value of broad knowledge, it becomes still more meaningful if you know that he uses the word *amateur* in the original or root sense of "a lover." Our English word comes from the French, which in turn comes from the Latin, *amator*, "to love." That is, an amateur is one who does something, not as part of a salaried position and for the monetary reward, but because the activity itself *is* the reward. She or he is *in love* with the subject.

Jack Horner has long been a professional paleontologist and educator. He concludes his book *Dinosaur Lives* by referencing an earlier time: "On a more personal note, for many years I was an amateur collector. If certain aspects of my life had gone differently, I'd still be traipsing through the badlands of Montana searching for dinosaur fossils, motivated by nothing more than the desire to witness something I hadn't seen before—to be surprised—which, come to think of it, is the same thing that motivates me today."

An amateur in natural history, then, is not necessarily one with extremely limited knowledge; the main characteristic possessed is that of having a love for this wondrous world of nature, and love will lead to knowledge in one degree or another. Should we not grant that all of us are called to be amateurs in something, and should we not all have in common this interest in the wider world on which we depend for absolutely everything, including life itself? May we never lose that loving sensitivity to the planet we call home.

For it can be lost. A character in an H. G. Wells novel confessed, "There was a time when my little soul shone and was uplifted by the starry enigma of the sky. That has now disappeared. I go out and look at the stars now in the same way that I look at wallpaper."

Again, this definition: A naturalist is one who studies nature for the purpose of greater understanding; who seeks to help or enhance, not harm, the world's natural processes, and who loves the natural world. All of that hinges on a prior condition, i.e., that a naturalist has a *conscious* relationship with nature. In 1845, Thoreau wrote those wonderful words, "I went to the woods because I wished to live deliberately, to front only the essential facts of life, and see if I could not learn what it had to teach, and not, when I came to die, discover that I had not lived."

All human beings, in common with all other living things, are enmeshed, or embedded in the natural world, are utterly dependent upon the whole, and exist only as a part of it. Most of the time, we are oblivious to that. We are like the whaler in Herman Melville's *Moby Dick*, who "out of sight of land, furls his sails, and lays him down to rest, while under his very pillow rush herds of walruses and whales . . ."

Therefore, children have to be taught that bread is grain in another form, that milk doesn't come from bottles, that meat doesn't just appear in the refrigerator, and that behind the grocery store there is a complex and fertile world that brings all of these products into being. We live, most of the time, in controlled environments that make it all too easy for us to forget about the sustenance of what used to be called Mother Earth. In many parts of the world, the raw earth is now seldom underfoot. We have, in fact, become largely an asphalt animal, existing in environments that insulate us from *the* environment. For most of us, our waking and working hours are spent in buildings designed to shield us from all external factors. Encapsulated therein and bathed in artificial light, we are seldom conscious even of whether the world has rolled into darkness. The forces of nature are mollified by central heating and air conditioning so that we seldom experience even the weather, except as a minor inconvenience when a drizzle spoils the picnic or a snowfall moves us to shovel the sidewalk. Artificiality encompasses us to the extent that it is the *real* world no longer seems real.

None of us wants to go back to the cave, but any thinking person must surely grant that the comforts of modern life have had effects, not all of which are positive. We are the first people in history to live so thoughtless of the elemental forces that sustain us.

From time immemorial, the eternal rhythms of night and day have reminded people of their total dependence upon the source of heat and light. Each second, the sun burns some 637 million tons of hydrogen in the fusion reaction to create 632 million tons of helium and, in the process, floods space with radiant energy. It is the equivalent of a million ten-megaton hydrogen bombs exploding every second. It has raged thus for some 5 billion years, and it likely will do so for still another 5 billion years.

Ancient peoples, of course, had no idea of the details supplied by modern physics, but they knew that light was life. Therefore, most of them viewed the sun as a god and worshipped the golden orb in the heavens. As in the words of W.H. Auden, people of old saw all of nature as being full of meaning and message,

> And heard inside each mortal thing
> Its holy emanations sing.

Now, insulated and distanced from nature, we no longer hear it speaking, for music is nothing if the audience is deaf. In the Victorian novel *Middlemarch*, George Eliot described herself and all of us most of the time, when she wrote: "If we had a keen vision and feeling . . . it would be like hearing the grass grow and the squirrel's heart beat, and we should die of that roar which lies on the other side of silence. As it is, the quickest of us walk about well-padded with stupidity." In Picasso's great painting, *Guernica*, the sun in the heavens has been replaced by an electric bulb, and one suspects the message is not salutary.

Part of the problem is the frenetic pace of life for most of us in the Western world. The sculptor Rodin said that slowness is beauty. We have, judging from much evidence, another outlook. Signs shout, "Why Wait? Get It Now: Pay Only a Dollar Down! Cars Washed: Two Minutes." In our grocery stores, the old slow, three-minute oatmeal has gone farther back on the shelf, unable to compete with the itch for the instantaneous. It is hard to wait for anything to ripen on the vine. (The spirit is typified by a sign on a golf course: "Members will refrain from picking up lost balls until they have stopped rolling.") When we hurtle along in tight traffic four lanes wide, and do so daily, the universe is narrowed to the width of the road. The grand world of sky and land and sea is compressed between the ditches. Devouring "fast food" on the run, we seldom enjoy it. A wise man of India said, "You have the clock, and we have time."

Literature of the twentieth century gave brilliant commentary on the accelerating pace of modern life and its consequences. Ray Bradbury's novel about life in the future, *Fahrenheit 451*, points to a logical development: "Have you seen the two-hundred-foot-long billboards in the country beyond town? Did you know that once billboards were only twenty feet long? But cars started rushing by so quickly they had to stretch the advertising out so it would last."

In such an atmosphere, pressure is intense for work to consume more and more of our lives. How many of us live at the corner of Work & Worry? *Babbitt*, the 1922 novel by Sinclair Lewis, is a portrait of a harried and conformist social climber that is not, by any means, out of date:

> Men were hustling to catch trolleys, with another trolley a minute behind, and to leap from the trolleys, to gallop across the sidewalk, to hurl themselves into buildings, into hustling express elevators. Men in dairy lunches were hustling to gulp down the food which cooks had hustled to fry. Men in barber shops were snapping, "Jus' shave me once over. Gotta hustle." . . . Men who had made five thousand, year before last, and ten thousand last

year, were urging on nerve-yelping bodies and parched brains so that they might make twenty thousand this year; and the men who had broken down immediately after making their twenty thousand dollars were hustling to catch trains, to hustle through the vacations which the hustling doctors had ordered.

Adding to the pace is the noise. Ambrose Bierce gave us a brief dictionary definition: "Noise. n. A stench in the ear. The chief product and authenticating sign of civilization."

Still further, we are preoccupied with various individual or personal issues and problems, triumphs and defeats, obstacles and enjoyments. In order to deal with all these, the mind raises a wall between oneself and things beyond. Psychologically, we engage in a perpetual evasion of the here and now, screening, managing, and toning down our sensory impressions, lest we be shocked or disarmed by them. We evade living on the surface of our skins, where we would more immediately encounter the things that are. So it is that to truly notice our surroundings is rare. John Ruskin, the English writer of the nineteenth century, affirmed, "The greatest thing a human soul ever does in this world is to *see* something and tell what he *saw* in a plain way. Hundreds of people can talk for one who can think, and thousands can think for one who can see. To see clearly is poetry, prophecy, and religion all in one."

Impressionist art seeks to portray this more immediate world given to us by the senses before the mind breaks it up and reorganizes it according to its preconceptions. Lisel Mueller, in her poem "Monet Refuses the Operation," imagines the artist responding to his optometrist, who wants to "correct" his vision to be in line merely with the flat surface of things shown by a camera:

> Doctor, you say there are no haloes
> around the streetlights in Paris
> and that what I see is an aberration
> caused by old age, an affliction.
> I tell you, it has taken me all my life
> to attain the vision of gas lamps as angels,
> to soften and blur and finally banish
> the edges you regret I don't see,
> to learn that the line I call the horizon
> does not exist and sky and water,
> so long apart, are the same state of being.
> Fifty-four years before I could see

Rouen cathedral is built
of parallel shafts of sun,
and now you want to restore
my youthful errors: fixed
notions of top and bottom,
the illusion of three-dimensional space
wisteria separate
from the bridge it covers.
What can I say to convince you
the Houses of Parliament dissolve
night after night to become
the fluid dreams of the Thames?
I will not return to a universe
of objects that don't know each other.

Thus, distracted by the pace, clutter, and din of a congested society, as well as by our own individual preoccupations, the primal world is, for us, opaque and mute. In such a culture, to relate with any sensitivity to nature does not come naturally; rather, one must put forth a conscious, deliberate effort to be aware of the wider world beyond our utilitarian purposes.

In the process, however, anyone who observes the world of nature also must struggle against the compulsion to label and categorize. It is more than easy to think that such lists and logs represent understanding. Instead, mere identities penned and collated distract us from, say, the grace of the hawk on the wing or the heron's arrowed thrust.

Imposing our own framework on the natural world hinders seeing what is there, such as when people "see" things in the clouds or in rock formations. The bedrock, the foundation of the world, protrudes. We observe it, climb it, mine it, but, sooner or later, we must use words, and we often do so to make the unfamiliar overly familiar. A sandstone cliff becomes a face in profile or a rocky spire a "castle," a horizon is entitled "the Sleeping Giant." Think of the Grand Tetons of Wyoming, which were named by mountain men. (There is consensus that they had definitely been in the woods too long.)

Go on a tour through a cavern filled with limestone forms built by the slow accretion of minerals in the trickle of water. The well-intentioned guide will point to the stalagmites and stalactites with a well-rehearsed monologue on how they resemble cartoon characters. Cheap chatter fills the silence between the glistening forms, as though we should not be allowed to be uneasy when confronted by such mystery. In the words of geologist David Leveson, "The guide's patter can only be distracting—but perhaps it is meant to be, for we have lost our sense of the religious, the numinous. Somehow we never let ourselves get beyond being uncomfortable when faced with the mysterious or powerful—we giggle nervously and try to reduce it to the mundane." Some message other than the one prepared for us in advance may reach us, a message from the earth itself.

We can be insulated from that message also by our relative afflu-ence. Ordinary people in the western world are wealthy beyond what most in former ages could even begin to imagine. It need not be the case, but this fact alone so often shields us from beholding nature. The old rhyme has it that "The world is so full of a number of things / I'm sure we should all be happy as kings." The trouble with that statement is that kings have never been known for their happiness, and mere power or control over things has never guaranteed it. In 1689, King Louis XIV of France ordered for his garden at Versailles, among many other items, 83,000 narcissus and 87,000 tulips to go with his 1200 fountains. We may make, if not the *same* mistake, at least the same *kind* of mistake with other things, using material goods as a way to measure our supposed status. Not many are of the mind of Socrates, who, by tradition, while strolling in the marketplace of ancient Athens, threw up his hands and exclaimed, "O, gods, who would have dreamed there are so many things I do *not* want!" Yes, who really needs so many of the things we buy? In the assessment by J. W. Krutch, the desire to be envied is almost surely what King Louis had in mind: "'It will be evident to all,' so he said to himself, 'that no one else in all the world can have as many tulips as I can, and they will envy me—though God knows, the whole eighty-seven thousand of them look dull enough to me!'"

We easily become jaded by more than we need. Shakespeare, in *King Henry IV,* described the syndrome in relation to the public seeing too much of Richard II, but it has a wider application, does it not?

> They surfeited with honey and began
> To loathe the taste of sweetness, whereof a little
> More than a little is by much too much.

In addition, in a culture of abundance, the perfectionist mentality lies close at hand. I recall a concert performed by a large city's symphony orchestra. It was a marvelous program of several pieces of classical music of great difficulty, and it was performed almost flawlessly. I say "almost" because midway through the clarinet solo of Brahms's First Symphony the reed in the instrument stuck, and the result was a sour note. After that, the soloist and the rest of the orchestra went on to play expertly for more than two hours. Following the concert, my wife and I went out looking for a place for dinner; almost every restaurant was filled with people who had been at the same event. It was interesting—amazing, really—that most of the overheard conversations were not about the superb renditions of the score and of how, with precision, timing and true finesse, several dozen men and women had produced for our enjoyment some of the world's greatest music. Instead, out of the hundreds of thousands or millions of notes, that which captured people's attention was the single one that was slightly "off." The object of one's focus does make a difference.

Something similar happens to many of the affluent millions who live in the suburbs and who take to the road to "experience nature," led to do so by the advertising that presents the land as a commodity, a package providing entertainment. Many of the 3 million people who visit Yellowstone National Parking Lot each year are disillusioned. Nature, as visualized on glossy and oversaturated photos on calendars, cannot live up to expectations. Barry Lopez summed it up: "People only able to venture into the countryside on annual vacations are, increasingly, schooled in the belief that wild land will, and should, provide thrills and exceptional scenery on a timely basis. If it does not, something is wrong, either with the land itself or possibly with the company outfitting the trip."

When you travel on a train, you can sometimes watch small children peering out the windows and saying, "Look, Mom, a cow! Look, Mom, a horse!" Parents are often tempted to apologize for that attitude, as did one by saying to the other passengers, "You know, she still thinks everything is wonderful." Well, not everything is wonderful, but many things are.

There was a person who was tired of living in the same place for many years and decided to move. She wrote an advertisement to put her house up for sale, in the process listing its attributes. She described its convenient features, a great location, the view, and so forth. When the newspaper came out, she read the ad and decided that it described a place as good as any she could ever imagine, and she cancelled it. All it took was a fresh pair of eyes, something that surely holds in relationship to the wider world around us.

If we can simply perceive things for what they are, even the most ordinary part of the world is far from ordinary. Ronald Reagan said, quite famously, "When you've seen one redwood, you've seen them all." We can give thanks that he did not speak for everyone. Elizabeth Barrett Browning writes, "Earth's crammed with heaven, and every common bush afire with God. But only he who sees takes off his shoes." Emerson, in his essay on art: "Though we travel the world over to find the beautiful, we must carry it with us, or we find it not."

In, with, and under the ordinary is the extraordinary. There is an entire literature of mystical experience that speaks of a deeper perception called *enlightenment*. Annie Dillard, in *Pilgrim at Tinker Creek*, says that "although it comes to those who wait for it, it is always . . . a gift and a total surprise." She described an experience thus:

> I saw the backyard cedar where the mourning doves roost charged and transfigured, each cell buzzing with flame . . . The flood of fire abated, but I'm still spending the power. Gradually the lights went out in the cedar, the colors died, the cells unflamed and disappeared. I was still ringing. I had been my whole life a bell, and never knew it until at that moment I was lifted and struck. I have only very rarely seen the tree with the lights in it. The vision comes and goes, mostly goes, but I live for it, for the moment when the mountains open and a new light roars in spate through the crack, and the mountains slam.

Insight varies: between people and, from time to time, for all of us. Robert Bateman is considered one of the world's greatest wildlife artists. He tells of how, as a teenager in the 1940s, he sat down one spring morning in a thicket of wild plums, his senses saturated with fragrance, and let the birds come to him. First, quiet. Then, there was the buzzing of insects. Then, there was what he calls a symphony of songs from yellow warblers, catbirds, and chipping sparrows. Then, a ruby-throated hummingbird vroomed in from nowhere and hung in the air in front of his face. Bateman says, "At that moment, the glowing cup of life was filled to the brim and overflowing. I have been very lucky in my life, in my travels and my adventures in nature, but I have never surpassed the special glow of that morning in May." A simple event it was, but it played to a receptive heart. It happened in a small slice of time to one who was paying attention.

Michelangelo, who said that he lived and loved in God's peculiar light, was the genius sculptor who was often able to see great possibilities in raw materials that had been overlooked by other artists. Many pieces of rock lay abandoned in local quarries due to some peculiar grain or other aspect, but he would take these back to his studio and use precisely those same qualities to capture in stone a unique shape that existed in his mind. This he did with a battered block of marble that had been disfigured by another sculptor forty years before, and, out of it, he made the colossal *David*. We now owe to his unique vision what the world counts as some of the very greatest works of art.

Most people know of the paintings of Andrew Wyeth, which are not colorful; instead, they are presented in drab tones of grays and muted browns. The subject matter, too, is unspectacular: a common tree, the wall of a farmhouse, a doorway and lantern, a curtain in a window, a bleak Pennsylvania hill. These portrayals of ordinary things, which usually go unnoticed, evoke in us the awareness that, in fact, they are filled with beauty and dignity. Looking at these canvases, we find ourselves moved to a deeper appreciation and we may think of similar things, "Why did I not see that before?" We are reminded that, while sight is a faculty, seeing is an art.

John Muir was another who deliberately, consciously cultivated that art in relationship to nature. He became the early twentieth century's most ardent spokesperson for conservation and was instrumental in the establishment of Yosemite National Park. (President Theodore Roosevelt spent several days with him in the area of the giant sequoias, calling the last "the best day of my life!" They slept in the open on evergreen boughs, and Roosevelt later wrote of "the enormous cinnamon-colored trunks rising above us like the columns of a vaster and more beautiful cathedral than was ever conceived by any human architect".)

As an example of Muir's desire to see, to know, and to truly experience the natural world, he once climbed a hundred feet up to the top of a Douglas fir tree, this in the midst of a storm. He relates the event, saying,

> Never before did I enjoy so noble an exhilaration of motion . . .
> bending and swirling backward and forward, round and round,
> tracing indescribable combinations of vertical and horizontal
> curves, while I clung with muscles firm braced, like a bobolink

on a reed . . . The storm tones died away, and turning toward the east, I beheld the countless hosts of the forest hushed and tranquil, towering above one another on the slopes of the hills like a devout audience. The setting sun filled them with amber light and seemed to say, while they listened, 'My peace I give to you.' As I gazed on the impressive scene, all the so-called ruin of the storm was forgotten, and never before did those noble woods appear so fresh, so joyous, so immortal.

Each and every day is filled with wonders. Consider the sorts of things that are happening all the time. Perhaps now, all at once, while you are reading this fleeting line of thought, a tree falls to the ground in the Adirondacks, an osprey catches a fish on the coast of British Columbia, a baby born to a woman in a grass-roofed hut in Zambia gives its first cry, as a bee lands on a flower in Mexico and a rocky cliff high in the Alps gives way. These, and uncountable billions of other events are happening every instant, and on and on, and at no time are they ever the same. Every moment, everything, all the time, is *unique*. In fact, strangely, to be unique is the most common thing in the world, causing many of us to think that God must love diversity in all its many forms.

The Psalmist wrote, "This is the day that the Lord has made; let us rejoice and be glad in it." The poet E. E. Cummings (who wrote in lower case and without most punctuation marks) had similar thoughts, which he expressed in the following manner:

> I thank You God for this most amazing
> day: for the leaping greenly spirits of trees
> and a blue true dream of sky; and for everything
> which is natural which is infinite which is yes
> . . . (now the ears of my ears awake and
> now the eyes of my eyes are opened)

6

Things Change

If by some fiat I had to restrict all this writing to one sentence, this is the one I would choose: The summit of Mount Everest is marine limestone.

John McPhee

IT IS AMAZING, BUT true. In the grasslands of central Montana, one walks on the surface of a portion of the planet now elevated about four thousand feet above sea level, yet evidence abounds that you are walking on what was once the bottom of the sea.

In the foothills of small mountain ranges in the area, deep strata of sedimentary rock have been thrust up at an angle. From such layers, curious objects have been eroding continually and litter the scene. Black and smooth, they resemble nothing so much as large-caliber bullets, two to four inches in length. They are, instead, the "pens" or hard parts of ancient squids, the fossils known by the scientific name *Belemnites*. Squids are found in huge schools in the oceans today, and the form of living things with tentacles goes back to the dim past. The ones I find on the rain-washed slopes are from creatures that filled the seas in the Jurassic Period, when the largest of dinosaurs dominated the land some 150 million years ago.

The seas came and went, and came again several times. The surface of the prairies of the region, away from the mountains and just beneath the thin skin of sod and grass, is composed of younger marine shale formations of the Cretaceous Period. Here, "younger" means 75 million years in age. On lands to the east and west, the last of the dinosaurs were flourishing, but in the central seaway that went through the heart of the continent were all manner of ocean creatures. This we know because strictly marine fossils are there in abundance, eroding out of fields and hillsides, ditches and gullies. Many are contained in so-called concretions, roundish limestone rocks a few inches to a foot or two in diameter.

I kneel beside one such rock and place the point of a chisel against it, hitting it soundly with a hammer. A crack opens and another blow splits the rock into two pieces. Lifting the top, a gem is exposed: the coiled and lustrous shell of an *ammonite*, virtually unchanged from when it settled to the bottom of the sea all those ages ago. These were highly evolved cephalopods—the word means "head-foot"—related to the octopus. Today, the octopus lacks a shell, but its ancient relatives, the ammonites, developed complex shells composed of many hollow chambers. Literally thousands of species have been found around the world, and they are often used as indexes in helping to date the various formations in which they occur.

We get an idea of what these creatures were like from a closely related one that survives today in the Indian Ocean as a kind of "living fossil," the chambered nautilus. A cutaway of its shell showing the geometric spiral within has long been used as a paragon of beauty in the natural world, as well as an example in mathematics of a pure "equiangled spiral," wherein a line from the very center to any point on the expanding shell will always intersect at exactly the same angle. Oliver Wendell Holmes imaged the nautilus in a poem that compares our mental and spiritual development to the expanding shell in which the tentacled animal lived; as the creature moved forward and sealed compartments behind it as it grew, each of those was larger than the one before:

> Build thee more stately mansions, O my soul,
> As the swift seasons roll!
> Leave thy low-vaulted past!
> Let each new temple shut thee from heaven with a dome more vast,
> Till thou at length art free,
> Leaving thine outgrown shell by life's unresting sea!

The shells of the ammonite are composed of many layers. Light refracting through them produces an iridescent effect of pinks, blues, and greens, and the shells are highly prized by collectors. The once-hollow chambers have usually been filled with silt that has turned to stone, but, when cross-sectioned, some of the fossils are revealed to have the chambers filled with gem-like minerals and crystals. Ammonite shells have been found in the graves of Stone Age peoples. It was the Ancient Egyptian god Ammon, symbolized by the coiled ram's horns, that inspired the name of the fossil.

There were variations on the theme. Some, of the genus *Baculites,* instead of fashioning a coiled shell, produced long, straight ones. In some areas, they are found in large numbers, being among the most abundant fossils in the Great Plains. Native American peoples took special notice of broken pieces of these shells, which fractured along the wavy lines of the chambers' divisions, since this resulted in a section of the shell that, in profile, vaguely resembled a buffalo. The stony image was used in amulets and medicine bundles to do homage to the animal that sustained the prairie tribes for untold generations. Thus, a sea of quite another kind was linked with the sea of grass over which moved the great herds.

Today, tractors plow the sea-bottom. Foundations for houses are dug in the ocean silt. We build cities, drive, walk, and do commerce without a thought to the fact that we are like deep-sea divers, living and moving on the now dried-out floor of a once-watery realm that lasted millions of years. In the words of Tennyson:

> There rolls the deep where grew the tree.
> O earth, what changes hast thou seen!
> There where the long street roars, hath been
> The stillness of the central sea.

The ancient sea had creatures related to those that still swim in our oceans today. I walk through an area of eroding stream channels and pause to pick up a small remnant from those days: a shark's tooth. Several more are strewn about here and there. I locate the source, which is a one-inch band of sandy sediment just two feet wide, somewhat darker in color than its surroundings, and likely representing a small pocket or low spot on the seafloor into which the waves concentrated loose debris. Carefully digging out the pocket with my hunting knife reveals more teeth. I take from my pack a fine screen and sift the sand through it, revealing teeth of four or five types of sharks. The largest measures an inch, representing a shark some eight or ten feet in length;

this is about the size of the ones we usually see swimming around on the television screen.

The sand that will not go through the screen is "concentrate" and is taken home for closer examination. (Later, our two daughters would spend many enjoyable hours peering into a low power microscope and sorting through the debris with dental picks and tweezers in order to find the ancient marine fossils, and each tiny tooth was a discovery, for them, equal to that of a new planet.) On following trips to the site, other such zones would be located and several thousand teeth collected. In all, the teeth of more than twenty kinds of sharks, sawfish, and rays would be found, most of them new to science. (The specialist who wrote up the descriptions in a scientific paper designated one of them as *Cretorectolobus olsoni*, which is how you Latinize a Scandinavian name.)

In addition to the sharks, there are indications of other predators, including the large marine reptiles. At the top of the food chain was the *mosasaur*, a huge lizard perfectly adapted to life in the sea. Resembling a crocodile in form but with limbs modified into slim steering organs, its long tail sculled from side to side to propel it forward. Some were twenty feet in length, some were thirty, and the largest was forty. Attacking in a rush, the mosasaur would have been a ferocious opponent. Its diet must have included fish, sharks, turtles, other reptiles, and ammonites, since shells are sometimes found showing puncture marks that match the mosasaur's sharp teeth. Fossils of the mosasaur have been found around the world, including hundreds of skulls, many of these in the badlands of western Kansas. Over the course of 15 million years, they proliferated into numerous species, only to die out with the dinosaurs.

A mile or so away, I come upon another eroded area. A few shark teeth are bleaching in the sun, but that's not all. Also visible are a few scattered vertebrae from the other large marine reptile of the times, the *plesiosaur* (sometimes called "swan lizards" in the old books, an allusion to the extremely long and slender neck). Once again, there were several types, but the very largest ones could be forty feet long and their necks had the most vertebrae of any known animal, more than seventy! Rather famous from its association in the popular media with the supposed Loch Ness monster, plesiosaur remains are much rarer than that of the mosasaur. In fact, while isolated skeletal elements are found in eroded landscapes, only a dozen complete skulls of the extremely long-necked varieties are known worldwide.

Protruding from a small ravine is a plesiosaur humerus, or upper arm bone, that is fractured into several pieces. This means that, as is often the case, a plaster jacket will be needed in order to remove and transport it without causing further damage. There is, however, a problem. Between the plaster and the bone, something is required to function as a separator, such as tin-foil, paper, or fabric, in order that the protective plaster will not stick to the fossil itself. Somehow, none of those items were included in my pack for this hike, but instead, are back in the truck a couple of miles distant. All is not lost, however, for under my blue jeans are a pair of shorts that, if necessary, I can get along without for a day. And, I conclude, it is necessary. So, I tear them up, use them in the plaster jacket, and they work just fine. Sometimes, in the pursuit of fossils in the West, "a man's gotta do what a man's gotta do."

A few yards away are a couple of plesiosaur vertebrae showing on the edge of a small drainage. Digging with my pick and knife exposes more of them linked together. After a time, ribs appear and, off to the side of the rib cage, one of the oar-like paddles composed of numerous hourglass-shaped finger bones. I brush the last fine layer of dirt off the ribs and see beneath them a pile of several dozen shiny black stones, unlike any found naturally in this region. They are *gastroliths* or "stomach stones" that were ingested by the animal to serve as a kind of grinder to aid in processing its food, and, perhaps, as a kind of ballast to help it dive to deeper levels. Some dinosaurs, also, had gastroliths, and many modern birds swallow tiny stones to aid in digestion.

With more digging, the vertebrae keep going, grading into the neck. However, after a dozen more, they end. Many years later, I would find a complete plesiosaur skull, but not on this day. The skeleton had come apart before burial and there is evidence of scavenging by sharks, so no more of it is found.

It is now late afternoon and several hours having passed since this process began. I lean against the coolness of the dirt bank, contemplating the future logistics of removing the specimen. The August sun beats down, heat waves blur the hazy blue-toned mountains in the distance, and all is still. At that moment, the air is split by a sonic boom! A delta-winged jet fighter roars overhead, out on a training exercise from the Air Force base ninety miles away and making practice runs over these remote badlands. I look up at that steel bird, paramount symbol of modern technology, as it hurtles through space. I gaze down at the remains of the prehistoric creature so unlike anything alive today, and it is as if the time separating the two—750,000 centuries—has been spanned in an instant. Unimaginable transformations have occurred since the plesiosaur oared its way through the waves. Continents have separated, mountain ranges have risen and been worn away, oceans have come and gone, and tens of millions of species have disappeared, only to be replaced by tens of millions of others, including ourselves. When a similar span of time will have passed again, what will the earth be like? Surely, everything we know and can imagine will have also passed away. In such a future age, will some creatures of high intelligence discover ocean liners, their vacant portals staring at the sky, eroding out of the then uplifted strata of our seafloors like immense index fossils for the Age of Humanity?

The easternmost boundary of the marine interior edged as far as Minnesota. The open pit mines in the Iron Range of the northern part of the state cut through strata dating from this time, and this overburden was put in spoil piles so the deeper iron-bearing rock could be reached. In those piles are marine fossils of the Cretaceous Period.

Farther south, and not far from where I grew up, are marine sites of quite a different sort. In exposures of granite bedrock at the surface, and in a few granite quarries, clues to the vanished sea can be found. There are, of course, no fossils in the granite itself; it represents once-molten rock of the earth's crust that has cooled gradually at great depths. However, once the bedrock was exposed at the surface, cracks and fissures a few inches wide developed, and, as the Cretaceous Sea encroached upon the land, shale was laid down, shale that included marine fossils. Most of the sediments of this age have either been scraped away by the glaciers or buried by a layer of glacial till. However, in the few exposures of granite still at the surface, sediments trapped in those fissures are preserved. Therein, the silt, sand, and water-worn gravel of an ancient beach tell of an environment that likely represented offshore islands. In those crevices in the granite are pieces of wood, again indicating a near-shore situation. There are worn plesiosaur bones and teeth, abraded from having been pounded in the surf. There are fish bones and scales and there are shark teeth—lots of shark teeth.

Some of the teeth are the sharp, pointed ones similar to those of today's mako sharks. A variety of sizes are found, but those of one species measure two inches, which calls to mind a shark of at least eighteen feet in length and weighing three thousand pounds, comparable to the largest great white sharks in the oceans of today. Other teeth are blunt and grooved; multiple rows of them existed as a solid pavement in the mouth of rays that crushed clams for a living.

Waters lapping on rocky islands in a subtropical climate, the seas filled with fish, long-necked plesiosaurs, and sharks—it is difficult to imagine a setting of greater contrast to the heavily settled farmland of today. Time moved on, and, over time, things changed.

A brief work by Byrd Baylor is entitled *If You Are a Hunter of Fossils*. In it, she describes the West Texas hill country, where the rocky outcrops there also were once the bottom of that same long-vanished sea. From a high vantage point, she takes note of a windmill and a pickup truck down below, but those have an air of unreality about them:

> Up here, what's *real* is the shallow warm Cretaceous sea and all these seashells knew. On this mountain, every rock still holds the memory of that time. When you are here, you hold it, too. The ocean's salt is in your blood. Its lime is in your bones. Its waves rise slow and green around you and you feel the pull of the tides. It never seems to be *now*. Here, time flows back and forth so easily that any day can be wrapped up inside some other day that came and went a hundred million years ago.

For most people, shark teeth have a certain mystique about them, no doubt having to do with sharks' reputation as fearsome predators. None was more fearsome than the largest of them all, *Carcharocles megalodon,* sometimes called the megashark. Known from its huge fossil teeth found in coastal deposits worldwide, it lived within the last 20 million years, only to die out perhaps 2 million years ago (even though monster movies try to convince us that there may still be some out there). A monster it was. The movie *Jaws* revolved around an exaggerated great white that was twenty-five feet long and had teeth of three inches. Numerous serrated *megalodon* teeth of five to six inches have been found, and the record is more than seven. That translates into a shark sixty feet long, as large as a sperm whale, as big around as a school bus, and weighing something like 100,000 pounds. Among the very largest carnivores ever, it very likely specialized in hunting and scavenging whales.

The fossilized teeth are found on coastlines from California to Maryland, in phosphate mines in Florida, and scuba divers find them by touch in the murky bottoms of some of the large rivers near the coasts of Georgia and the Carolinas. They are found in Mexico, Peru, Chile,

Argentina, France, the Netherlands, Italy, the island of Malta, Australia, and have even been located at the edge of Antarctica. Clearly, these giants were abundant, and our modern seas are quite different without them; no doubt, their absence allows us to be a bit more comfortable on the water, knowing we need not look over our shoulders for this, one of the largest predators of all time.

In the depths of a mountain cave, I was looking for another predator, of which one does not expect to find even a trace in this part of the world: a lion. Today, the lion, *Panthera leo*, is confined to Africa (except for one small remnant of a previous population in India). However, as recently as biblical times, there were lions in the Holy Land. "The wolf shall dwell with the lamb, and the leopard shall lie down with the kid, and the calf and the lion and the fatling together, and a little child shall lead them." (Isa 11:6) There are ninety references to the lion in the Bible. In Mesopotamia, the lion appears often in relief carvings in the palaces of ancient Persia, as at Susa and Persepolis, and the kings hunted them with chariot and spear. There are many references to lions in the Greek epics of Homer and its bones have been found at Troy.

It is thought that it was about 700,000 years ago that the lion expanded out of Africa, beginning a truly extensive migration. Ice Age paintings in the caves of France and Spain show lions among the reindeer, horses, wooly mammoths, and rhinos. With more water being locked up in the continental glaciers, the oceans were perhaps three hundred feet lower than today, so the lion was able to reach England. In addition, where the Aleutian Islands are now, between Siberia and Alaska, stretched the thousand-mile wide land bridge known as Beringia. Mammoths and bison came over it to join the saber-toothed cats that are so dramatically preserved in the La Brea Tar Pits in the heart of what is now Los Angeles. With them also came the lions, of which nearly a hundred have been found at La Brea. Conditions of exceptional preservation, such as that, are exceedingly rare. Still, there is abundant evidence of lions in the permafrost of Alaska, so it must have been common there, and its known range extended even to Peru. Thus, by 10,000 years ago, when they died out along with most of the larger Ice Age mammals, lions had existed on every continent except Antarctica and Australia. As scientists studying the Pleistocene Epoch tell us, "At the peak of its success, the lion ranged from Africa through Eurasia and North America into South America and appears to have been the most wide-ranging wild animal of all time." No single species, other than man, with his rats and domestic animals, has occupied so wide a territory nor proved so adaptable, finding a home from the verdant grasslands and lush jungles of Africa to the bleak tundra on the other side of the world. The title of King of Beasts has been rightly bestowed.

One of the few environments conducive to preserving remains of creatures that do not frequent the water is that of the cave. Lion bones have been found in goodly numbers in the caves of Northern Europe, where the cold-adapted subspecies was even larger than the African variety. A sinkhole in Wyoming has produced lion, as well as a cheetah, again, larger than today's. So-called Jaguar Cave in Idaho also had a lion. However, such finds in the contiguous United States are fragmentary and rare, indeed. Thus, when I heard of some unidentified bones found by a spelunker in a mountain cave here in Montana, "I was all ears."

Following up on such reports most often leads nowhere, but this was different. On the table in front of me were several pieces of the front portion of a white skull, including both of the large canine teeth, as well as most of a lower jaw, complete with teeth. Decades ago, the man who had found them was a teenager. He and others had been exploring the cave and, squeezing through a narrow passageway, he found himself crawling over a skeleton; he picked up these fragments and had never returned since. I borrowed the specimen and located a complete skull of a modern African lion, with which to make comparisons. Placing them side by side, there was no doubt: we had lions in Montana.

Could more of the specimen be found after all these years? Three of us, including the discoverer, obtained permission from the landowner and crawled through a small opening in the wall of a limestone cliff. It quickly opened up into a large room, and almost as quickly, all illumination from the outside world was gone. Going into such a place, as much as several hundred yards back into the mountain, was not something I took lightly. In fact, I carried almost every light known: a headlamp, a gas lantern, a large battery lantern, a sizeable flashlight, and a small one—plus matches. All that was missing was a torch of the kind the peasants used in storming the castle of Dr. Frankenstein.

Turning out the lights produced an inky darkness unlike any other. It could be day or night outside, no matter what, but it is perpetual night in there, like the far side of the moon. Thousands of years ago, the ambient temperature had settled in at fifty degrees. We could see our breath in the air of 100 percent humidity, and a film of wet dust covered every rock, making the going slippery and treacherous. The passageway wound and turned, going in and down, widening now and again into large caverns. We clambered over huge blocks and boulders, some of them the size of railroad boxcars, which had fallen from the cave's ceiling. Most of them had likely been jarred loose in earthquakes that have rocked the region over time. If one should occur now . . .

Still farther in we went, climbing up and down, around, and among the rock debris to find a path. Alone, if one had a single light and would slip and fall, to break either a leg or a bulb, the chances of finding the way out of the labyrinth would be nil.

Something like that must have been the situation of the lion. It had been drawn to explore the depths, but had gone too far into the utter blackness for even its keen senses to be able to locate the route to the surface. Perhaps, after searching for a way out for days, finally dehydrated and exhausted, it lay down in that narrow space to sleep in the endless night. Curiosity had indeed killed the cat.

After seven hours of our searching for the rest of its bones, nothing more turned up. Was that first discovery simply too long ago for the finder to remember the shadowy landmarks? Had other cave explorers found the skeleton and carried it off, not realizing what they had? Or, had the site been buried by one of those numerous rock-falls? In any case, it was a relief when we finally climbed out again into the light of day, realizing, in a more profound way than ever before, how much we take it for granted.

In spite of our finding nothing more, just the fragments of the skull are significant and remind us, as do so many fossils, of how greatly the tree of life has been transformed over time. Heraclitus of ancient Greece said that no one can step into the same river twice. We have all seen the videos of lions chasing and bringing down zebra, wildebeest, and Cape buffalo on the African savannahs. It seems odd to think of them attacking, instead, bison, white-tail deer, and elk on our western plains and in the Rocky Mountains. Yet, this is the scene that must have been enacted countless times.

And, now, the lions are gone, at least from our part of the world, just as the ammonites, giant sharks, and marine reptiles are gone from the entire planet. Things change.

7

The Big Picture

If the stars would appear one night in a thousand years, how men would believe and adore and preserve for many generations the remembrance of the city of God they had been shown.

Ralph Waldo Emerson

A PHOTOGRAPH OF NORTH America taken at night from a satellite reveals the continent to be ablaze with light. Only in the western interior of the U.S. is there anything like darkness. The eastern seaboard is lit up from New York to Miami, and it is not difficult to imagine the predictions of a future that includes one continuous city between those points. Even in small towns, the streetlights obscure the stars and create the illusion that our little part of the world is most of what exists. You have to drive out into the countryside, away from the lights of our own creation, to see the lights of the cosmos, the lights our ancestors saw every night of their lives over almost all of human history. From the entrance to their cave shelters, after the fires had died, they gazed upwards at the stars and planets that tracked across the sky from dusk until dawn, and wondered.

I drive for five or six miles outside of town to a little-used road and stop the car. The Milky Way stretches from one horizon to the other, a vast river of stars. It's an edge-on view of the galaxy, a view from within. The hub or center is where sky meets the mountains to the south. From there, the trailing arms wind around and under the earth into the opposite sky, lost there in the daylight of the other side of the world. At night, the galaxy is lost in the glare of the streetlights in town, also; however, out here, it shines in all of its glittering splendor. I always spend a few minutes simply standing beneath it all, without binoculars, telescope, and maps, the way people have everywhere for countless generations. Walt Whitman knew:

> When I heard the learned astronomer,
> When the proofs, the figures, were ranged in columns before me,
> When I was shown the charts and diagrams, to add, divide, and measure them,
> When I sitting heard the astronomer where he lectured with much applause in the lecture-room,
> How soon unaccountable I became tired and sick,
> Till rising and gliding out I wander'd off by myself,
> In the mystical moist night-air, and from time to time,
> Look'd up in perfect silence at the stars.

A meteor streaks across the sky. Blazing into the atmosphere at speeds of over forty miles per second, the tiny bit of cosmic rock announces its presence in a dramatic burn that takes only a second or so. Afterwards, its dust and ashes will settle out to mingle with the crust of our planet. It is estimated that more than a hundred tons of meteoritic dust are added to the earth each day by such hail on the roof of the world. It means that at least some of what the farmer plows is "stardust."

It takes about thirty minutes to set up the telescope, which is equipped with a mirror that will gather more than 800 times the light than can my unaided eye. That light is focused to one tiny spot, and eyepieces of different powers are then used to magnify the image and reveal what is otherwise unseen. The trickiest parts are getting the tripod base level and then aligning the scope with the celestial pole. Were an axle run through the rotating earth from pole to pole, one end would point very near to the so-called North Star, i.e. Polaris, which is the end-star in the Little Dipper. A camera's wide-angle lens trained on this spot and left on time exposure for only fifteen minutes shows star trails making arcs around that point, thus tracing the rotation of the earth.

With the scope aligned parallel to the earth's axis, I plug it in to a portable power source that feeds the clock-drive, this in order to slowly rotate the base of the telescope to compensate for the rotation of the earth and to keep the object observed from drifting out of sight.

Centering the scope on a star, I refine the focus, and then, as usual, cannot resist pulling the plug to the power source. The star begins to drift, and, in just a couple of minutes, has passed completely out of my field of view. It's a way to sense the rotation of planet earth. Disconnecting the power is like letting out the clutch, and, with the right effort, one can almost feel the dynamo of the earth begin to spin. At this latitude, such planetary motion is carrying me toward the eastern horizon at speeds of something like 800 miles per hour, almost causing me to lean a bit into that trajectory.

When, instead of a rotating sky, the idea was first proposed of a rotating earth, the common sense obstacle to it was the fact that people could not feel it. After all, if one is spinning at a thousand miles an hour at the equator, why do you not feel the wind of the strongest hurricane times four? The answer is, of course, that the atmosphere encounters no resistance from empty space and, therefore, rotates along with the earth. Just so, as you drive your car sixty miles an hour, a fly up against the windshield need not go sixty-one to stay in position, because the atmosphere in the cab is already moving along with the rest of the vehicle.

Sensing the earth's rotation is the easy part. There are lots of additional motions. Beneath the earth, on the opposite side, is the sun, large enough to contain a million of our planet. Around it, our little earth is hurling along at some 70,000 miles per hour, 1100 miles a minute, eighteen miles a second. It is rushing ahead in a straight line—almost, that is. For every eighteen miles, the earth's path turns inward toward the sun a ninth of an inch, giving just a bit of an idea of how vast is the earth's orbit, that such a minimal gravitational tug takes a full year at that speed to close the ellipse and keep the planet in orbit.

Additional motions are more complex, such as wobbles and "precessions," wherein the earth's poles track a small circle of change in the course of 23,000 years. However, the really big motions involve the Milky Way itself. The sun, with its entourage of planets, is itself revolving around the galactic core. Like some gigantic flywheel, 200 billion such suns in the spiral arms are turning, spinning, flying along at 150 miles a second. The size of the galaxy is almost beyond any comprehension, for, even at that astonishing speed, it is believed to take more than 200 million years to make one revolution. The sun has made less than half a trip around since the passing of the dinosaurs. Light, traveling at some 186,000 miles per second, takes 100,000 years to traverse the Milky Way from one side to the other. How naive, even now, we are about the scale of things. Consider that when the astronauts came back from the moon, one of them stood up in the U.S. Senate and said that we are masters of the universe, able to go anywhere we please. When they kicked out of earth orbit and headed for the moon, they did so at what seems to us a horrendous speed: 25,000 miles per hour (seven miles a second); however, at that rate, the time it would take to reach the nearest star is—125,000 years!

In its flight through space, the Milky Way may have close encounters with other galaxies. Its near-twin, Andromeda, is closing in on us at more than seventy-five miles per second. The photographic plates taken by the giant lenses at mountain observatories and the images beamed back by Hubble Space Telescope have shown galaxies interacting: colliding, being distorted, and sometimes being swallowed by others. However, much of the time, it is thought, they pass right through each other, their stars light years apart and able to continue undisturbed in their courses.

Still another motion exists. The light from distant galaxies is stretched toward the red end of the spectrum, which indicates they are all speeding away from us. It's the velocity imparted by the big bang of cosmic genesis. Earth was edged from the center of things by the Copernican revolution, but at least our galaxy seemed to be the center, for everywhere you looked in the night sky, galaxies were rushing away from us, or so it appeared. "Appeared" is the key word; it was not long until someone took a balloon, marked it with dots, and inflated it. As more air was put in and the balloon expanded, every dot became farther from every other one. A micro-person on *any* dot would perceive itself to be the center with everything moving away from there. No single point can be determined to be central.

So the galaxies hurtle outward, the farthest ones going the fastest, until they edge closer to the speed of light itself. With a radius measured now at nearly 14 billion light years, the universe "grows" every time a more sophisticated instrument is invented for such measurement. Is there an edge to the universe at all?

I turn the telescope on a star-like object, brightest of anything in the southeast at this time of year. Unlike the stars, all of which twinkle a bit, it shines steadily: the giant planet Jupiter. Larger than all the other planets combined, it could contain a thousand earths. Jupiter has more than sixty moons. The largest four can be seen with the simplest of telescopes, and it was Galileo who first saw them in the year 1610. The moons, shuttling around the planet like a miniature solar system, changed positions from night to night, giving him the convincing analogy of all the planets revolving around the sun, i.e., their dance was typical and, by extension, was the way the entire solar system worked: as those four moons orbited Jupiter, so the earth moved around the sun. Later forced to recant that conclusion, he is reputed to have murmured under his breath, "Nevertheless, it moves." (If he didn't, he should have.)

Next, I train the scope on the planet Saturn. The rings are tilted for optimum view. Magnified fifty times, they are discernible; at eighty, the planet reminds one of a tire and hubcap. Space probes have provided gloriously detailed pictures of the rings, resolving them into dozens and confirming the fact they must be made up of countless small particles that have sorted themselves into different orbits with spaces between the different rings. Yet, such photos are no replacement for seeing the small and far less vivid image of Saturn glimpsed through a telescope in real time. Numerous people who have looked through my instrument have expressed some amazement that Saturn actually is out there, hanging in space, and that they can see it.

Those heavenly objects have been variously regarded in different periods of history. Astrology was the polytheistic religion of ancient Babylonia that held that the planets were intelligent beings, i.e., gods who influenced, if not determined, our affairs. That view also became prevalent in ancient Greece and Rome. Mars was the god of war, Venus the goddess of love, and Jupiter the king of all the gods. Astrology, the superstition of the stars, still flourishes; horoscopes appear in hundreds of newspapers.

It is excusable, given the knowledge of the times, that Alexander the Great consulted astrologers before every major decision and battle. Now that we know that the stars and planets are not deities but thermonuclear reactors and chunks of rock, it should be so no longer. Science has demonstrated that it is ridiculous for modern people to hold such beliefs. Thus, there was huge and justified outrage when it was learned that Nancy Reagan routinely consulted an astrologer on behalf of her husband, the President of the United States, for the scheduling of conferences, travel, and meeting with world dignitaries.

Speculation concerning the possibility of life on other worlds goes back to early Roman times, when Lucian of Samasota wrote a piece that he called "The True History," wherein he described, in science-fiction style, a voyage to an inhabited moon. In the history of the West, it is often assumed that thoughts of life elsewhere are very recent phenomena, beginning, perhaps, with the twentieth century, but that is not the case. In fact, the first edition of the *Encyclopedia Britannica*, published in 1771, virtually assumes that the Big Picture includes extraterrestrial life, affirming that it simply went against reason that a creator god would put all animals and vegetables in one place and leave the other planets barren.

The idea of extraterrestrial life can be cast in either positive or negative terms. Tradition attributes this remark concerning the stars to Thomas Carlyle: "A sad spectacle. If they be inhabited, what a scope for misery and folly. If they be not inhabited, what a waste of space!" In any case, over the last few centuries, the idea of life elsewhere did not strike most people as inconceivable. Instead, it seems that many were predisposed to a belief in life on other worlds.

There are many events illustrating this point but none better than those involving England's great nineteenth–century astronomer, Sir William Herschel (1738–1822) and his son John. William began as an impoverished church organist who dabbled in astronomy with instruments he built himself. Using those, he discovered the planet Uranus in 1781. That single discovery, of the first planet added to human knowledge since ancient times, brought him the favored and well-financed appointment of "The King's Astronomer" to England's King George III. Sir William made the best use of the telescopes of that era. He and his sister Caroline polished eighteen- and twenty-inch mirrors and then set out to cast a metal mirror three feet in diameter. No foundry would touch the project, so they decided to do it themselves. To cast such a mirror required a mold of some sort, a form into which the metal could be poured. For this purpose, they settled upon horse manure. For days, for the sake of starlight and science, they pounded this substance into shape, but, upon pouring, the heat cracked the mold and the family had to run outdoors to escape the molten metal. The limits of amateur telescope building had been reached.

However, the King of England took over, funding a forty-eight-inch mirror that weighed a ton and had to be housed in a tube forty feet long. Quite limited in maneuverability, with its use requiring climbing a scaffold fifty feet high, it nevertheless represented a huge step forward in telescope design. In keeping with its size, it was dedicated by royalty, and it is said that the king took the arm of the Archbishop of Canterbury with the words, "Come, my Lord Bishop. I will show you the way to heaven."

Until this time, John Herschel, the son, had made no major discoveries of his own, but he did benefit from his father's reputation. In January of 1833, two years after his father's death, he set sail for Capetown, South Africa, to study the stars of the Southern Hemisphere. A year and a half later, no word had been received from him.

Then, in August of 1835, the *Sun* newspaper of New York began several installments written by a reporter named Richard Locke, who detailed Herschel's findings by claiming to reprint articles from a so-called supplement to the *Edinburgh Journal of Science*. The subject was introduced thus: "In this unusual addition to our journal, we have the happiness of making known to the British public, and thence to the whole civilized world, recent discoveries in astronomy which will build an imperishable monument to the age in which we live, and confer upon the present generation of the human race a proud distinction through all future time."

Herschel had, it seemed, built a powerful new telescope with a light-collecting lens, not a mirror, an astonishing twenty-four *feet* in diameter. (In reality, not until the mid-twentieth century, nearly a hundred years later, would California's Mount Palomar instrument have the largest mirror in the world, at seventeen feet.) Not only that, Herschel had devised his telescope on radically different optical principles, enabling it to cast an image on a screen, which could then be examined with a microscope at an effective magnification of 42,000 times! Such a system could not possibly work, for as an image is greatly enlarged, it becomes fainter and, finally, fuzzy in the extreme. However, the *Sun's* readers learned Herschel had overcome this difficulty with a method of "transfusing artificial light" in order to brighten the image, which was then examined with a "hydro-oxygen microscope." Readers awaited the next installment to learn what he had discovered when the wondrous new telescope had been focused on the image of the moon. It was under this same moon that lovers in every age had sighed and pledged their undying devotion; the same moon that now hung over the high buildings of their bourgeoning city of New York; the same glowing disc that now looked, for all the world, like *another* world.

The stories in the *Sun* about the moon did not disappoint. Readers learned of the astronomer beholding oceans with brilliant beaches, pelicans, and shaggy bison-like beasts. However, a beaver was a creature with differences; the creature lacked a tail and carried its young in its arms. In addition, judging from the smoke arising from its lodges, it had mastered the use of fire. Next, there appeared a creature much like a goat but with a single horn.

The unicorn had provided a riveting ending to the second install-ment; by the third, paperboys were selling issues of the *Sun* like the pro-verbial hotcakes. Circulation would boom to 19,360, which made the upstart newspaper the best-selling one in the entire world, even though, at the time, London was four times the size of New York. The fourth article kept it coming: miniature zebras, bears with horns, blue pheas-ants against hills of yellow quartz, as well as sheep-like animals having an unusually long neck and spiral horns, white as polished ivory.

At last, the news was delivered of men on the moon! The mighty telescope enabled astronomers to be "thrilled with astonishment to perceive four successive flocks of large winged creatures, wholly un-like any kind of birds, descend with a slow, even motion from the cliffs on the western side and alight upon the plain." These creatures walked like human beings: "Certainly they *were* like human beings, for their wings had now disappeared and their attitude in walking was both erect and dignified . . . They possessed wings of great expansion, similar in construction to those of the bat, being a semi-transparent membrane united in curvilinear divisions by means of a straight radii, united at the back by the dorsal integuments." (Note the linguistics of science.) Later, the creatures swam in a lake, and one detail after another was given of their eating, flying, lounging, and bathing. The description then turned to nomenclature. "We scientifically denominated them the Vespertilio-homo or Bat-man; and they are doubtless innocent and happy creatures, notwithstanding that some of their amusements would but ill comport with our terrestrial notions of decorum."

The need was felt by the discoverers half a world away to enlist oth-ers to attest to the veracity of their astonishing reports. Thus, we are told, Dr. Herschel invited civil and military authorities of the South African colony, as well as several Episcopalian, Wesleyan, and other ministers, to witness these wonders and to attest to their truth, all on the condition of secrecy, of course. The Scottish journal states: "We are confident that his forthcoming volumes will be at once the most sublime in science, and the most intense in general interest, that ever issued from the press."

A marvelous temple constructed of sapphire was observed, built, it was assumed, by another species of moon men, described as being of infinitely greater personal beauty, like angelic beings. It was also intimated that the newspaper possessed forty pages of mathematical calculations that had accompanied the Scottish journal, but these it would refrain from printing because of their difficulty for the general reader.

In that summer of 1835, the readers of the *Sun* were bedazzled by the news of extraterrestrials. Of course, some doubted, but very little was known about the moon, new scientific discoveries were being publicized regularly, and there were those citations in scientific-sounding language from a science journal to bolster everything and these, in turn, buttressed by the authority of the prestigious Dr. John Herschel.

It was, of course, all a hoax. The paper tried to keep the act alive to boost circulation, maintaining for another two weeks that the stories were authentic but, at last, the truth came out: it was all a fabrication forged by a single reporter. In fact, Herschel had no telescope with an aperture of twenty-four feet, and no one had heard from him. He remained in South Africa, concentrating on his star survey and giving no reports until twelve years later in 1847. In them, there was nothing of unicorns and nothing of Batman, either.

The source for the above quotations from the *Sun* newspaper stories is from an 1877 book by astronomer Richard A. Proctor titled *Myths and Marvels of Astronomy* written four decades after the hoax. (By then, the false reports had migrated around the world, taking on, as we say, "a life of their own.") Near the end of the chapter concerning the lunar lie, Proctor remarked on the great difficulty that scientists continued to encounter when asked to prove, for example, that the earth is *not* flat or the moon *not* inhabited, for, he says, "the circumstance that such a question is asked implies ignorance so thorough of the very facts on which the proof must be based, as to render argument all but hopeless from the onset . . . The conclusion at which I have arrived, is that to make a rope of sand were an easy task compared with the attempt to instill the simpler facts of science into paradoxical heads." The astronomer's comment from more than 130 years ago is instructive concerning the uncritical will to maintain foregone conclusions (and is not unrelated to issues explored in Chapter 10 of this work).

Even today, the predisposition to believe in extraterrestrials is not far beneath the surface, for it has been there all along. In 1938, on the night before Halloween, thousands panicked when they tuned in to Orson Welles' radio dramatization of *The War of the Worlds* and believed it to be a descriptive of what was actually happening, that Martians in spaceships were landing in New Jersey and that alien creatures were wreaking destruction at every path.

The serious astronomer Percival Lowell spent the early part of the twentieth century studying the planet Mars from his observatory in Arizona. He produced numerous drawings showing "canals," which he surmised were produced by drought-stricken Martians trying to channel water from icecaps at the poles. Now, we know that the canals were an optical illusion and that the planet is a red desert.

Universe is a film by the National Film Board of Canada released in 1960. After describing the workings of a giant telescope, it goes on to survey the solar system, and then, objects of deep space. Superbly executed, it won all sorts of major awards for film-making; even today, it remains a fine artistic achievement, one that articulates very well the state of astronomical knowledge in the mid-twentieth century. One sentence of the narration, in the strictly scientific description of Mars, is particularly revealing of the spirit of the times: "It is *reasonably certain* that the markings on its surface, greenish blue in the summer and turning dark brown in the Martian winter, *represent vegetation.*" In that era, there was a strong desire in the scientific community to find life beyond our own world, and conclusions were occasionally drawn that edged somewhat beyond the evidence. There was this immediate qualification about conditions on Mars: "But no creatures like men could live here, 140 million miles from the sun."

The report of a crashed flying saucer near Roswell, New Mexico, spurred huge numbers of believers. In the 1950s, conventions were held at Giant Rock in California's Mojave Desert, where as many as 5,000 people of the same mind would gather to exchange information. Many gave reports of their own travels aboard such crafts, one saying he had made over 350 trips to Venus and a planet named Clarion. Another described friendly saucer people as looking like us and that the men had clothes very similar to our Greyhound bus drivers. Beginning in the 1960s and peaking in the 80s, there surfaced the so-called alien abduction syndrome, wherein people reported being kidnapped by large-headed, big-eyed "grays" of more sinister intent. Estimates range as high as 3 percent of the American population—i.e., several million people—believing they have been abducted by aliens. Almost all who study such things see this as manifestations of psychological needs that, in previous ages, were clothed in different images: the same phenomena, now in space-age dressing.

In our time, the desire to receive some sign from, or better yet, some contact with, unearthly beings has been ratcheted up, and whole industries are built around it. As Robert Baker says, "For the average person walking down the aisle of a modern bookstore or passing through the checkout lane at the nearest supermarket, it would be easy to conclude that aliens from outer space not only are here but have also joined the Baptist church, have put their kids in school, and belong to the Rotary Club." Almost any night, you can turn on the television and see documentaries on purported UFOs. As of late, these have been making their way onto channels that we once thought were reserved for factual reporting of the discoveries of science. One hour's programming on the History Channel may concern the history of Arctic exploration and the next may be about ghosts or about supposed ancient astronauts who built the pyramids. (After actively promoting such bizarre conclusions, these so-called documentaries usually have a near-inaudible disclaimer of the sort that was used by other newspapers at the time of the moon hoax to inform their own readers that, on the issue of truth or falsity of stories about the bat-men on the moon, they should decide for themselves.) Thus, whether such things are cause or symptom, there exists now a widespread inclination, a strong predisposition, to accept the incredible.

In keeping with the spirit of the times, otherwise respectable scientists, too, occasionally draw conclusions that go far beyond the evidence. Consider the 1996 announcement made at NASA headquarters and reported by television all around the world. Hailed as "the find of the century," it concerned a rock of quite mundane appearance, which those holding the press conference proclaimed had a remarkable history. Their explanation was that it was part of the crust of the planet Mars, formed over 4 billion years ago. Then, some 16 million years ago, a comet or asteroid impact blasted it clear of the gravitational pull of its home planet and into outer space. Out there, between Mars and Earth, it swung in orbit until about 13,000 years ago, when it entered our atmosphere and fell on the ice sheet of Antarctica. There, it lay in the ice-desert until 1984, when it was hoisted aboard a snowmobile and taken back to be analyzed in the United States.

That scenario is remarkable enough. However, what had occasioned the press conference was the idea that within cracks in the meteorite there were seen to be microscopic structures that likely indicated the presence of life on Mars—not little green men, but tiny bacteria. Held up as evidence were carbonate globules, which were compared to by-products of bacteria on earth. There were polycyclic aromatic hydrocarbons, which can be a chemical result of organic decay. There were also microscopic structures that looked like fossilized bacteria themselves.

Numerous other experts disagreed. Scientists from UCLA noted that the so-called bacteria were one hundred times smaller than the smallest bacteria on earth and that the chemicals in question can be formed inorganically: PAH, for instance, is found in car exhaust. There was also the announcement of twenty-five years before, in which investigators made similar claims for a meteorite that had fallen in France, and that turned out to be without basis.

Overall, the so-called evidence was circumstantial, tentative, and pointed to a very slight possibility of extraterrestrial life. However, any reservations or qualifications were all but forgotten by the press, where the reaction was often in the vein of "Yahoo, we're not alone!" (There may have been a spike in alien-invasion movies, also.)

There were questions, as well, in the broader scientific community concerning why this specimen, which had been around for years, had been brought out now. Many had the sense that the timing had something to do with shoring up public support for a new round of costly NASA missions to the red planet in a time when interest in such things had waned. Few are in a position to answer that question; however, concerning the science itself, the slogan popularized by Carl Sagan is applicable that "Extraordinary claims require extraordinary evidence." As a planetary scientist and public educator in the realm of astronomy, no one would have enjoyed finding evidence of extraterrestrial life more than he. However, he never saw any evidence even approaching that standard; hunches and "maybes" are not science, any more than are the numerous anecdotal reports of "sightings."

Some scientists used the find as a launching pad for both related and unrelated themes. I watched one so-called rocket scientist state that the find "demonstrates now" that life is abundant in the universe *and* that such life is *not* due to a series of rare events or miracles "as we may have been taught as children." Life is, he said, simply natural and ordinary. The subtle implication is that any talk beyond what is ordinary or natural is somehow childish, and that grown-ups like him have left that behind. Of course, a finding of life elsewhere would not demonstrate that life processes are purely mechanical or natural. Again, there is the desire to leap from thin, suggestive indicators to firm conclusions that are much beyond the evidence.

The same is true with arguments made on a purely statistical basis, i.e., that the universe is so large, has so many galaxies, which must have so many suns, which have so many solar systems, etc., that, *ergo*, surely life is abundant. The so-called Hubble Deep Field photograph is a montage or composite view of 342 pictures taken by the Hubble Space Telescope of deep space. The view is through a little patch of the sky in the region of the Big Dipper's handle and covers an area about the size of the head of a match held at arm's length. In just that tiny window to the heavens shines the distant light of some 1,500 other galaxies, and such density seems to be typical of the rest of the entire sky. It is an astounding picture and unimaginable just a few years ago. But does it mean that we are "*definitely* not alone" and that "the universe is *surely* teeming with life?" It may indeed be true that life abounds elsewhere, but estimates concerning the abundance of galaxies, stars, and planetary systems do not force that conclusion. UCLA astronomer George Abell grants the possibility of life beyond earth. However, he states in his college textbook *Exploration of the Universe,* "On the other hand, we do not know how life began on our own planet and have no objective means of assessing the probability of life beginning elsewhere, much less of evaluating the likelihood of the critical steps of evolution which may lead to intelligent beings. Life may abound in the universe, or it may be unique to the earth; on this topic we can do no more than speculate."

Speculation led to including a message to "out there" on the space probe known as *Pioneer 10*. Launched on March 3, 1972, the craft photographed Jupiter and Saturn and then kept going. It has now passed beyond the orbit of Pluto, out of the solar system. In *The Cosmic Connection,* Carl Sagan describes the attached six by nine-inch, gold-anodized aluminum plaque that was attached to the craft, giving the position of earth in relation to the other planets, as well as a representation of the binary number 1 and "a schematic representation of the hyperfine transition between parallel and antiparallel proton and electron spins of the neutral hydrogen atom," supposedly things a technologically advanced civilization elsewhere might understand. In addition, our sun is located in relationship to a number of rotating neutron stars, or pulsars. Sagan said, "We believe that a scientifically sophisticated civilization will have no difficulty understanding the radial burst pattern as the positions and periods of 14 pulsars with respect to the Solar System of launch." Also, among the engravings are the bodies of a man and woman, their figures based on the classical models of Greek sculpture and set against a diagram of the spacecraft for scale.

A few months after the launch, NASA convened a symposium on the subject of life beyond earth. One of the panelists was the renowned anthropologist, Ashley Montagu, who said, "The simple truth is that before we can communicate with others successfully, we must first learn to communicate with ourselves, and we are a long way from achieving that . . . We have landed on the moon. It might not be such a bad idea if we tried landing on earth. When asked by a European inquirer what he thought of Western civilization, Gandhi paused awhile, and wryly smiling, replied, 'I don't think it would be a bad idea.'"

In a way, the launching of *Pioneer 10* was like a shipwrecked sailor casting his bottled message into an ocean—only the ocean is incredibly vaster than any ocean we know. Odds are that this cosmic greeting card will be the longest-lived artifact of the human race, preserved in the cold vacuum of space for millions of years. The chances of it being picked up by an intelligent being elsewhere are *next* to zero.

When the launch was publicized, it provoked wide-ranging responses. *Natural History* magazine published the *Pioneer 10* picture and invited readers' responses. In an article titled "Waiting for the Phone to Ring," John P. Wiley wrote, "If we do send further messages, what shall we say? Charles Bigelow of Portland, Oregon suggested, 'It is difficult to say what messages to send or guess what we might receive when as yet we know so little of communication on earth. What stories do the crows tell on winter evenings in their city-like roosts? What would the ants say of their vast altruistic and totalitarian societies? And do porpoises discuss the currents and blooms of the oceans, as farmers gather to talk about the weather and crops?'"

Another person had a reference to the hand of the man in the picture, which was upraised in a greeting of goodwill, saying such a venture was dangerous. We had already broadcast World War II pictures of the Nazis with a similar salute; thus, the residents of outer space might conclude that all earthlings are alike and that it is best to extinguish life on such a planet. A women's liberation organization thought the woman looked too passive. Predictably, others were upset at the images of the nude figures. In response, a newspaper columnist imagined the outrage of residents of another planet receiving such obscene mail and then covering with tape the naked *feet* of the man and woman.

The message was a mirror. Sagan said, "It is a kind of cosmic Rorschach test, in which people see reflected their hopes and fears, their aspirations and defeats—the darkest and the most luminous aspects of the human spirit . . . The greater significance of the *Pioneer 10* plaque is not as a message to out there; it is as a message to back here."

I turn the dials on the telescope, peer through the finder-scope, and center the crosshairs on a star. Then, looking into the eyepiece and focusing the image at high power, the star is resolved into not one but two. It is estimated that at least half of the stars we see in the heavens are actually two stars, so-called *binary* systems, wherein the stars are in orbit around each other or, more accurately, around a common center of gravity.

Next, I swing the scope almost straight up and locate the great globular cluster, M-13 in the constellation Hercules. One of the best objects for amateur telescopes, the dense cluster appears reminiscent of an exploding popcorn ball and contains an estimated half-million stars. Such clusters are within our own Milky Way system and represent some of the oldest stars therein. Years ago, a radio message inquiring whether anyone was home was sent to the Hercules cluster. Because the object is approximately 22,000 light years away, it was felt that the radio beam would broaden out just enough to cover most of the cluster's stars—lots of bang for the buck. The down side, of course, is that, assuming anyone is there, we will have to wait 44,000 years for a response.

Charles Messier of France completed his famous *Nebulae and Star Clusters* catalog in 1781. Searching for comets, he would also describe "nebulous" objects that came into his telescope's view, drawing and plotting them so they would not be confused with the comets that were his main concern. Of the 102 objects he listed, some of them were gaseous nebulae, lit by stars forming within. Others have turned out to be the debris of supernovae explosions. Some are globular clusters, like M-13. Most of them, unknown to Messier or anyone else at the time, are galaxies. Astronomers of the early twentieth century would go on to collect their starlight in hours-long exposures on glass plates to reveal their splendor. They come in several shapes: round-ellipticals, spirals trailing either tightly or loosely-wound arms of billions of suns, and those of irregular shapes. All of them were thought to be part of *the* galaxy, the Milky Way, and the one-and-only. Not until the 1920s, when techniques were found to measure such remote distances, did it become known that they represented systems outside our own, that they were, in fact, *other* galaxies: huge continents of stars separated from our own and from each other by endless seas of night and sailing over distances wherein even light itself grows old.

I turn the barrel of the scope to find a galaxy. As I do so, I think of the two so-called Clouds of Magellan, which are really smaller galaxies in orbit around our own and which were first seen with the naked eye by the great explorer in 1520. Only visible from the Southern Hemisphere, I will likely never see them. I make a mental note to myself to send a star map showing their location to our son serving in the Peace Corps in Southeast Africa; it would be a grand sight, I think, for him to see them with the naked eye, like Magellan, and know what he is seeing.

The galaxy I have chosen is M-33 in the constellation Triangulum. It is a loosely coiled spiral that appears flat-on to our line of sight and is close enough to nearly fill the telescope's field of view, if the "seeing" is good, i.e., if conditions in the atmosphere are stable as well as clear. We have been spoiled by all those long-exposure prints from the big observatories, yet the faint image in real time has an allure. It comes and goes, so one needs concentration, as well as the so-called averted image technique (putting it just off the eye's central focus, thereby avoiding the so-called blind spot of the optic nerve where it enters the retina). With that, the faint star clouds of the the immense whirlpool of billions of shining stars appears, confirming to me the words attributed to Michael Faraday, "Nothing is too wonderful to be true." The evidence is in the eyepiece.

And with it comes that idea whether life, so resilient and filling every conceivable niche on earth—and doing so in such abundance—is also out there. Are there creatures beyond our imaginings looking back the other way? In all of time, in all the galaxies of the far-flung universe, how many beings have stared into the same night sky and posed the same question?

The Big Picture may or may not include life Out There. If it exists, we may or may not verify it, and, given the distances involved, may never establish communication. However, we seem to think, it is not entirely inconceivable that other worlds exist that harbor life. And it would not be too amazing, would it, for, when you think of it, what is more amazing than this world, this life we know here and now? In fact, as incredible as we are finding the vast universe to be, there is a sense in which it is even more incredible that the human mind can contain it, encompass it within itself, and seek to understand it by asking the question.

The galactic image is fading. My eyes are tired, and there is a thin coating of dew beginning to settle on the glass, so it's "time to call it a night." And a Good Night it has been. It's time, now, to go back home for a few hours sleep before returning to the world of family: people sharing love in a tiny slice of time and eternity. Time to go back, also, to the world of work, to the routine of various gatherings, committees, and meetings. Time to go back to other sources of excitement and joy and beauty, but, also, to that mundane world where noble thoughts are so often shadowed by ignoble realities. Time, now, to return to ambiguity, occasional tragedy and, sometimes, outright evil. Therefore, whether on the world scale of nations or on the small scale of communities and individuals, progress is sometimes nonexistent. When it is real, it is usually very slow in coming, and it is almost always invisible—except for a lens.

I find myself recalling the thought of philosopher George Santayana: "The problem of darkness does not exist for a man gazing at the stars. No doubt the darkness is there, fundamental, pervasive, except at the pinpoints where the stars twinkle; but the question is not why there is darkness, but what is the light that breaks through it so remarkably; and, granting that light, why we have eyes to see it and hearts to be gladdened by it."

I disassemble the equipment, load the trunk, and head the car for home along the winding dirt road. The headlights punch little holes in the dark.

PART II

Issues and Implications

8

Nature Is . . .

There is nothing more difficult than to become critically
aware of the presuppositions of one's thought.
Everything can be seen directly,
except the eye through which we see.

E. F. Schumacher

MANY PEOPLE IN THE western states have fine collections of arrowheads, flint points they have picked up; some have found hundreds. Over the years, I have spent most of every summer vacation out
in the hills of those same regions, and I have found only three. But I've
found hundreds of dinosaur teeth and bones.

What you find depends so much upon that for which the eye is cali-
brated. Paleontologist Jack Horner says that he has walked into trees while
looking for dinosaurs, so focused does he become on the object of his
search. In some basic sense, what you see is what you get, and what you
see depends on that for which you are looking in the first place. We follow
self-made paths through life, in search of that to which we are predisposed
by expectations, temperament, or personality. Thus, the categories of the
mind, formed by experience, education, prejudice, and a host of intangibles, frame our world, and it may well be that we can reverse a familiar
cliché to have equal truth: "We'll *see* it when we *believe* it."

Consider how six individuals approach the identical forested
mountain landscape but see it differently. A hiker goes there for physical training and finds its contours and elevations conducive to that. A

geologist explores its rocky outcrops for clues to the age and history of the formation. A lumberman goes there to assess the economic value of his lease in terms of board feet. A developer focuses on the best locations for the roads and houses he would like to build. A biologist is charged with protecting and preserving the wildlife and other components of what is, to her, an entire ecosystem. An artist comes with paint and brush, intent upon capturing something of the beauty of the scene. It's one and the same forest, but the frame of reference for each of those viewers varies so much that they *see* very different things.

Seeing can be distorted. Sometimes, we do not see what is there and, in that case, glasses may help. We can also "see" what is not there. Consider individuals who have become paranoid. Their suspicions make perfect sense—if you accept their basic presuppositions or starting points; then, one thing follows another in a kind of hyper-rationalism. It is, of course, those initial assumptions that are skewed, illustrating, again, that perception is far from a simple thing. How we regard the world is colored by all sorts of things, factors that sometimes have our recognition but, most often, are simply assumed. Thus, we say that beauty is in the eye of the beholder, but so is everything else.

To be awake is to be exposed to everything around us, which is more than any human being can handle, so, in the most basic sense, the mind must be selective in order to comprehend. Virginia Stem Owens suggests an interesting image: "Consciousness has already made up a shopping list before the brain ever begins its daily marketing." The result is that nothing ever just *is*. It always exists *as seen* from a particular vantage point. Since what we call reality is filtered through a lens of usually unexamined assumptions, there really is no such thing as an immaculate perception.

Beyond the basic constrictions that are necessary in order for our perceptions to make sense, there exist larger mental frameworks that make up what we call our worldview, and these often determine the things we notice, expect, and the kinds of questions that we ask. Most of the time, we are looking through these glasses colored by our collective history and individual experiences, our values, religion, or philosophy of life, and, in large degree, these determine what we find—or don't find, as in Frederic Farrar's words:

> O, where is the sea? the fishes cried,
>   As they swam the crystal waters through.

We have heard from of old of the ocean tide,
  And we long to look on the waters blue.

Thus, every waking minute, we are barraged by all kinds of bits and pieces of sensory data coming from every direction. The temperature of the room, the buzz of the florescent lights, the cricket dimly chirping under the floorboards, the beating of our heart, the itch of our shirt collar: all these the mind senses and knows—these and a thousand other things—but the mind is able to screen them out and move them to the side, so that it can focus on a few more important things. To do that, it opens certain windows on experience, their shape and direction usually taken for granted. The view is assumed (either consciously, or more often subconsciously) to be of what is "out there"; it is, however, a personal worldview or frame of reference, something often called a *paradigm*.

The term itself comes from Thomas Kuhn's 1962 book, *The Structure of Scientific Revolutions*. Kuhn began to wonder how the genius Aristotle could be so wrong about so many things concerning how the world actually works. Finally, he decided to put himself in Aristotle's mental shoes and see the world as it was known at the time. Then, Aristotle's ideas on all sorts of things were seen to make sense and to consist of facts, as he saw them. "As he saw them," is the key. Kuhn then focused on what controls the type of questions asked by scientists, the kind of experiments they conceive, and he found those were influenced and controlled, even, by the conventions of the times. "Fad" is perhaps too strong a word, but such unscientific conventions and constraints funnel and control what questions are regarded as worthwhile and, even, what is seen to be real.

The situation might be at least vaguely analogous to that black and white figure that virtually everyone has seen. At first, it may appear to be a white flower vase against a black background. Then, by the flick of some mental switch, it appears as the black silhouettes of two heads in profile view and facing each other. (One thinks, too, of that old story of the man who goes to the psychiatrist and takes the inkblot test, which consists simply of miscellaneous abstract shapes, and a person imposes a meaning upon them. The fellow sees everything in sexual, even pornographic, terms. The doctor says, "You really have a problem here." The viewer answers, "Me?"—*You're* the one with all the dirty pictures.")

The "faces and vases" remind one of what happens when paradigms shift. Kuhn references the mental revolution created by the Copernican way of looking at the world, which opened up previously unanticipated questions. The ideas of Darwinian evolution, the expanding universe of the big bang, and new ideas of quantum physics dealing with subatomic particles did the same. Seemingly well-established views were overthrown. By way of illustration, Kuhn describes experiments in psychology and perception, whereby a person is fitted with goggles having inverting lenses to make everything appear upside down. Amazingly, after a time of initial confusion, the mind is able to "flip over" the visual field to make things appear normal once again. "Literally as well as metaphorically, the man accustomed to inverting lenses has undergone a revolutionary transformation of vision." So it is with one's view of the world.

Many times, when people thought they had the truth, what they had, instead, was one way of looking at a reality that is capable of being seen through many different lenses. The problem comes when we think our lens is the only one or that ours is the only one with value. That is not to say that all is merely relative and that some are no closer to reality than are others; it is simply to affirm the existence of all those oft-unexamined glasses, lenses, or paradigms.

What *is* nature? Many people, in former ages, have thought that they knew. Many people, today, are quite certain that they know. Goethe said that nature is the living, visible garment of God. When Fernando Belaunde Terry was the president of Peru, he closed a speech by saying, "Nature is our enemy, and nature can be overcome." It would be difficult to find two points of view more in opposition than those. There are, however, a number of additional options.

∼

One position is that nature is simply all there is. In it, reality is summed up by the universe; nature exists but nothing supernatural. This, of course, is the position we call *atheism*. Some have arrived at it after a long and difficult struggle with trying to make sense of the presence of evil in all its many forms. Others hold atheism as a kind of creed, a kind of religion; when they say there is no god, they display something of an inner certitude that goes beyond arguments for or against. A character in Graham Greene's novel, *The Power and the Glory*, illustrates it well: "There are mystics who are said to have experienced God directly. He was a mystic, too, and what he had experienced was a vacancy—a complete certainty in the existence of a dying, cooling world, of human beings who had evolved from animals with no purpose at all. He knew."

Some try to evict God from their concept of nature because their exposure to religion has been to that of the worst sorts: simplistic or legalistic, superstitious or ignorant, and, indeed, these can be found in relative abundance. When someone tells me they have come to be an atheist, I often ask them to describe the God in whom they don't believe, and, after they do, almost always, my response is that neither do I believe in that kind of God. Where do a great many people get their ideas of religion? Some have not been involved in the church and so have little experience with religion as it is actually practiced; others were involved only as children and left the church before they were old enough to appreciate the concepts; few have studied them as adults. Is it any wonder that many people have, therefore, a childish conception of religion, one that cannot possibly stand up in the real world? The concept of God as an exaggerated man, or the Little Old Man on Cloud Nine, is not totally a satire, something illustrated by a test done years ago, wherein students were asked to respond immediately, without any reflection, to this question: "Does God understand radar?" In most cases, the response was "No." There was laughter as they soon realized how absurd this would be. However, it did reveal that at the back of their minds was a very inadequate concept of God, of one who had perhaps been quite a power in a former day, long ago, when everyone viewed the earth as a flat disc set on pillars but who could not possibly be expected to keep up to an advanced and technologically sophisticated society such as ours.

Some who claim atheism are fixated on the kinds of evidence for God that religious people cannot provide, and which, again, involves a naïve concept of the deity. Fingerprints of the creator cannot be found on the world—*ergo*, God does not exist. In the 1960s, the Soviet Union, an officially atheistic state, sent the first cosmonauts into space. It was widely reported that when they came down from orbit they gloated that, since they did not *see* God up there in the stratosphere, God does not exist—case closed.

There may be still other, more subtle, reasons why some are rather eager to embrace atheism. The agitated German atheist, Friedrich Nietzsche, was unusually candid about what accepting the reality of God might entail. This author of the ego-over-all "superman" concept, which was employed so powerfully and so destructively by the Nazis in the next generation, wrote in *Thus Spake Zarathustra*, "But that I may reveal my heart entirely unto you, my friends: *If* there were gods, how could I endure it to be no God? *Therefore,* there are no Gods."

Atheists often suggest that belief in God is easy comfort. Rather, if you suggest that reality includes a god who is not indifferent to the human adventure, then there is the implicit need to analyze one's own life in relationship to that. The natural inclination, however, is to want to determine such things in autonomous fashion (an idea explored in Genesis chapters 2 and 3). In a culture often regarded as individualistic and focused on self-fulfillment with few strings attached, the recognition of something greater than oneself implies a transformation of thought and action in the light of a higher and less individualistic ethic. That there might be such a need for such could be affirmed even without seeing the festivals sponsored by MTV for students on spring break in Cancun, where the young hedonists sing, "We're only mammals / So let's do it like they do it on the Discovery Channel." God is not a factor for anything like ethical behavior, if you are "only a mammal."

Others would simply not be bothered, and, to avoid the complexities, take the simpler route of deleting the divine from the equation. Cynicism is easy. In the words of Frederick Buechner, "Unbelief is as much a choice as belief is. What makes it in many ways more appealing is that whereas to believe in something requires some measure of understanding and effort, not to believe doesn't require much of anything at all."

Those subscribing to atheism often seek to justify that position by referring to those occasions when acts of evil have been perpetrated by those claiming religion. Pascal said, "Men never do evil so completely and cheerfully as when they do it from religious conviction." There have certainly been many such times; oppression and persecution by a religious establishment has surely existed and should be openly and strongly acknowledged as a perversion of its creeds.

However, atheism, also, has a tendency to see itself in possession of exclusive truth, and has often been more than zealous and strident in promoting conformity to its dogmas. A few decades ago, it was fashionable in some quarters to acclaim atheism as a liberator for the oppressed. When the Berlin Wall fell in 1989, it set in motion the process whereby western scholars could examine what had been the secret archives of the Soviet Union. That revelation put to rest any notion that atheism is always a tolerant and gentle worldview. In fact, the publication of *The Black Book of Communism*, a volume based on official records, indicates a death toll under Stalin at between 85 and 100 million! After citing this fact in *The Twilight of Atheism*, Oxford's Alister McGrath, himself a former atheist, concludes, "Communism promised liberation from the illusion of religion; it ended up with a body count exceeding anything previously known in history." Human nature is one and the same and can be led down tyrannical and destructive paths by a creed that is corrupt or by the supposed absence of any.

~

Somewhat related to atheism is *agnosticism*. The term was coined by Darwin's friend and advocate Thomas Huxley from the Greek word for knowledge, *gnosis*. Adding the negative prefix, *a*, gives the meaning: that one does not have enough knowledge to make up one's mind one way or another, so one remains undecided and uncommitted. (Trilobites are ancient ocean fossils. Some have huge and compound eyes like a bumblebee; however, one is blind, having no eyes at all. It is named *Agnostus*.) Being a position of suspended judgment, there is not much to say about the agnostic stance, except that it is often not permanent. The old saying that there are no atheists in foxholes is not entirely true, but, I think, neither are there as many agnostics as one might assume. The trials and tribulations common to life have a way of forcing us to choose.

~

Another position is that of *pantheism*. In contrast to atheism, which maintains that all that exists is nature, this says that *all that exists is God*. Nature and God are identical. The world, the universe, the totality of it all, is divine—nature *is* God. In this conception, we ourselves are part of one vast organism of nature. Just as we are made up of cells, which could be looked at individually and that go about their business thinking, if they could think, that they are something separate, so this idea says that we go about what we take to be our business, but we are simply cells in the larger organism of the universe. Every atom, tree, star, flower, person, is thus a part of God. We have limitations, problems, and know suffering, but this is only because we are such a small part; in the grander scheme, those do not exist. (Most of us likely find this semantic redefinition of evil to be trivializing and quite inadequate to deal with what we experience in daily life.)

In the West, the great "amateur" philosopher from Amsterdam, Spinoza (he was a lens-grinder to pay expenses), developed the idea of pantheism. Of his system of thought, he wrote, "How would it be possible, if salvation were ready to our hand and could without great labor be found, that it should be by almost all men neglected? But all things excellent are as difficult as they are rare." Thus, the very complex and abstract formulations of Spinoza about the nature of reality attracted very few.

It is in the East that pantheism is ardently believed and practiced by hundreds of millions. *Hinduism* has no founding individual; instead, this religion consists of a vast accumulation of teachings, traditions, and practices with a history of more than four thousand years. Hinduism has thousands of gods and goddesses, but they are all expressions of *Brahmin*, the one who is incomprehensible and indescribable and "before whom all words recoil." Hinduism's primary text, the *Bhagavad-Gita*, contains this seminal passage about the place of nature: "All living creatures are led astray, as soon as they are born, by the *delusion* that this world is real." All is God.

Unity with Brahmin is the goal of life. The deepest part of one's self, what many call the soul and what Hindus call the *atman*, is really God, also, and salvation is for the individual's soul to make its way back through successive embodiments or reincarnations, escaping, at last, from the turning of this wheel to be absorbed by the impersonal but infinite center of being. It is the drop of water returning to the ocean. In the final stage, one renounces all material things, all earthly attachments, and all feelings. (Christian missionary E. Stanley Jones once told of visiting a holy man in a cave who said to him, "I haven't thought about a woman in thirty years!" Jones said, "Isn't it strange that this was the *first* thing he told me?") Far from easy, this dying away from all that a person holds dear—love, family, community—this renunciation is preparation for eternity. Thus, in India, you see the holy men sitting endlessly in the yoga position with the far-away look in their eyes. The entire external world is seen to be of no account and has ceased to matter.

Buddhism began with a Hindu who had a transforming experience. Siddhartha Gautama was born to the aristocracy and shielded from suffering on every hand. His first exposure to the wider world, where he saw rampant poverty, disease, and death, shook him to the core, and he responded by discarding his royal robe, leaving his wife and child, and entering the forest to seek enlightenment. Under the Bo tree, he became the Buddha, the awakened one.

The briefest summary of his teachings: All things in this world involve suffering and sorrow. The desire for personal or individual fulfillment is the root cause of sorrow. The cure is to overcome such desire, to become indifferent, until, with all individuality erased, one enters *nirvana,* a word that means, "to extinguish." Deprived of fuel, the fire goes out. This applies to desires, but to the person, also. It is the drop in the ocean, again, and the idea has much in common with the pantheism of Hinduism. Is nirvana God? If that means a personal being, one who created the universe and who cares about us, then nirvana is not God and Buddhism is atheistic. You can say what many things in this religion are not, but it is difficult to say what very many are. Buddhism is famous for its ambiguity and obscurity. This much can be said: nature, as in Hinduism, is not seen as something real in and of itself. Nature is illusory, merely an appearance.

Christians reject pantheism and affirm *creation.* God and nature are to be distinguished; they are not the same things. God is transcendent over nature. If you total up all the elements of the universe, you do not get God. For you, they may *point* to God, but God they are not. St. Augustine must have been dealing with this issue in the fourth century, for, after describing in elegant prose the pleasures of sight, sound, and touch that fill human experience in the world, he asked what was it that he loved, in loving God:

> I asked the earth; and it answered, "I am not He"; and whatsoever are therein made the same confession. I asked the sea and the deeps and the creeping things that lived, and they replied, "We are not your God, seek higher than we" . . . I asked the heavens, the sun, moon, and stars: "Neither," say they, "are we the God whom you seek." And I answered unto all these things which stand about the door of my flesh, "You have told me concerning my God that you are not He; tell me something about Him." And with a loud voice they exclaimed, "He made us!"

Very few cultures have held, as did the ancient Greeks, that nature itself is eternal, without beginning or end. The idea simply lacks force and runs counter to human experience that individual physical things owe their existence in a causal relationship to other things, i.e., something always comes from something else. There is simply no evidence that supports the view of nature as everlasting and self-sufficient. Whether you start with the scientific account of the primordial fireball of astronomy and physics or the biblical account that "In the beginning God created the heavens and the earth"—and many of us would say they are not talking about two different things but simply the same thing in different ways—the universe had a beginning. Nature is *created*.

∾

Nature is also *good*. The first creation story in the Bible (there are several) affirms this repeatedly in the course of the "days" of creation. From light to the waters and the dry land, to the vegetation, to the sun, moon and stars, and all manner of creatures in sea and on the land, including humanity—these are all declared good. Finally, "God saw everything that He had made, and behold it was very good" (Gen 1:31).

Nature, in spite of that, is ambiguous. It can be as beautiful as a rose or a sunset, but it can also be as deadly as a tsunami. It may speak of order but is also red with tooth and claw and indifferent to human concerns. The germ, the parasite, the cancer, the avalanche, and the earthquake: these, too, are nature, and they crush and kill. So, if one seeks to find God in nature alone, to have a kind of nature-god or a god of beauty, eventually, one becomes disillusioned, as did the Buddha, by the world's suffering and pain. That is why the Christian faith speaks not only about creation, but also about redemption, the cross, resurrection and about re-creation on a cosmic scale. St. Paul's Letter to the Romans says that "the whole creation has been groaning in travail" (Rom 8:22), and the book of Revelation points to a consummation yet to come wherein there will be "a new heaven and a new earth" . . . and God himself will be with them; he will wipe away every tear from their eyes, and death shall be no more, neither shall there be mourning nor crying nor pain any more, for the former things have passed away" (Rev 21:1, 3b–4).

Yet, nature, in its entirety and at its deepest level, even now, remains good. The volcanoes that can obliterate a city were instrumental in creating our atmosphere. Comets have the potential to cause mass extinctions when they collide with our world, but they also may have brought most of the water on which all of life depends. The movement of the continental plates that shakes the earth is an effect of the inner heat-engine of the planet, and without such geologic activity, earth would likely resemble the moon, unchanging and sterile. There is an overall goodness, then, that surpasses any judgment about any particular part of the system and its usefulness to humanity. If the various parts and processes of the whole have worked together to produce this astounding biosphere, then we cannot pick and choose. Aldo Leopold, in his justly famous book, *A Sand County Almanac*, writes, "The last word in ignorance is the man who says of an animal or plant: What good is it? If the land mechanism as a whole is good, then every part is good, whether we understand it or not." That is a perspective that is promoted today by virtually everyone in the biological sciences, but it is as old, really, as Genesis chapter 1. The affirmation that creation is good is necessary to state, because the idea that the world is less than good has a long history and is still around. The Zoroastrians and Manichaeans of ancient Persia were *dualists* in the extreme, i.e., they divided reality into two realms, one evil, one good, with each ruled by a deity with the same qualities. The intangible realm of the soul was good and the material world was evil. However, it was in Classical Greece, from which western civilization received so much in terms of language and concepts and ideas, that such a dichotomy gained the most traction.

Plato was one of the towering intellects of history and surely one of the most influential. His system of thought is dualistic, dividing reality into the mental and the material, and it affirmed that, by far, the most real is the mental. Plato believed in the primacy of ideas and was the founder of a whole school of philosophy called *Idealism* that has continued to the present time.

Modern Idealism might be illustrated by a story Margaret Moorman tells of the art critic, Leo Steinberg. He had an uncle who was a philosopher. When Leo was about six years old, he asked his uncle what philosophy was all about and was told, "A philosopher is one who thinks about philosophical problems." Not to be put off, the boy asked what such problems might be. The uncle said, "Well, I'll give you one: Suppose an architect builds a house, using 10,000 bricks. After awhile, a brick crumbles and has to be replaced. Then another, and another, until all the bricks have been replaced by new ones. Is it now a new house or is it the old house?" Leo said immediately, "It's a new house." However, when the uncle came to visit again a couple of weeks later, Leo said he had changed his mind and that he now believed it to be the *old* house.

The uncle turned to the boy's father and said, "Congratulations! Your son has moved from materialism to idealism in two weeks!" Plato, also, would have been proud. Is it not the case that the Idea, the form, the mental construct of the house, not its construction material, is its essence? The idea was in the mind of the architect before the carpenter gave it shape. Form is prior to fact.

Idealism in that vein has a long and noble history in philosophic thought. The astrophysicist James Hopwood Jeans, famous for his discoveries relating to the interior processes of stars, is also known for suggesting that the universe is beginning to look less like a great mechanism and more like a Great Thought.

Plato, however, went much further. In his famous analogy in *The Republic*, he likens the unenlightened, those in a state of "thoughtlessness," to prisoners in a cave who can see only flickering shadows of things on the wall and who mistake those for the things themselves. Material objects are merely the shadows, Plato said, while Ideas, sometimes termed Eternal Forms, are what is real. You know when something is beautiful because you already have in your mind the Form, the Idea or Ideal of beauty; you recognize beautiful things insofar as they partake of that ideal quality that exists in another superior, immaterial, and eternal realm accessed by the mind. Perhaps it can be illustrated, also, by saying that you know what a person is and how to judge him/her because you have within your mind the built-in or innate idea of "personhood." All individuals are more or less flawed copies of the Idea. (One cannot help but be reminded of the fellow who went to a psychiatrist to lay out his problems, faults, and deficiencies of personality—and they are many. The doctor says, "You don't have an inferiority complex—you simply *are* inferior!")

It was almost inevitable that Plato's focus on the mental would get out of balance and depreciate the physical. Virtually everything was divided into those two realms: spirit and matter, soul and body, the immaterial and physical, and the conception had implications in almost every area. In another of his works, *Phaedo*, Plato quotes his mentor Socrates concerning death: "And is this anything but the separation of soul and body?" For them both, the soul was immortal, while the body was transient, mundane, and an outright hindrance to the higher life of the soul. Death, in this conception, was a release of the soul, so that it could be free of material limitations, a kind of shuffling off the mortal coil that weighed it down.

This idea was handed down and mingled with other ideas in Western thought and is now often confused with biblical Christianity, distorting it in the process. The old song, "John Brown's body lies a-mouldering in the grave, but his soul goes marching on," is really a Platonic hymn, not a Christian one. The latter perspective is, instead, that a person is an organic whole, indivisible, a psychosomatic unity, much as modern medicine understands it. Thus, traditional Christian teaching does not speak about an indestructible soul, immortal no matter what. Instead, it talks about resurrection of the whole person, i.e., re-creation, and this totally as gift. Thus, it is the whole being, including the body, that is good, and it is the entire world, not just some spiritual part of it, that is good.

Some length has been spent on this, because it is all too common in our culture to depreciate this earthly realm of nature in favor of some nebulous, otherworldly reality. The consequences of this are many, including an insufficient value placed on our environment, the world of here and now.

The dualistic view can edge over into seeing nature as the enemy, even, as illustrated in *Moby Dick*, which is widely regarded as one of the most substantial novels to come out of America in its first two hundred years. Therein, Captain Ahab reveals to his shipmate that he is after the great white whale, not only because it had bitten off his leg, but also because he views it as representative of the evil he sees lurking beneath the surface of all things:

> All visible objects, man, are but as pasteboard masks. But in each event—in the living act, the undoubted deed—there, some un-known but still reasoning thing puts forth the mouldings of its features from behind the unreasoning mask. If man will strike, strike through the mask! How can the prisoner reach outside, except by thrusting through the wall? To me, the white whale is that wall, shoved near to me! . . . I see him in outrageous strength, with inscrutable malice sinewing it. That inscrutable thing is chiefly what I hate; and be the white whale agent, or be the white whale principal, I will wreak that hate upon him!

The fear and terror of the crew is partly due to their knowledge that to regard nature as evil is a blasphemous view, one utterly different from that taught either by Scripture or by common sense. So, they know they are on board with a crazy man at the helm, this even as they watch the dolphins and fish and the great leviathans of the deep sporting and cavorting in the waves as testimonies to the fullness and goodness of creation.

~

Another point of view on nature is that it is a *machine*. The Age of Enlightenment began to look upon nature in a way that was very different from most previous cultures. In prior ages, nature was seen to be animated, alive, even enchanted with spirits, gods, and goddesses moving throughout. Scientists looking for causal relationships began to change that. The work of Isaac Newton in describing the laws of gravity and motion by which the paths of the planet are governed was a supreme achievement along those lines, so much so, that his epitaph became:

> Nature and Nature's laws lay hid in Night:
> God said, Let Newton be! And all was Light.

The universe was said to operate as a vast machine obeying invariable laws of cause and effect. It was like a billiard table in which God had imparted the initial motions and, if you knew every angle and force of the matter involved, you could predict where things would be in the indefinite future. The immense popularity of clocks in this era provided the paradigm for nature itself, so that the image that came to dominate was that of a clockwork universe of gears and levers and hinges. (Emperor Charles V retired so he could spend years trying to synchronize thirteen clocks to keep time together; he never succeeded.) Newton allowed that it might be necessary for God to do a little tinkering, every 50,000 years or so, to keep small instabilities from getting out of hand. However, his laws of motion were so comprehensive in describing the way nature works that it was not until Einstein's concept of relativity that much new was added concerning all of this, and for most things, those prior formulations of natural law continue to work very well. On one of the early space shuttle ventures, after lift-off and well into the flight, mission control asked the astronauts, "Who's flying the plane?" The pilot answered, "Isaac Newton."

Newton's ideas were inflated by others to become part and parcel of an entire worldview called *Deism*. This is a variety of *Theism*, or belief in God, but with a particular twist. In the beginning, it said, God had created the clockwork of the world, wound it up and set it running, and it has been operating ever since only by natural law. Deists believed in a deity, but only as a kind of first cause or prime mover of the vast mechanism that is nature, an image first developed by Aristotle. Thus, after creation, God did not intervene; the clock ran by itself, so to speak. In contrast to the Christian faith, therefore, Deism ruled out miracles and the incarnation. A supreme being existed, but only as remote instigator and, for some, as a judge in the afterlife; in the meantime, the world ran strictly as a machine.

This view was prominent among aristocracy of the Enlightenment in France and that, in turn, influenced the aristocracy in America. Benjamin Franklin, Thomas Jefferson, and a number of the framers of the Constitution were Deists. Thomas Paine played a key role in the American Revolution by editing the pamphlet, *The Plain Truth*, with which he fanned the flames. Paine also gave Jefferson many of the best-known statements in the Declaration of Independence. Written in Paris, Paine's 1794 book, *The Age of Reason*, spells out Deism: "The creation is the Bible of the Deist. He there reads, in the handwriting of the Creator himself, the certainty of his existence and immutability of his power, and all the other Bibles and Testaments are to him forgeries . . . This knowledge is of divine origin, and it is from the Bible of the creation that man has learned it, and not from the stupid Bible of the church, that teacheth man nothing." Knowledge of morality is confined to every person's conscience, while "the groveling tales and doctrines of the Bible are fit only to excite contempt." You can still see Jefferson's Bible, wherein he took his razor and literally cut out passages from the Gospels that refer to the miracles of Christ or to any assertion that God was present in and through him. Jefferson was left with Jesus as merely a great humanistic teacher, since God was only a creator who could not be involved with the world here and now.

How ironic, therefore, that the religious Right today often urges the need to "get back to the religion of the Founding Fathers" and that "America was founded by great Christians." They know not whereof they speak. Virtually all the founders believed in a supreme being, but not all concepts can be termed Christian. God was, to some, instead, the Great Clockmaker, or—in deistic images that survive today in certain secret societies—the Master Builder or Great Architect of the material universe, period.

For some Enlightenment thinkers, the mechanistic view meant that living beings were themselves machines. René Descartes (1596–1650), as mathematician, did pioneering work on calculus. As philosopher, he speculated on many things, including going so far as to say that animals did not have souls or minds or feelings or anything remotely resembling what goes on inside of us. They were, instead, merely complex physical mechanisms, so that, if you stuck a needle into a dog's paw and it howled, you could not say it had pain; that was just a mechanical response. His followers conducted cruel experiments on animals based on this assumption, contrary to all common sense, that the creatures had no feelings at all. In 1651, Thomas Hobbes published his essay on government, in which the image of the machine was extended to man, "For seeing life is but a motion of limbs . . . For what is the heart, but a spring; and the nerves, but so many strings, and the joints, but so many wheels?"

In the image of the machine, nature had no life of its own. Peoples of antiquity, Stone Age man, as well as later peoples in Africa and elsewhere that the Europeans called primitive, viewed all objects in the world as having a spirit. Nature was animated, i.e., had an *anima* or spirit running through it. Nature was alive. In effect, and in great contrast, Europeans rewrote the fable of the maiden who found an ugly toad by the edge of the pond. The toad said, "Help me, sweet maiden. I am really a handsome prince who has been put under a spell by a wicked witch. Take me with you, hold me close all night, and you will break the spell." Therefore, she took the toad to her cottage, held it close all night, and, when she awoke the next morning—she had warts! Nature was now *dis*enchanted. Of course, the typical person of that era would not have been familiar with the reasoning of Descartes or Hobbes; however, the implications of their views trickled down. It is usually the case with paradigms or worldviews that they are not objects of reflection; instead, they are assumed: "Why, everybody knows that!"

Also, if nature really were a machine, then the more you learned about how it worked—and science was becoming *the* way to do that—then you could manipulate it, control and contrive it for your own purposes, for as a collection of inanimate objects, nature had neither souls nor goals of its own. *The Platypus and the Mermaid*, by Harriet Ritvo, deals with the efforts in the eighteenth and nineteenth centuries to classify newly discovered animals. In it, she cites an 1824 work by George Graves entitled *The Naturalist's Companion, Being a Brief Introduction to the Different Branches of Natural History*. It recommends that "on procuring an Animal with which we are unacquainted, the first point . . . is to ascertain whether it is . . . applicable to the uses of Man . . . or should its habits be detrimental or obnoxious, what measures are pursued to destroy the species." Nature was something to be used by man, the tool-using animal, and culled to his own liking. Nature was the impersonal setting for the human drama; it was merely the stage or backdrop for human adventure and history. The stage had no real value in and of itself; it was simply there so the actors could play their parts, and there was no doubt about who was the main player.

Thus, nature as machine implied that it was also tool box, storage chest, treasure chest. It was there for peoples' taking: there *for* them, there for consumption and exploitation, as well. This was the view of the great majority of those who, in this same age, set out in ships to explore the world beyond the vast oceans. Those who followed Columbus found a continent with astonishing natural endowments. The historian Frederick Turner tells us, "The men of Henry Hudson's *Half Moon* . . . were temporarily disarmed by the fragrance of the New Jersey shore, while ships running farther up the coast occasionally swam through large beds of floating flowers. Wherever they came inland, they found a rich riot of color and sound, of game and luxuriant vegetation . . . Had they been other than they were, they might have written a new mythology here. As it was, they took inventory."

In the New World, such a point of view was not obvious to those who were already here. Instead, the Europeans' lens stood in sharp contrast to that of the Native Americans whom the explorers encountered on these shores.

≈

Native peoples had been here for many thousands of years already. There was a time, of course, when the continents of the Western Hemisphere were empty of human habitation. Then, at the end of the last Ice Age, when the sea level was perhaps 300 feet lower, people from Asia migrated across the land bridge to Alaska. They may have made the trip also by sea, following the western coast of North America. Archaeologists are presently rewriting this story, pushing back the earliest migrations from 12,000 years to perhaps even 30,000. In any case, they moved down, one generation after another, and in just a few thousand years settled from the Arctic to the tip of South America and, in the process, developed different languages and cultures. In North America, the white man would encounter such groups as the Pequot, Seminole, Sioux, Ojibwa, Salish, the Comanche, and dozens of other tribes.

It is easy to glorify or romanticize the past just because it is past; it is easy to idealize pre-Columbian native peoples, also. The English playwright, John Dryden (1631–1700) wrote, "I am as free as Nature first made man, / Ere the base laws of servitude began, / When wild in the woods the noble savage ran."

For all our cultural contrasts, human nature is alike. Thus, native peoples had their wars and, we may assume, all kinds of other failings and imperfections. Yet their view of nature deserves special attention. Each tribe had distinctive beliefs, but two generalized statements may be said to apply to all.

In the first place, *the land cannot be owned*, either by individuals or by groups. Native people belonged to the land and not the other way around. There was no idea of boundaries as applied to the earth. The little red and blue lines that are all over our maps do not occur in nature and native peoples could not conceive of them in any fashion. Goods such as those gathered or fashioned by people could be traded, but not the land itself; one could have individual property such as this or that tepee or knife or horse, but the land was no commodity. It was not theirs to sell. Mother Earth was not real estate.

The white man not only bought and sold the land; he bought and sold life, including human life, in the terrible slave trade. The founders of our country, such as Washington and Jefferson, while they could write about the inalienable rights of every human being, had slaves themselves until the days they died. So deep is the mind-set of an age that, decades after these presidents, the Capitol Building in Washington, DC was built partly by slaves.

For Native Americans, the unified and organic whole that is the land could not be portioned out. Nature, its rocks and soils, trees and all living things: these could not be owned by human beings, the fundamental reason being that they all belong to the Creator Spirit. The idea is not different from that of the Psalms: "For every beast of the forest is mine, the cattle on a thousand hills. I know all the birds of the air, and all that moves in the field is mine" (Ps 50:10–11).

Contrast this with the sense that dominates our modern society, with its boundaries, fences, deeds, titles, and title-searches, its constant litigation over property lines and "water rights," even. Land is now being sold for thousands of dollars a shoreline-*foot* on the great Flathead Lake in Montana, this in the very home of people who had not the slightest idea that you could divide or sell anything of the natural world.

Put all this in the context, also, of the long history of the earth. When you see a prairie or mountain landscape that has been here for millions of years before we got here and that will likely be here for millions more, the image of people holding little paper deeds and loudly proclaiming, "This is mine!" is fairly ludicrous. We brought nothing into the world and we shall leave with the same, but the world will remain. It is not our possession; rather, we belong to it, and it all belongs to the Creator, as the Native Americans knew.

In the second place, and intimately related, is the idea that *nature is sacred and must be treated with respect.* Instead of property, the earth is provider. Directly and indirectly, Mother Earth feeds all her children. The Sioux medicine man, Black Elk, said of his people's view, "It is the story of all life that is holy and is good to tell, and of us two-legged sharing in it with the four-leggeds and the wings of the air and all green things; these are children of one mother and their father is one Spirit." Other creatures are seen as "relatives," a phrase that occurs time and again in Native stories. All are bound together in a single circle that has mystical ties between sun and moon and stars, the undulating prairie with its waving grasses and flowing rivers, and the creatures that lived in, with, and under it all. Chief Luther Standing Bear explained: "We do not think of the great open plains, the beautiful rolling hills, and winding streams with tangled growth, as 'wild.' Only to the white man was nature a 'wilderness,' and only to him was the land 'infested' with 'wild' animals and 'savage' peoples. To us it was tame. Earth was bountiful and we were surrounded with the blessings of the Great Mystery."

The movie *The Last of the Mohicans* opens with the chase scene between hunters and game. The Indians and the frontiersman Hawkeye, adopted son of the tribe, dash through the trees to intercept the running deer. With a single shot from the long-rifle, the antlered buck hurtles down a knoll and slides into the fallen leaves, dead. Afterwards, there are no "Yahoos" and high-fives, as are common in the autumn woods today. The hunter's foot is not on the creature's neck with talk of having conquered a trophy. Instead, there is a long moment of silence. There is reverence before the great animal, now still, the animal that was so fleet, vital, and full of energy just a few minutes before. Honor is paid to the holy character of both life and death and to all those numinous forces, both known and unknown, which sustain us in the natural world.

~

What *is* nature? How our ancestors answered that question, consciously or not, determined how they treated the world and the same is true for us today. It is seldom that a frame of reference that has become dominant is questioned. The buffalo hunters of the plains, who in just a few years killed off thirty million for hides, saw them simply as a resource to be exploited as fully as possible and did so to the very edge of extermination. "Resource management" is a modern term familiar to everyone in our culture. It retains something of the connotation of nature as merely a means to human ends: nature as raw material for all those products we make or covet, this, instead of something that has its own reason for existing. So, we look at the world and what we see is a reflection of our inmost selves. It is said that the writer Ring Lardner stood on the rim of the Grand Canyon and quipped that it seemed like it would be "a good place to throw used razor blades." What can one say in response to such a mentality?

Yet, occasionally, a voice reminds us of the circle of life upon which we depend and of which we are not a spectator but a part. Occasionally, a voice reminds us of the eternal mystery of things, which is the real nature. In 1920, Henry Beston published his book, *The Outermost House*, a chronicle of a solitary year spent on the beach at Cape Cod, a year during which he came to know the turning of the heavens and the ceaseless rhythms of the seasons, of wind and sand and sea, the migrations of birds, and the sacredness of all life:

> We need another and a wiser and perhaps a more mystical concept of animals . . . We patronize them for their incompleteness, for their tragic fate of having taken form so far below ourselves. And therein we err, and greatly err. For the animal shall not be measured by man. In a world older and more complete than ours they move finished and complete, gifted with extensions of the

senses we have lost or never attained, living by voices we shall never hear. They are not brethren, they are not underlings; they are other nations, caught with ourselves in the net of life and time, fellow prisoners of the splendour and travail of the earth.

9

The Two Books

Science & Religion

There are two books of God: the book of God's Word and the Book of God's Works. They are not to be confused in their nature, language or purpose, and we must not unwisely mingle or confound these learnings together.

Francis Bacon (1605)

The most beautiful thing and deepest experience a person can have is the sense of the mysterious. It is the underlying principle of religion as well as all serious endeavor in art and science.

Albert Einstein

A N ASTRONOMER AND A theologian were seated next to each other on a plane. After the introductions and small talk, the scientist said, "So, you're a theologian. Well, religion is really pretty simple, isn't it? Doesn't it all come down to 'Do unto others as you would have them do unto you?'" The theologian replied, "So, you are an astronomer. Well, let's see: astronomy is really quite simple, isn't it? Doesn't it all come down to 'Twinkle, twinkle, little star, how I wonder what you are?'"

Of course, neither science nor religion is so simple, and surely not their relationship, interaction, and implications for one another. Religious ideals have affected the uses to which the findings of science have or have not been put, and there's no question that scientific discoveries have altered and enlarged our concepts of God, as well as that of the natural world. In a truck stop restroom in Nebraska, someone put this graffiti on the wall: "The earth is flat—signed, 'The Class of 1491.'"

However, much of the public has accepted with little questioning the oft-heard idea that religion and science have, over the centuries, been involved in a kind of warfare. As historians of both science and religion are demonstrating these days, that conclusion, like Mark Twain's obituary, which he read in the newspaper, has been greatly exaggerated. Despite the difficulties Galileo encountered with leaders of the church of his day, science was seen as a way to know the mind of God. Galileo wrote, "There is only one truth, but it is communicated in two forms: the language of the Bible and the language of nature. Both are God's languages." The early discoverers of the laws of nature were the true creationists; they read the text of the world and paid reverence to the creator with every new discovery and strove, like Bacon, ". . . with humility and veneration to unroll the volume of Creation." In the 1600s, Johannes Kepler, a schoolteacher, passionately devoted his spare time to astronomy and became the first person to figure out that the orbits of the planets did not trace a circle but an ellipse. He said that he was "but thinking God's thoughts after Him." It was the same with Isaac Newton, as he penned his elegant formulas. Their work was worship, and, in a sense, they viewed all science as theology, inasmuch as it revealed more of the power and the creative activity of God. Christopher Wren was the architect who designed St. Paul's Cathedral in London. On a plaque to his memory are the words, "If you would seek his monument, look around you." In the largest sense, applying it to God, this could have been the motto of most of the workers in the various sciences in those decisive early days. When the great Austrian philosopher, Immanuel Kant, wrote that two things filled him with wonder and awe, "the starry heavens above and the moral law within," this was without any sense whatsoever of those being mutually exclusive realms; rather, those realities pointed to twin components for the full experience of life.

Darwin's theory of evolutionary descent brought reaction. When *On the Origin of Species* first appeared in the booksellers' windows in 1859, this remark, supposedly, was overheard: "Let us hope that it is not true; but if it *is* true, that not many find out about it." However, opposition to the idea has often been greatly overstated. After all, Darwin's funeral was held in London's Westminster Abbey cathedral, and his tomb is inside the church, next to that of Newton. Thus, when he died in 1882, the Church of England had already largely come to terms with the new knowledge, accepting it as a description of the forces, the mechanisms, and the laws by which creation is sustained and diversity achieved in nature. For evolution deals with secondary causes, not primary ones; i.e., it concerns the process, the details, not the ultimate source. Many people believed then, as millions do now, that God created life, and evolution was the way God did it.

In our own time, millions have looked through the window provided by modern science, respected the methodology, and appropriated the view that science has afforded, this without diminishing in the least their reverence for a creator behind creation. Carl Sandburg awoke in the middle of the night to gaze out over the skyscraper peaks of Chicago and later penned these lines to the poem "Glass House Canticle":

> Bless Thee, O Lord, for the laws Thou hast ordained holding fast
> these tall oblongs of stone and steel, holding fast the planet Earth
> in its course and farther beyond the cycle of the sun.

~

With this background, how did we get into a situation where many people continue to see science and religion in terms of polarization, if not conflict? Simply witness that almost any story in newspapers or websites concerning even the most obscure discoveries in the realm of biology are met with online blogs that quickly degenerate into shouting matches between creationists and atheists.

Such a syndrome might be said to begin with two books published in the late 1800s here in America: John Draper's *History of the Conflict between Religion and Science* and Andrew Dickson White's *A History of the Warfare of Science with Theology in Christendom*. Both books were polemics, mostly against the Catholic Church, which they despised. Both works were extremely popular in their time, but they have been thoroughly discredited by modern scholarship. Yet, their labels entered the mindset of the culture and perpetuated what is, for the most part, the myth of the conflict/warfare scenario. John Hedley Brooke points out that "much of the conflict ostensibly between science and religion turns out to have been between new science and the sanctified science of a previous generation."

Quite to the contrary of the warfare model, many historians of science are now positing that there was a strong connection between the rise of science in the western world and the Christian worldview. One of the great philosophers of the twentieth century was Alfred North Whitehead, who expressed this line of thought in *Science and the Modern World*, wherein he points out that before you could have science, there needed to be in place an assumption that the world is rational, capable of being understood, i.e., that there are laws that function uniformly. In other words, you need the presupposition that the world is not ruled by gremlins and capricious spirits—not multiple gods each with their own agenda—but a single creator (monotheism) who does not act upon whim nor constantly interferes with the forces and laws that have been set in place. Thus, there could be no chemistry if the scientist had to worry about leprechauns coming into the laboratory every night and turning the hydrochloric acid into water. As stated in Loren Eiseley's book, *Darwin's Century* (published in 1958 on the eve of the centennial of the *Origin* and still one of the best explications of evolution and those who discovered it): "It is the Christian world which finally gave birth in clear and articulate fashion to the experimental method of science itself . . . It is surely one of the paradoxes of history that science, which professionally has little to do with faith, owes its origins to an act of faith that the universe can be rationally interpreted, and that science today is sustained by that assumption."

Along the same lines, Timothy Ferris has indicated that the idea of the universe as a single system ruled by uniform laws was derived from the Judeo-Christian-Muslim belief in one God. Eric Hoffer continued the discussion in his essay, "Jehovah and the Machine Age." Mathematics, he said, was God's style: "Nature was God's text, and the mathematical notations were His alphabet . . . It is as if the Occident had first to conceive a God who was a scientist and a technician before it could create a civilization dominated by science and technology."

Added to this is the idea that those religions held that nature, created by God, is good but not itself divine, in contrast to many other ancient cultures (such as those that assumed pantheism). Therefore, nature itself was not to be worshiped, and it was permissible, instead, to examine it and experiment with it. The linear biblical conception of time, as outlined in a previous chapter, also played a part.

Thus, there was a connection between the worldview of medieval Europe, which included a certain conception of God, and how all of this graded into the Renaissance. One way to describe it is to say that the conception of an orderly creation by a dependable creator is what gave strong impetus to scientific inquiry.

At the same time, over the course of the last five centuries and concurrent with the development of formal science, there has been an erosion of a number of religious beliefs, this due to what Walter Lippmann calls "the acids of modernity," so that "there is gone that ineffable certainty that once made God and His Plan seem as real as the lamp-post." Some of us doubt that the religious impulse ever had certainty to such degree, else it would not be called faith. It is also the case that many of us would consider quite a number of those shed beliefs to be extraneous, at the fringe, and some of them even outright distractions to the core of it all. People can believe all sorts of ridiculous things, and "faith" is far from always an unqualified good. Therefore, it has not all been loss, by any means.

There have always been the village atheists, of course, but there are a lot more of them now. Richard Dawkins has become famous for holding that human beings are mere robot vehicles for the survival of selfish genes. He is strident in maintaining that all religion is due to ignorance and that science and religion are diametrically opposed, representing completely incompatible worldviews. The evolutionist Stephen Jay Gould knew better; in *Rocks of Ages: Science and Religion in the Fullness of Life*, he critiques such simplistic exaggerations by saying, "I do get discouraged when some of my colleagues tout their private atheism . . . as a panacea for human progress against an absurd caricature of 'religion' as a straw man for rhetorical purposes."

In such discussions, one often encounters the term *naturalism*. A parenthesis is necessary here to distinguish two kinds. There is, first, *scientific naturalism*, which simply means that science must seek and deal with causes and effects in the material world: matter and energy are the subjects to which the scientific method is applied. Thus, when Napoleon asked LaPlace what part God had in his theory of the formation of the planets, LaPlace replied, "Sire, I have no need of that hypothesis." In so doing, he was not denying God. The statement has often been misconstrued as one of atheism, but he was simply operating as a good scientist, confining the method to such things as are within its scope and not confounding it with supernatural explanations. Science deals with natural objects and natural causes.

There is also, however, *philosophical naturalism*, which is a world-view, one that goes far beyond methodology and says that all that *exists* are those things that are the subject of science: the mindless, material forces of matter and energy. In this view, it is not just that science is the only satisfactory or reliable way to investigate the workings of the physical universe; it is that there is nothing else *besides* the physical universe. So, geneticist Richard Lewontin of Harvard says that it is a "hopeless" task to educate the public in all the findings of modern science; therefore, the goal is to get the public "to accept a social and intellectual apparatus, *Science*, as the only begetter of truth." He is unusually candid about it, saying, "It is not that the methods and institutions of science somehow compel us to accept a material explanation of the phenomenal world, but, on the contrary, we are forced by our *a priori* adherence to material causes to create an apparatus of investigation and a set of concepts that produce material explanations . . . Moreover, that materialism is absolute, for we cannot allow a Divine Foot in the door." Confined to material explanations, ideas of purpose and meaning are to be replaced by a mechanical universe displaying nothing but blind, empty indifference. However, the expectation and the conclusion are intertwined.

Such nihilistic views were outlined by philosopher W. T. Stace in a 1948 article written for the *Atlantic Monthly* titled "Man Against Darkness." Long before, Thomas Hobbes had stated that what we call good and evil are simply "names that signify our appetites and aversions." Stace expresses much the same sentiment, and, in so doing, accurately describes a kind of malaise that affects the modern world. Great progress has been made in things technical, but this does not inform our ideals: "No one any longer effectively believes in moral principles except as private prejudices." This, he presumes, comes from the picture of the universe presented by science: "The world, according to this new picture, is purposeless, senseless, meaningless. Nature is nothing but matter in motion." A person's behavior is thus seen as being determined by multiple causes, much as other phenomena in nature. Therefore, "Not moral self-control, but the doctor, the psychiatrist, the educationist, must save us from doing evil. Pills and injections in the future are to do what Christ and the prophets have failed to do." As a description of the depersonalizing influences of our time, the assessment could be considered to be rather accurate; however, it is very much in line with his personal views as well. Most philosophical naturalists stop short of the above sentiments, but Stace deserves credit for pursuing this line of thought farther than almost anyone else, so that all can see where it leads. (Even he hedges a bit by trying to wring out a little hope that civilized people can "walk straightly and to live honorably without the props and crutches of one or another of the childish dreams which have so far supported men." Yet he fails to mention what the terms "straight" and "honor" signify and why those have either meaning or appeal in the lifeless scheme of things that he has outlined.)

Interestingly, a naturalism of this stripe relieves the holder of any effort toward making the world a better place, since words such as "better," "right," "wrong," or "ethical" describe either irrational impulses or convictions held merely as the result of conditioning. Those words are, like the universe, without any meaningful content and cannot be said to be true or false any more than can an itch or a reflex. In this view, there exist no foundations whatsoever for ethical values; they can claim to be nothing more than mere opinion. (However, naturalists espousing such a view will strongly object if someone steals their car, credit cards, their spouse, or their idea for a book. If they are to be logically consistent, they should not object, but in fact—quite irrationally—they do.) One must go further and maintain that the logical extension of the idea that neither good nor evil exist means that it doesn't matter whether your neighbor greets you or shoots you. Indeed, some of the "senseless acts of violence" of which we often hear in the news occur because the perpetrators have adopted the conclusion that the world makes no sense. But why should one do anything at all, why even get out of bed, if it is just that everything is mere molecules in motion? It shouldn't matter to the molecules, because *nothing* matters. Hobbes' description of life as "solitary, poor, nasty, brutish, and short" would seem to be a "natural" consequence of *this* sort of naturalism.

As a method, science consists of the observation of facts and collection of data, the formulating of hypotheses, experimentation to test them, and then generalizations formulated to describe how the world appears to work. As such, the employment of the method is entirely compatible with the way most of us see religion. Ideology masquerading as science is a different tune. Here, science has become scien*tism*. Personal predilections, likely held for any number of reasons, are portrayed as necessary consequences of what science tells us about the world. Religion does have conflict with a distortion of science that becomes totalitarian, dictating conclusions to questions that can never be properly addressed by its own methodology, such conclusions as would contribute to an artless debasing of humanity.

Peter Dodson of the University of Pennsylvania is a geologist, an anatomist, an evolutionary biologist, and one of the world's foremost dinosaur paleontologists. He also highly values religion. In an essay published by The Paleontological Society entitled "Faith of a Paleontologist," Dodson gets at the issue: "An evolutionism or scientism that teaches in the name of science that there is no God, no soul, there is no ultimate purpose to life, and no such thing as free will, is no friend of society . . . Science discounts human experience, while religion is about human experience. When forced to choose between a religion that enriches human experience and an evolutionary science that ignores human experience and minimizes humans as a species, people will unhesitatingly choose the religion that gives meaning to their daily struggles." They will, indeed, and, I would add, this is true even if it means choosing some form of religion that is ultimately less than helpful, which many will consider is the case with fundamentalism.

In 2005, an individual named Chris Norris of Connecticut wrote a letter to the Editor of the science magazine *Discover*, saying he was once a student of Dawkins at Oxford. Greatly appreciative of the science he learned there, he combines an acceptance of evolution with a personal faith in God and says he has been "alternately amused and saddened by Dawkins' subsequent antics." Norris says his former teacher has become a mirror image of the religious extremists he decries: "He and the religious fundamentalists have ended up saying the same thing—namely, that religious belief and science belong in the same intellectual arena and that it is legitimate for one to comment on the validity of the other. Thinking that there is a real debate to be had between the two fields ultimately opens the door to equal time for creation science . . . and is something that every scientist—religious, atheist, or agnostic—ought to reject."

Science is a wonderful tool. Every day, we all benefit immensely from its discoveries in ways that need not be detailed here. However, when its methodology is inflated to an exaggerated, all-embracing authority on virtually everything, then it is deficient in the extreme, leading to the false expectation that all has been understood *via* our mechanisms, technologies, and techniques. As described above, scientism pursued with all the ardor of religious zealots is indeed another kind of fundamentalism. That syndrome is a broad thing that has perverted many a religion, but other systems of thought, also, can become rigid, narrow, and dogmatic in the extreme.

The British philosopher David Hume (1711–1776), in his *Inquiry Concerning Human Understanding*, uplifted empirical investigation (read "science"). He spoke against all metaphysics (read "religion") and said of any such writing: "Commit it then to the flames: for it can contain nothing but sophistry and illusion." When he penned those words, reason and its child, science, were being similarly extolled across the English Channel, and the 1789 French Revolution was just a few decades away. In it, the world was to be saved not by God but by the guillotine, and thousands were forced to bow to it in the overthrow of the old order. In Paris, nobles and priests were first in line. "Were you not a noble?" asked the leader of the tribunal of the accused. "Yes," was the reply. "Enough; another," the judge would intone as the long line of victims proceeded through the court. In the so-called "Reign of Terror," in one space of just seven weeks in 1794, the total of those beheaded was 1,376. In the midst of such slaughter, it was declared that the revolution should not rest until it had "dethroned the King of Heaven as well as the kings of earth." Churches were closed and their treasures confiscated by the state. Bells were melted down into cannon. In many cemeteries, all emblems of hope were obliterated, and over their gates were inscribed the words, "Death is eternal sleep." In place of all supposed superstition, a celebrated beauty personifying the Goddess of Reason was paraded through the streets of Paris and set on the stripped altar of Notre Dame Cathedral as an object of worship. The lunacy culminated in the leaders turning upon one another with the same thirst for blood as they had toward their perceived oppressors. (Upon the shambles of it all, Napoleon would rise to emperor.) All of this madness—at the height of the so-called Enlightenment with its proclamation of the primacy of reason and committed in its name—was anything but rational. It may well be that the greatest of illusions is to be conscious of none.

~

Science honors the *empirical principle*, appealing to the kinds of facts that can be put in the test-tube, connected to the meter, or weighed on the scale. The dogmatic extension of this is to say that such facts are the only ones that count. Science utilizes the *quantitative principle*, describing reality with units and numbers; "If there's no numbers, there's no science." Scient*ism* says that which cannot be subject to such is not real. Taken together, the exclusive focus on the empirical and quantitative principles becomes full-blown materialism. Thus, Harvard entomologist E. O. Wilson, who has done highly admirable work in things ecological, sometimes goes beyond that to write as if science is the arbiter of all things. In *On Human Nature* he says, "The final, decisive edge enjoyed by scientific naturalism will come from its capacity to explain traditional religion, its chief competitor, as a wholly material phenomenon." In addition, the mind itself will be explained simply as "an epiphenomenon of the neural machinery of the brain."

Of course, the brain is a physical thing, and there is no doubt that it teems with electrical and chemical reactions that make possible thought and emotion, but is the mind reducible to that? Obviously, a painting by Cezanne or Rembrandt can be analyzed in terms of its material constituents: the canvas, oils, and pigments, etc., but is that the end of it? Is it, again, all simply hurrying electrons and ultimately meaningless? Is what is going on in a symphony by Mozart or Beethoven "a wholly material phenomenon"? If so, then must not the same be said of Wilson's science, rendering it ultimately without foundation? Or is it not, rather, that if we design instruments to measure, ask questions, and solve problems that have to do *simply* with things physical and quantifiable, then that's the only sort of thing we will find? Nature itself, in that mode of apprehension, is poor substitute for the wild, wondrous, and mysterious realm that many of us know. W.H. Auden's summary is concise:

> The glass-lens
> desanctified Sight: men believed
> they had seen through Nature.

We overlay the world with our concepts in the attempt to manipulate and understand it, but, in so doing, it is possible to mistake the map for the territory. Simply consider that countless other creatures perceive the world in quite a different fashion than we do. The Clark's nutcracker is a bird found throughout the conifer forests of the Rocky Mountains. (It was first described in the journals of the great westward expedition of Lewis and Clark.) This inquisitive and handsome jay feeds almost entirely on the seeds of pinecones, and, to ensure its survival throughout an entire year, it collects thousands of seeds and buries them in hundreds of places over a wide area. When the seeds are needed for food, the bird is able to find almost all of them. Some of us can't find our keys. Clearly, the nutcracker's brain is adapted to see the world in a different fashion than is ours.

Many creatures see the world in ultraviolet light, a part of the spectrum closed to us. The honeybee cruising among red flowers is not drawn to them by the vivid colors that attract us; instead, it sees the ultraviolet rendition, wherein red appears to be more nearly gray and is devoid of brilliance. On the vast stage of life, whose is the real show?

Thus, it would be naïve to think that our theories, perceptions, and observations are equivalent to the world itself, and the simplistic and cocksure descriptions of what reality does or does not include are just that. In *The Mind's Sky*, Timothy Ferris points to everlasting mystery with the words, "Outside our frame of reference forever hovers something else—the larger reality, embracing every bird's egg and mud puddle, every star and planet, every poem and crime in the gigantic and eternally incomprehensible universe."

So, our methods of investigation are human constructs to order our perceptions and, as such, may tell us as much about ourselves as about any objective external reality. Sir Arthur Eddington was the brilliant British astrophysicist who confirmed some aspects of the theory of general relativity with observations taken on an island off the coast of West Africa during the solar eclipse of May 29, 1919. He was one of the few capable of transmitting the idea of relativity to a wider audience. He concludes the book *Space, Time and Gravitation* with the thought that science gets out of nature that which the mind first puts into it: "We have found a strange footprint on the shores of the unknown. We have devised profound theories, one after another, to account for its origin. At last, we have succeeded in reconstructing the creature that made the foot-print. And Lo! It is our own."

In *The Philosophy of Physical Science*, he also describes the tools of scientific inquiry and their results with his wonderful parable of an ichthyologist studying life in the deep sea, this with a net having a two-inch mesh. After hauling up numerous samples, he found no fish smaller than two inches. Should the conclusion be that there are no such fish in the sea? No: "There are plenty of sea creatures under two inches long, only your net is not adapted to catch them." The graphic illustration suggests that the results are determined in advance by the method. If the method is limited—and science certainly is—the results will not be a complete picture. (Eddington filled out at least part of the remainder of the picture with religion; he was a Quaker, regularly attending gatherings at the Friends' Meeting House.)

A similar point with broad application was made by John Steinbeck, who had been a student of marine biology. In 1961, he published his book, *Travels with Charley*, in which he described his trip across America in his pickup camper with his dog "to find the truth about the country." He learned that to uncover such truths and to convey them was far from easy. Therefore, he wrote, "I carried in my head and deeper in my perceptions a barrel of worms. I discovered long ago in collecting and classifying marine animals that what I found was closely intermeshed with how I felt at the time. External reality has a way of being not so external after all." Again, "What you see is what you get," and what you see is influenced by all sorts of things.

～

Science continually deals with the *mechanical principle* of cause and effect. This is the kind of understanding a child might seek when he or she tries to figure out the workings of a watch. Why do the hands move? The back is pried off in the effort to see what makes it tick, i.e., what is the cause of this or that effect? (True or not, I remember hearing of parents who gave their young son a drum for Christmas and proceeded to go almost "dingy" from the constant pounding. They put a knife in his hands and asked, "I wonder what is *inside* the drum?") Questions of *what* and *how* are the questions of science. Modern medicine and technology in general are monuments to the success of asking and answering those sorts of questions; the process has transformed our world in many positive ways. Push the mechanical principle far enough, however, and you have *determinism*. The ancient world knew the concept of fate, well expressed by Persian poet Omar Khayyam in *The Rubaiyat*:

But helpless Pieces of the Game He plays
Upon his Chequer-board of Nights and Days
Hither and thither moves, and checks, and slays,
And one by one back in the Closet lays.

The Fates have been replaced today, in some quarters, by biological determinism, wherein all is merely stimulus-response, understood in physical-chemical terms. In that line of thinking, we are completely determined by forces beyond our control and free will is an illusion, as indeed some of the writers quoted above openly stated. All this is in spite of the fact that every legal system in the world depends upon the understanding that we are responsible because we are free. (The truth of this is confirmed by our feelings when someone throws a rock through our window—or does worse. We do not just say, "Well, he couldn't help it.") It is convenient to assume that every aspect of human behavior, including even the most horrific, is simply rooted in our animal nature and dictated by our genes, since that means that ethical lapses of every sort should occasion no guilt. It also implies that the poor and hungry masses of humanity have only themselves or their genetic material to blame and that we need not lend a hand. The psychiatrist Karl Menninger writes, "The present world miasma and depression are partly the result of our self-induced conviction that since sin has ceased to be, only neurotics need to be treated and the criminals punished. The rest may stand around and read the newspapers."

The response of microbiologist René Dubos is fitting: "The mechanical definition of human life misses the point, because what is human in man is precisely that which is not mechanical." (In addition, he is doubtful it applies to animals, and points to Harvard biologist George Wald's framing of what has come to be known as the Harvard Law of Animal Behavior: "Under precisely controlled conditions, an animal does as he damn pleases!")

The determinist could be disarmed in simple fashion, although the disclaimer must be that the specific technique is "not actually recommended." When you encounter one who maintains that free will does not exist and that everything we do is the result of heredity, genes, chemical reactions and electrical impulses in our brains and bodies, the result of stimuli-response and social conditioning—you could simply lean over the coffee cup and punch him or her in the face. The assaulted one would no doubt get upset. You could then simply explain that you had no choice in the matter, that you were conditioned, controlled, and determined, and thus it was all perfectly "natural" and that, therefore, the other person should not be upset at all.

Further, if the logic of determinism were to be consistent, it must be the case that a person's ideas regarding the issue would themselves be determined: those ideas are simply the products of genes, hormones, and chemistry, and they could not possibly have a claim to the status of *truth*. Of course, determinists *will* want to claim such ideas as true and are often vociferous in such claims. Everyone else may be determined, but not them and not their "science."

Thus, some of those claiming support from science far exceed its sphere of competence and draw conclusions that are far beyond the evidence, even though, supposedly, they are based on facts. The first chapter of Charles Dickens' novel *Hard Times* is titled "One Thing Needful." Schoolmaster Gradgrind opens the tale with these words: "Now, what I want is the Facts. Teach these boys and girls nothing else but Facts. Facts alone are wanted in life. Plant nothing else and root out everything else. You can only form the minds of reasoning animals upon Facts: nothing else will ever be of any service to them . . . Stick to the Facts, Sir." It is a rather good picture both of an impoverished education and of the indication that, in knowledge, we always are dealing with human selectivity.

Owen Gingerich was professor of astronomy and the history of science at Harvard for decades, as well as a senior astronomer at the Smithsonian Astrophysical Observatory in Cambridge. He writes, "As a scientist, I work within a mechanical framework . . . because the system of prediction and explanation is so powerful and successful. There is much about myself that can be profitably understood as a mechanical product at the end of a four billion-year chain of evolution. But as a human being, I am also entitled to believe that these are not the ultimate answers. Not only am I entitled to believe that human beings are more than machines, I proclaim it!"

C. S. Lewis proclaimed it, also, to a prior generation. His not-so-subtle reaction to some of his materialist and reductionist colleagues speaks for many of us: "This astonishing cataract of bears, babies and bananas: this immoderate deluge of atoms, orchids, oranges, cancers, canaries, fleas, gases, tornadoes and toads—how could you *ever* have thought this was ultimate reality?"

Such affirmations, again, are needed in the face of oft-heard sweeping generalizations supposedly based on science when, in reality, many of them grow out of naturalistic presuppositions imported into the discussion. Such presuppositions, of course, cannot be verified using the tools of science itself. Science writer Eugenie C. Scott affirms, "We must remember that science is not equipped, methodologically speaking, to tell us whether or not there is any 'point' to the universe. If scientists undertake nevertheless to hold forth on such matters, they must admit in all candor that their ruminations are not scientific declarations." No less an organization than the National Academy of Sciences states the issue in clear terms: "At the root of the apparent conflict between some religions and evolution is a misunderstanding of the critical difference between religious and scientific ways of knowing. Religions and science answer different questions about the world."

One of the premier evolutionary biologists of the twentieth century was Stephen Jay Gould, who held that the two enterprises were entirely different. He viewed science as dealing with the facts of the natural world and developing theories that explain and coordinate these facts, while religion centered in the equally important, but quite different, arena of human meanings and values. As he stated in a lecture titled *Darwin's Revolution in Thought*: "To say it for all my colleagues and for the umpteenth millionth time (from college bull sessions to learned treatises): science simply cannot, by its legitimate methods, adjudicate the issue of God's possible superintendence of nature. We neither affirm nor deny it; we simply can't comment on it as scientists."

Eric Cornell was awarded the Nobel Prize for Physics in 2001. In 2005, he wrote an article titled, "What Was God Thinking? Science Can't Tell," wherein he spoke to the question, "Why is the sky blue?" and indicated that there are two answers. (1) The sky is blue because of the wavelength dependence of Rayleigh scattering; (2) The sky is blue because that's the color God wants it to be. They are two different answers, he said, but neither replaces the other. The religious answer is a supplement to, but not a substitute for, the scientific one. "We may now, if we care to, think of Rayleigh scattering as the method God has chosen to implement his color scheme." In trying to preserve science from its friends, as well as its foes, Cornell offers this: "Should scientists, as humans, make judgments on ethics, morals, values, and religion? Absolutely. Should we act on these judgments, in an effort to do good? You bet. Should we make use of the goodwill we may have accumulated through our scientific achievements to help us do good? Why not? Just don't claim that your *science* tells you 'what is good' . . . or what is God.'"

Science does not replace religion; neither do religious answers replace those of science. An anecdote concerning the great English journalist G. K. Chesterton tells that he was once asked if he were stranded on the proverbial desert island and could have only one book with him, which one he would choose? Chesterton was an openly religious person, and therefore, it was thought he would say the Bible, the Book of Common Prayer, a volume of readings on the faith, or some such thing. Instead, he answered, *"Taylor's Guide to Home Boatbuilding."* There are things for which religion is not much use. Prayer is a substitute neither for mechanics nor for CT scans and surgeries. Most people don't need to be told that.

Again, back on the other side of it, neither does science do away with the need for things of the spirit, for meanings and values. Indeed, no one does live only by the empiricist creed; no one forms conclusions based strictly upon observation. I think of the story of the physicist who took a ride in the country, and upon his return he was asked if the sheep had been shorn yet. His reply was not "Yes" or "No" but, rather, "As far as I could see, all the sides of the sheep presented to me had been shorn." No one functions like that, do they?

The physical and natural sciences excel in taking things apart and examining the pieces. Year by year, the pieces get smaller and smaller, and such focus has led to numerous advances. However, science is far from equally competent in considering those larger realities that are emergent from the whole, all those realities where the sum is greater than the total of the parts. In the process, a total picture, a coherent narrative, something more than an accumulation of facts, is missing.

∼

Life consists largely of issues *other* than those engaged by science. Thus, you don't analyze a piece of pie for its specific gravity—you could, but the scientific method is inappropriate for such an item. Instead, you taste it. We don't apply statistical analysis to the statues of Michelangelo; what could that possibly tell us about art? An x-ray gives important and accurate information of the human body, but there is no one who keeps an x-ray on the dresser as a portrait of the beloved. You could go to a wedding with all sorts of analytical tools and measure the physical stress on the floorboards as the wedding party comes down the aisle or the force of the sound waves from the organ speakers bouncing on the walls; you could measure the respiration and pulse-rate of the bride and groom. In so doing, you will have gained a multitude of facts and acquired a certain kind of truth, but in the process you will have missed, and rather badly, what the ceremony is really about.

Thus, what we would call the deepest issues of existence—matters of life and death—do not lend themselves to detachment. Any satisfaction in relation to them comes from personal involvement, which is the very opposite of the methodology employed by science. A person may work in the laboratory all day, but by evening goes home to spouse and family to deal with issues and feelings that are on quite another level: those of love and commitment, of hopes and dreams, of value and meaning, i.e., levels of existence that open themselves only to engagement. These are issues not of science but of religion in the broadest sense. Nobel Prize-winning physicist and mathematician Richard Feynman was quick to maintain that "There are some things left out, for which the scientific method does not work. This does not mean that those things are unimportant. They are, in fact, in many ways the most important." The hard-nosed empiricist philosopher Wittgenstein maintained that even if it were possible to answer all scientific questions with certainty, the basic issues of life would not be touched at all. At bottom, everyone knows that. No one is more than a part-time scientist, but everyone is a full-time human being.

Because this is true, the mass of people on the planet recognize intuitively that there is not a single method for discovering truth, i.e., science, but that there are, in fact, different ways of knowing, each appropriate in its own realm and each existing in a complementary relationship to the others. In the words of Jane Goodall in *Reason for Hope*, "Yes, there are many windows through which we humans, searching for meaning, can look out into the world around us. There are those carved out by Western science, their panes polished by a succession of brilliant minds . . . Yet, there are other windows." She goes on to speak of a profound experience of her own: "I had known timelessness and quiet ecstasy, sensed a truth of which mainstream science is a small fraction. And I knew that the revelation would be with me for the rest of my life, imperfectly remembered yet always within."

Thus, who knows the sea better: the analyst who breaks down the water into its constituent elements or the sailor, who, with John Masefield, loves

> . . . a tall ship and a star to steer her by,
> And the wheel's kick and the wind's song and the white
> sail's shaking,
> And a grey mist on the sea's face and a grey dawn
> breaking?

The theologian Paul Tillich wrote that verification of a truth is, in fact, most often "experiential in contradistinction to experimental." Surely, it is the case that the largest part of our knowing is like that: simply by experience. If the method and the results are not as precise as those provided by science, this is because the subject is less trivial, i.e., much more complex and vast. Therefore, Thomas Aquinas taught, "The slenderest knowledge that may be obtained of the highest things is more desirable than the most certain knowledge obtained of lesser things." Limiting ourselves to the kind of knowledge that can be confirmed as being true beyond much doubt means minimizing the risk of error; however, it also means we will be missing what are the most subtle, crucial and rewarding elements in life. The love of another, the loyalty of a friend—these are not subject to empirical demonstration (in fact, that might destroy them), but they are among the most real things we know. Pascal must have been thinking along such lines when he wrote in his *Pensées*, "The heart has reasons, which reason does not know. We feel it in a thousand things."

It is because such realities constitute our most significant experiences that we find words to be inadequate to express them and that we are drawn to use other modes of expression. Thus, in music and art, for example, the fact that they are not subject to precise analysis or quantification is precisely their value. Van Gogh wrote to his brother: "Tell them I long most of all to learn how to produce those very inaccuracies, those very aberrations, reworkings, transformations of reality, as may turn it into, well—a lie if you like—but truer than the literal truth."

When we do speak, we thus take account of the fact that religious and scientific ways of speaking are each appropriate within its own realm but cannot be interchanged. Call to mind the child's nursery rhyme: "Twinkle, twinkle, little star / How I wonder what you are / Up above the world so high / Like a diamond in the sky." Here is a "scientific" version, author unknown: "Scintillate, Scintillate, globule vivific / Vain would I fathom your nature specific / Loftily poised in ether capacious / Strongly resembling a gem carbonaceous." It's not the same thing, is it?

By involvement and immersion in life, we have perhaps not a comprehension—the biggest issues of life are never *solved*—but an apprehension. Truth, in that sense, does not tumble out at the end of an equation, but instead, is self-authenticating. Not reducible to facts and formulas, a pulse of certainty nevertheless beats through many religious encounters. Emerson wrote, "Our faith comes in moments; our vice is habitual. Yet there is a depth in those brief moments which constrains us to ascribe more reality to them than to all other experiences." William James in *The Varieties of Religious Experience* contended that our normal waking and rational consciousness is but one special type, "while all about it, parted from it by the filmiest of screens, there lie potential forms of consciousness entirely different." Mystics in every culture know what he means. Jewish theologian Abraham Joshua Heschel speaks of "moments when we are stirred beyond words, of instants of wonder, awe, praise, fear, and radical amazement," and says that religion, awareness of the divine, "is the result of what one does with one's higher *in*comprehension."

On the morning of December 6, 1273, while saying Mass in Naples, Aquinas had a singular moment of transformation. He had written thousands of pages of theology and philosophy; he had explicated the thought of Aristotle and related it to the historic Christian faith in a process that took decades and made him into one who is still regarded as a towering figure of the Middle Ages. That morning, he cut short the service and, from that moment on, never resumed the role in which he had so excelled. He finally explained that he could do no more, saying, "All I have written seems to me like so much straw compared with what I have seen and with what has been revealed to me."

Are there times when dramatic inner experience is delusional? Yes, indeed. But is this true of all such times? No one can get inside the mind of another, and therefore we cannot, without extreme bias, dismiss such things as being mere neural surges, mere static on the mental screen. They may be, instead, a more profound experience of a larger reality, one usually closed to us by the business, clutter, and preoccupations of daily life. In the words of the nineteenth-century French priest Joseph Roux, "God often visits us, but most of the time we are not at home."

Death. Surely this is the basic issue faced by all thinking or cognizant beings. It is the axial problem, the reality that stirs in people an awareness of the things that matter most; it also highlights the insufficiency of science in dealing with them. Science will not replace religion because, among other reasons, it cannot solve the problem of death. The mortality rate of the human race has never varied from a full 100 percent. We are the species that knows that life is terminal and that, as soon as you are born, you are old enough to die. Shakespeare's dirge is true, that "Golden lads and girls all must / as chimney-sweepers, come to dust," as are the words of Longfellow that

> . . . Time is fleeting,
> And our hearts, though stout and brave,
> Still, like muffled drums are beating
> Funeral marches to the grave.

We usually do our best to prevent this thought from crossing our minds. The old syllogism that some of us learned in basic logic, that "All men are mortal; Socrates is a man; therefore, Socrates is mortal," does not have our name in it. Carl Sandburg's verse, "Limited," well illustrates the syndrome:

> I am riding on a limited express, one of the crack
> Trains of the nation.
> Hurtling across the prairie into blue haze and dark air
> Go fifteen all-steel coaches holding a thousand people.
> (All the coaches shall be scrap and rust and all the men
> And women laughing in the diners and sleepers shall
> Pass to ashes.)
> I ask a man in the smoker where he is going and he
> Answers: 'Omaha.'

That additional and final destination is kept out of conscious reflection. As Sir Thomas Browne wrote, "The long habit of living indisposeth us to dying." Thus, the end takes us by surprise, as in the old English play, *Everyman*: "O death, thou comest when I had thee least in mind." Thus, not only teens and young adults have the illusion of immortality, so do most of us most of the time, until an illness, accident, or the infirmities of old age impinge upon us. In Leo Tolstoy's short story *The Death of Ivan Ilych,* the main character takes a fall, bruising his side. At first, it is just an aggravation. However, as time passes, Ilych does not get better; then, day by day, he gets worse. Finally, and incredibly, it is evident that he is going to die. He is then forced to review the manner in which he has spent his years, also keenly assessing the lives of those others who come to pay their obligatory last respects: "In them he saw himself—all that for which he had lived—and saw clearly that it was not real at all, but a terrible and huge deception which had hidden both life and death."

Consider a scientist who works for twenty years behind a microscope dissecting invertebrates or overseeing chemical reactions in the laboratory. Then, he receives the medical diagnosis indicating that very soon he is going to die. Is there anything in his science that is of much use in confronting that most pressing of all problems? No. The scientist, the garbage collector, the statesman, the farmer, teacher and shopkeeper are "all in the same boat," for the issue is of another and a higher order than that which any of those habitually deal in their vocations. The question is of a different *kind* entirely than the questions of *what* and *how* of science. Now, the scientist faces a religious question. It is *why*, and *who* am I, anyway, and *for what* has my life counted, and *where* am I going and is death oblivion and annihilation or something else? And no one can answer those questions for another. With issues of this magnitude, truth is not one item among many for objective and detached analysis. It is, instead, something one appropriates: it is personal.

Over the course of nearly four decades, I have conducted hundreds of funerals. Like others in my profession, I have sat by the bedsides of numerous people who were confronting death, whether from age, or illness, or accident. Each one has been different, and the responses to that situation have ranged from utter despair to profound joy. One is reminded of some more famous personages with their, also, varied responses. As death drew near, Rabelais, the sixteenth-century French writer, said, "Draw the curtain: the farce is ended!" Michelangelo: "I regret that I die just as I am beginning to learn the alphabet of my profession." Thomas Edison: "It is very beautiful over there." Artist Jean Carot: "In spite of myself, I go on hoping . . . there will be painting in heaven." John Wilkes Booth: "Useless! Useless!" Ballerina Anna Pavlova: "Get my swan costume ready." Queen Elizabeth I: "All my possessions for a moment of time." O. Henry: "Turn up the lights. I don't want to go home in the dark." Henry James: "So, here it is at last, the distinguished thing!" And, from the cross, Jesus: "Father, into thy hands I commit my spirit."

In the Roman Empire, at the time St. Paul was writing his letters that are contained in the New Testament, tombstones were sometimes inscribed with these words of Epicurus, "I was not; I became; I am not; I care not." There are many modern versions, also. What they have in common is that they are rather consistent with the reductionist and materialist view of philosophical naturalism that we are simply highly developed mammals who came from nowhere and are headed to the same: mere matter in motion.

There are no small numbers of others, however, who have experienced the end of this life as the last and best chance to be fully human. In the process, they have appropriated the conviction voiced by eighteenth-century playwright Joseph Addison:

> The stars shall fade away, the sun himself
> Grow dim with age, and nature sink in years,
> But thou shalt flourish in eternal youth,
> Unhurt amid the wars of elements,
> The wrecks of matter, and the crush of
> worlds.

Of course, this is not a conclusion of science, but science has neither expertise nor authority in the realm of these, the *ultimate* questions.

∽

As with death, the confrontation with nature, too, can give rise to transformational insights, something that is affirmed often between the lines of this book. Professional golfer Lee Trevino was out on the course when lightning struck a tree very near to where he was standing. Asked what he thought when the "bolt from the blue" hit, he said, "I learned that when God wants to play through, you'd better let him!" That is a humorous remark, but the incident itself would also generate reflection that is more serious. Like him, when most of us confront the natural world, it is not with tools for use in experiments but rather simply by direct and immediate encounter. Here, we are not in any manner above nature, superintending it for analysis and measurement; instead, we are simply there with openness and receptivity: nature happens *to* us. The poet William Wordsworth recorded such in his poem "Lines," which was written a few miles above Tintern Abbey in 1798:

I have felt
A presence that disturbs me with the joy
Of elevated thoughts; a sense sublime
Of something far more deeply interfused,
Whose dwelling is the light of setting suns,
And the round ocean and the living air,
And the blue sky, and the mind of man;
A motion and a spirit, that impels
All thinking things, all objects of all thought,
And rolls through all things.

⁓

This chapter on science and religion ranges widely, something that is necessary in order to do any justice to the nature of religion, for it is not one compartment among many. The great psychiatrist Carl Jung had these words of affirmation put over his doorway and on his tomb-stone, "Bidden or not bidden, God is present." Werner von Braun was the scientist who headed up America's Apollo space program to build the huge Saturn rockets that carried the astronauts to the moon. He re-ferred to what science might possibly reveal about God with the image that we need not light a candle to see the sun. Religion embodies less this or that subject than it does perspectives, i.e., the basic premises of religion are never "seen" directly; rather, they are the light in which everything else is seen.

It seems that the great Einstein, also, understood that. I have in-dicated that science and religion deal with different types of questions. However, beyond that separation of different sorts of inquiry and meth-od there exists a more basic unity, one that makes investigation of the world possible in the first place. Without that assumption, no science could proceed. Thus, Einstein spoke of "the religious basis of scientific enterprise." "Certain it is that a conviction, akin to religious feeling, of the rationality and intelligibility of the world lies behind all scientific work of a higher order." Further, "Try and penetrate with our limited means the secrets of nature and you will find that, behind all the discern-ible concatenations, there remains something subtle, intangible, and inexplicable. Veneration for this force beyond anything we can compre-hend is my religion." His religious sense included "rapturous amazement at the harmony of natural law" and a "deeply emotional conviction of the presence of a superior reasoning Power." He affirmed that the belief in the existence of basic all-embracing laws in nature also rests on a sort of faith: "Everyone who is seriously involved in the pursuit of science becomes convinced that a spirit is manifest in the laws of the universe— a spirit vastly superior to that of man, and one in the face of which we, with our modest powers, must feel humble." In response to questions about God from Jewish theologian Martin Buber, Einstein said, "What we physicists strive for is just to draw his lines after him."

Thus, scientists describe the workings of the larger dimensions of physical universe with differential equations, but that does not remove the mystery of why the differential equations work in the first place.

The Princeton physicist Freeman Dyson was entranced by the peculiar harmony between the way the universe is structured and the needs of life and intelligence and has written of the many "numerical accidents that seem to conspire to make the universe habitable." Before scrolling through many of them, from the nuclear forces within the atom to the expansion rate of the universe, he writes, "It is true that we emerged in the universe itself by chance, but the idea of chance is only a cover for our ignorance. I do not feel like an alien in this universe. The more I examine the universe and study the details of its architecture, the more evidence I find that the universe in some sense must have known we were coming."

Einstein and Dyson both viewed the trustworthiness of the universe, the uniformity of natural laws, and the fact that there can be some degree of comprehension of it all, as pointing to the universe being grounded in God. Einstein once spoke to a conference at Union Theological Seminary in New York about the scientists' faith in the rationality of the world. Walter Isaacson, in his recent Einstein biography writes, "The talk got front-page news coverage, and his pithy conclusion became famous: 'The situation may be expressed by an image: science without religion is lame, religion without science is blind.'"

Indeed, religion can be "blind." The Flat Earth Society is motivated by a commitment to the cosmology of three thousand years ago. In 1993, the supreme religious authority of Saudi Arabia, Sheik Abdel-Aziz Ibn Baaz, issued an edict or "fatwa" declaring that the world is flat and all who think that it is round should be punished. (The irony is that the idea that the earth is a sphere, first discovered by the Greeks, was transmitted to Western Europe in the Middle Ages by scholars who were Muslim

and Arab.) Religion has sometimes picked fights where no proper conflict need exist, sometimes becoming imperialistic, having lost sight of
its proper domain. It has often been manipulated by those with political
agendas. Too often, too, it has been small-minded and legalistic. In its
concern for the individual, it has sometimes become individualistic, losing sight of larger social issues. It has neglected the very first article of
the faith dealing with creation, and thus has been too feeble a voice in
environmental concerns. Religion has sanctioned ill-begotten wars. At
times, it has been subverted by extremism, and recent history provides
abundant illustration. All this is true because religion is human, and distortion and corruption exist in all human endeavors.

On the other hand, religion has also been a reservoir and preserv-
er of knowledge of all kinds. During England's industrial revolution,
most children living in the slums worked six days a week in mines and
factories; it could be said that public education had its beginning in
the so-called Sunday schools run by Christian congregations wherein
such kids were taught to read and write on their only day off. The first
universities were founded in Europe in association with the cathedrals,
and the first great universities of America, Harvard, Yale, Princeton,
and others, were begun by the church. Religion was the driving force
behind the foundation of hospitals and provided the impetus for hu-
manitarian efforts of many and varied kinds. It has built thousands of
nursing homes and done remarkable work in battling world hunger. It
was the prime mover behind ending slavery in one century and promoting integration and civil rights in the next. Religion has also em-
braced, and in some ways enabled, new discoveries about the nature
of the universe—discoveries that have only increased our sense of awe
and appreciation at the created order.

In the process, millions of believers have allowed the findings of
science to reassess our place in nature in a more realistic fashion. The
nineteenth-century invertebrate paleontologist T. A. Conrad is alleged
to have commented about a particularly ancient fossil that if the trilobites could speak, they would correct many a false theological dogma.
They were once the crown of creation; in the Cambrian Period, 500 million years ago, those ancient two- and three-inch arthropods were the
highest form of life. We, who have not been here very long and who may
not be here much longer, are forced to admit that the continents did not
move and the seas did not rise and fall just for us; the great branching

profusion of living things has had many expressions. If we say that this is God's creation, then clearly—given all those eons since the dawn of life—God has other concerns besides us (something you would not know by watching most religious programming on television).

Awareness of that immense depth of geological time, as well as the vastness of space with its countless far-flung galaxies, has caused most of us to reframe our notions of God's activity in ways that greatly enlarge the concept of the divine. A verse by Samuel Foss speaks of a provincial boy who "paced and ploughed his little plots and prayed unto his little god." New knowledge appeared, threatening his faith, but not for long:

> He saw the boundless scheme dilate, in star and blossom, sky and clod;
> And as the universe grew great, he dreamed for it a greater God.

Most forms of religion (fundamentalism excepted) have thus been greatly enriched by the modern concepts of the universe, our planet, and the complexities of life itself, as science has discovered them.

Science has transformed the world in a thousand ways for good, something that is abundantly clear and obvious enough to need no further expansion here. As a human venture—and this should not surprise us—it is also subject to human failings. The goal may be that of doing so-called "pure science," but those actually trying to do it know all too well about the excessive commitment attached to a pet hypothesis and about the turf battles and personality conflicts that can color the enterprise. In the understatement of paleontologist Mark Norell, "Science is not always a genteel world of polite discourse."

Science can be more than "lame." It can also be dangerous, a threat to civilization itself, as when it places its expertise in the service of twisted values. History records it to have been an instrument of barbarism on numerous occasions, and the potential for huge evil is always there. Victor Weiskoff has written of his work as a young physicist with Oppenheimer and the rest at Los Alamos on the Manhattan Project to build the atomic bomb. He describes the first test, there in the New Mexico desert. As the countdown began, the loudspeaker picked up the frequency of a nearby radio station, so that in the background of the cadence, Ten, nine, eight, seven, six . . . there was heard the music of *The Nutcracker Suite*. "Thus," says Weiskoff, "the countdown for this test of the most powerful weapon of war yet dreamed up was accompanied by the lyrical sounds of a waltz by Tchaikovsky." The meaning was not lost on many of those who had worked on the project: the terrible ambiguity of power. Knowledge can be used to bomb or to bless. It can be used to wreak and ruin or to uplift and inspire. Today, even after some reductions, there are more than 40,000 nuclear weapons. They lurk beneath the waves in holds of huge submarines, and they crouch in underground missile silos, waiting to spring into the daylight. Most of them are already programmed to destroy the major cities of "the enemy." In so doing, they would also destroy most of life on earth. After World War II, Winston Churchill visited the U.S. One of his speeches was to a large crowd at Fulton, Missouri, in which he warned, "The Stone Age may return on the gleaming wings of science." The warning is not out of date.

Of course, the tools of science *per se* are not the problem; as always, it is the manner in which the tools are used and the goals and values that are served. This means scientists cannot, with any conscience, separate their discoveries from how those are employed, but it also means that we need more than science. We must give as much attention to values and ideals, to those ethical and religious sensibilities that determine not just what *can* be done but what *should* be done. A world that spends more on weapons of war than on education and that lets nearly a billion people go to bed hungry each night is far from understanding that.

Pope John Paul II summed up much in a 1988 message by affirming that science can save religion from superstition and error, while religion can guard science from a commitment to false absolutes.

Thus, in both science and religion, as well as in every other human endeavor, we have great need for humility. That word has its root in the Latin *humus*, meaning "earth," with the connotation that humility keeps us grounded. The great Newton wrote, late in his life, "I do not know what I appear to the world, but to myself I seem to have been only like a boy playing on the seashore, and diverting myself in now and then finding a smoother pebble or prettier shell than ordinary, whilst the great ocean of truth lay all undiscovered before me."

Such a spirit is appropriate, because, in science, our explanations are not *explanations* at all. They are, instead, *descriptions*. Science attempts to describe *how* things appear to work, but *why* things work the way they do escapes us. Science discovers the laws of nature, but the laws and the realities to which they point are simply givens. The acorn and the oak tree can be taken apart and the process of the one developing into the other can be documented in specific detail, but why either exists at all cannot be explained.

We direct and manipulate the forces of nature, often to our own satisfaction. G. K. Chesterton noted in his essay "The Ethics of Elfland" that we can describe natural processes, "But we cannot say why an egg can turn into a chicken any more than we can say why a bear should turn into a fairy prince . . . When we are asked why eggs turn to birds or fruits fall in autumn we must answer exactly as the fairy godmother would answer if Cinderella asked her why mice turned to horses or her clothes fell from her at twelve o'clock. We must answer that it is *magic*." Chesterton reminds us that the world was once new—new and astonishing—to us all: "These tales say that apples were golden only to refresh the forgotten moment when we found that they were green. They make rivers run with wine only to make us remember, for one wild moment, that they run with water."

Thus, scientists delve into questions of cause and effect, and do so quite successfully, but when it comes to the much larger questions, they, like all others, can only speculate, since the methods employed by science only access what might be called a certain outer shell of things. While the public often assumes that more is comprehended than is the case, Einstein, again, exhibited great humility in the face of the unknown: "We see a universe marvelously arranged and obeying certain laws, but only dimly understand these laws." Timothy Ferris also takes note of the physicist and philosopher of science, John Archibald Wheeler, who wrote, "The vision of the universe so vivid in our minds is framed by a few iron posts of true observation—themselves resting on theory for their meaning—but most of the walls and towers in the vision are of papier-mâché, plastered in between those posts by an immense labor of imagination and theory." Ferris himself then concludes, "We are confronted, then, not with *the* universe, which remains an eternal riddle, but with whatever model of the universe we can build within the mind."

I think of an incident when I was a freshman student at South Dakota State University. The class was chemistry, and, in the middle of his lecture, our professor stopped and asked a friend of mine sitting in the back row (for good reason), "What is electricity?" Taken back, not having read the assignment, the student gave the standard reply that he *had* known the answer to that question, but he had forgotten it. At this, the teacher, a very demonstrative man, began pacing about and waving his arms. He even pounded his head on the blackboard several times, finally stopped, threw up his hands, and said, "Oh, no!—The only person in the history of the world who *knew* what electricity was, and he *forgot!*" (I can still see him after all these years.) In that superbly dramatic fashion, he made the point that, even though we have harnessed this energy and utilize it routinely, it remains, in essence, a mystery.

I think of those illusionists who perform on television and who, by some gigantic slight-of-hand, make even elephants seem to appear and disappear before our very eyes. It is, of course, only seeming. However, in a deeper sense, there's magic all around us. Ultimately, we don't know the what and the why of the universe; we don't know how life began or why flowers grow, so that the magic by the showman on stage is but a metaphor for the real thing. Thus, beyond the most superficial explanations, why is it that a heart can beat or a brain think, and why *is* there something instead of nothing?

As a young boy on our farm in southwestern Minnesota, I would often climb to the top of our silo to survey the surrounding countryside. Sometimes, unknown to my parents, the venture was at night, for it seemed the mere thirty feet of additional height brought me just a little closer to the stars. When looking at the horizon, it was often unclear whether the tiny points of light that shone in the darkness represented stars thousands of light years away or, instead, the farmstead lights of neighbors within walking distance. So, too, science and religion, in their respective ways, attempt to sort things out, but there are regions wherein the boundaries blur and answers elude us.

Symbols of unending curiosity, the largest telescopic lenses and mirrors in the world are perched on the highest peaks, staring into the darkness of outer space in order to spy out the very edge of the known universe. These are now supplemented by satellite eyes that soar in orbits high above the atmospheric haze of an increasingly industrialized planet. At the other extreme, scanning electron microscopes and other tools delve into the structure of matter itself, this in search of that which philosophers of a former age, in a grasping for words, called the underlying "substance" of things. In all this exploring, humanity is like the bear in the children's song that went over the mountain "to see what he could see."

In the glass of our instruments, both large and small, is the reflection of our own eye looking back into the recesses of our own selves. It is within that more nebulous inner space that religion, art, literature, and all the humanities seek to illumine what it means to be a human being. There, we find no answers in the back of the book. While we must allow others to trace the paths of subatomic particles or to collect light from a distant galaxy, in this endeavor, each individual in every generation must largely begin anew to find a place within it all: a living coherence of purpose, fulfillment, and relationships. Yet in this realm of what we call the things of the spirit, progress can be made. In an expanding universe, the mind can continue to expand and so can the heart and soul.

10

Creation, Evolution, and Creation*ism*

There is grandeur in this view of life, with its several powers having
been originally breathed by the Creator into a few forms or into
one; and that, whilst this planet has gone cycling on according to
the fixed laws of gravity, from so simple a beginning endless forms
most beautiful and wonderful have been and are being evolved.

Charles Darwin

THE BROADEST CONNOTATION OF the word *evolution* is simply that
of change in the course of time. In that sense, language evolves and
is doing so constantly. Think of the clichés that come and go among
teenagers. Last year's "in" words are soon passé and replaced by new
ones. No one says, "Swell!" anymore; that was replaced by "Far Out!"
and "Radical!" etc., and I do not know what might be the present equivalent. (Although it is curious that the slang "Cool," current when I was in
high school, is still around. It is a bit like the exceptional crocodiles that
survive from the Age of Dinosaurs.) Language evolves. Cities are not
invented; they grow and become what they are over the passage of time.
No one would deny the fact of such change, such "evolution."

Change and development also occur, said Darwin, in living things.
He noted how English farmers were able to carry on selective breeding
to produce, in a rather short time, low-slung dogs like the dachshund to
go down into the badger's den; he went to pigeon shows and saw some
birds with feathers on feet that resembled wings. It was *artificial selec-*
tion, and it stimulated this idea: "Can it be thought improbable, seeing

that variations useful to man have undoubtedly occurred, that other variations useful in some way to each being in the great and complex battle of life should occur in the course of many successive generations? . . . This preservation of favorable individual differences and variations, the destruction of those which are injurious, I have called *Natural Selection.*" Key factors in the process are population pressures, which force competition for a limited resource, such as food, and mutation and variation, which are constantly taking place, so that when there is a variant that is better suited to a new circumstance, it may survive, in contrast to those that are less suited. Over time, such changes result in differences sufficient to be termed new species. Evolution is thus like a sieve through which pass those living things that are best adapted to a current environment.

That, in the briefest summary form, is the core of Darwin's contribution. He did not "invent" the idea of evolution; that concept was around in the entire century preceding him. Many people believed evolution to be a fact. (Lamarck had a highly developed theory, and Darwin's grandfather wrote of evolution.) Darwin, along with others, said about a species what Galileo had said about the planet, that it *moves.* However, what no one before Darwin had adequately described was *how* it actually took place, i.e., the mechanism for it, which we now term natural selection.

The mechanism was discovered at virtually the same time by another amateur naturalist, Alfred Russell Wallace, but in view of the huge amount of supporting evidence published by Darwin, it is most associated with the latter.

In the course of more than a hundred and fifty years, the theory has been refined and modified in various details and supplemented by new discoveries in genetics. Still, the basic outline remains the same, that all living things are related branches on a single tree. The life we know today is of a continuum with the life that has gone before. It has descended from, or grown out of, previous generations of living things over an immense span of time in the process called evolution. (The word comes from a Latin term meaning to unfold or to unroll, as in the unrolling of a scroll.)

There are many lines of evidence that point to evolution. The ordered appearance of different sorts of creatures in the fossil record is one such line. If species had been created all at once, we would not find fossils in the sequential order that we do; instead, different sorts would be found all together. Or, if individual species were created one at a time in sequence, caribou and kangaroos could easily have appeared first, lowest down in the rock strata, then birds, then elephants, then fish, then trees, trilobites, bacteria, rabbits and sail-backed reptiles, etc. That is not what is found. Each group, each species, appears to have been preceded by an ancestor to which it is closely related, pointing to what Darwin called "descent with modification."

Suggestive, also, are what evolutionists call *homologous structures*. The skeletal structure of the human arm, the flipper of a whale, the leg of a mole, the wing of a bat and a bird: these are all markedly similar in form. They have been modified to perform different functions—grasping, swimming, digging, flying—but they share a similar underlying anatomy. A common ancestry is seen as the source of those similarities.

There are literally dozens of such lines of evidence that have been compiled by scientists, but what is compelling, even more than such individual lines of argument, is the evidence *overall*. Darwin himself indicated that his proposal rested not on this or that critical component of the theory, but instead, on what we might term the coherence of an entire body of facts and observations, what Darwin called "one long argument" and which he laid out in *On the Origin of Species*.

Almost every idea that is fundamentally new engenders reaction, discussion, and some opposition. However, over the course of the passing decades, most people appropriated the new information into their life-perspective. The French paleontologist and Jesuit priest Pierre Teilhard de Chardin, who discovered *Homo erectus* or Peking Man in China in the 1920s, wrote, "A process is at work in the universe . . . which can best be compared to the process of gestation and birth" and viewed humanity as "evolution becoming conscious of itself." In 1952, the Vatican Commission of Science spoke to the world's billion Catholics, saying the evidence for evolution appears to be overwhelming and that it may be regarded by the faithful as the likely *way* in which God created the diversity of living things we know today. That was followed, in recent decades, by two papal encyclicals making the same point. After all, the Apostles' Creed, in its ancient wisdom, simply says, "I believe in God the Father Almighty, creator of heaven and earth." There are no hundred footnotes about the details, something indicative of the writers' intuition that such ideas would change over time. Consider a statement of George Gaylord Simpson, one of the leading paleontologists of the twentieth century. In

The Meaning of Evolution, he indicates that while some forms of religion are not consistent with discoveries concerning evolutionary processes, others are. "I take it now as self-evident . . . that evolution and *true* religion are compatible. It is also sufficiently clear that science, alone, does not teach all truths, plumb all mysteries, or exhaust all values, and that the place and need for true religion are still very much with us."

~

Of course, not everyone has agreed that evolutionary science and religion can coexist. At the famous Scopes trial in Dayton, Tennessee in 1925, William Jennings Bryan, who in earlier years had been a social reformer of note and twice a presidential candidate, was the prosecutor. There, near the end of his life, he used his oratory skills to convict an educator of wrongful teaching and rallied fundamentalists to the anti-evolutionary cause. In the circus atmosphere of the trial, there were slogans, chants, songs, signs, and graffiti, all with the message that "You can't make a monkey out of me."

For several decades thereafter, such creation-evolution controversy seemed to be relegated to fringe groups, and one did not hear a great deal about it. Now, you do. Now, there are huge numbers of people, most of them fundamentalist Christians, who are for religion and against evolution, saying that you have to believe one or the other. You hear about the *creationist movement*, which claims to support something called "creation science," "Bible science," and "scientific creationism," all affirming that the Bible is to be understood, in addition to everything else, as an authoritative document concerning science. The first few chapters of Genesis are taken literally and the earth is seen as just 6,000 to 10,000 years in age. Everything is now as it was created then, except for changes made by the flood of Noah, which they read in a factual, historical, newspaper-reporting kind of way.

The resurgence of this viewpoint began about the time Ronald Reagan was campaigning in Texas and he was asked his views on the teaching of evolution. He replied, in what was an almost verbatim quotation of the position of Jerry Falwell's group, The Moral Majority: "It is a scientific theory only, and it is not believed in the scientific community to be as infallible as it was once believed. But if it is going to be taught in the schools, then I think the biblical story of creation should also be taught." Reagan continued, "I have a great many questions about evolution. I think that . . . discoveries down through the years have pointed up great flaws in it." He was quite wrong about that, but it is what the creationists want the public to believe, so they have been active in manufacturing flaws, distorting science, and quoting scientists out of context, an approach that has had results, not the least of which is pressuring school textbook printers to do little more than mention the dreaded "e"-word. Legislation has been introduced in more than thirty states to have schools teach both creation and evolution in biology classes. President George W. Bush came out in favor of it, for he always knew where his base stood in regard to such things. In 2005, Falwell could be seen on television saying, "I talk to the White House every week!" No doubt, some of what he talked about was creation *versus* evolution. (In that administration, the National Park Service even allowed its bookstores at the Grand Canyon to sell a publication that argued that this incredible gouge in the earth was created by the biblical flood in a matter of days just a few thousand years ago.)

Creationists are busy writing letters to newspapers and magazines and holding conferences attended by several thousand at a time. Surveys now show that nearly one-half of the American public does not accept evolution, this despite the fact that the concept is the cornerstone of modern biology and medicine. As Theodosius Dobzhansky, President of the American Genetics Society and himself a Christian, put it, "Nothing in biology makes sense except in the light of evolution." Indeed, every time you get a flu shot, you benefit from the science that takes seriously that this year's strain of flu is different from last year's; it has evolved. Thus, evolution is still going on, all the time, all over the place.

Peter and Rosemary Grant, biologists from Princeton, have spent thirty years re-studying the finches of the Galapagos Islands. Jonathan Weiner describes their conclusions in *The Beak of the Finch*, writing that Darwin "vastly underestimated the power of natural selection. Its action is neither rare nor slow. It leads to evolution daily . . . all around us, and we can watch." Weiner cites the work of Martin Taylor, an entomologist studying pesticide-resistant moths in the Cotton Belt, who says, "These people are trying to ban the teaching of evolution while their own cotton crops are failing because of evolution. How can you be a creationist farmer anymore?" The words of wildlife biologist Douglas Chadwick are appropriate, also: "All environments inevitably do change. The secret of life is that it can change with them and continue to thrive, and if I were searching for signs of an infinitely wise Creator, I might find them there."

But the creationists will have none of it. In simplistic black and white terms, it's either creation or evolution: either you are for the Bible or you are against it. Millions of people today are what might be called theistic evolutionists, but creationist Duane Gish says to them, "You really cannot believe the Bible and evolution both."

Nothing brings out the fundamentalist critique/attack like the fossils of dinosaurs. Some who criticize are clearly ignorant of paleontology, including the "Country Preacher," as he called himself in his weekly radio program based in Tennessee. He told of his visit to a natural history museum, where he was astonished to see the exhibits containing skeletons of those prehistoric beasts. His response is related by Conrad Heyers: "Now nothing prehistoric could possibly be Christian . . . So I tried then and there to plan how I might mount a crusade against this new devil religion of dinosaur belief. Dinosaurs are the work of the devil . . . Such godless, communist dinosaur information must be destroyed before it carries us all to perdition!"

The semi-illiterates have not been the only ones on the attack, either. Consider the words of attorney Judge Braswell Deen of Georgia: "This monkey mythology of Darwin is the cause of permissiveness, promiscuity, pills, prophylactics, perversions, pregnancies, abortions, pornotherapy, pollution, poisoning, and proliferation of crimes of all types!" Such paranoia somehow finds its focus in the idea of evolution.

Other creationists send hate mail to paleontologists and make hostile remarks to staff and docents at natural history museums. So much does this happen that, for the last several years, the Society of Vertebrate Paleontology has sponsored workshops at its annual meetings in order to better understand and respond to such confrontations.

A few years ago, the United States Postal Service issued a series of four postage stamps showing dinosaurs. Third graders wrote in to correct the name of one of huge beasts: *Brontosaurus* is now officially called *Apatosaurus*. They also pointed out that another creature pictured is not a dinosaur but a pterosaur, a flying reptile. However, there were also numerous letters from adults denouncing the USPS for even printing such things. The reason? "Dinosaurs promote the idea of evolution."

Along the highway near Los Angeles are two huge "roadside kitsch" concrete dinosaurs built in the 1960s that beckon to the traveling public.

The gift shop, located in the belly of the "*Brontosaurus*," sells toys of pre-historic creatures. Attached to each is a safety label warning to parents: "Don't swallow it! The fossil record does not support evolution." Robert Anderson, who described stopping there, says, "I was sad to lose the dino stop, but I realized the new owners had found the perfect outlet for their cause. If you're going to attack a basic tenant of modern science, do it through tacky highway attractions."

The warning label likely refers to the catchall objection often voiced by creationists to the idea of evolution, of supposed gaps in the fossil record. The perception that there exist "no transitional forms" is, however, the result of a campaign of disinformation. The famous *Archaeopteryx* is a perfect transitional form between reptiles and birds. The skeleton is of a small dinosaur with a long bony tail, but it has feathers, claws on its wings, and the rare and proverbial hen's teeth. Recent discoveries in China revealed a whole range of small, feathered dinosaurs that grade right into more modern birds. There are numerous other *non*-missing links, as well. However, as soon as a discovery along those lines is made, the creationist response is to complain that there is not a fossil filling the gap next to that one. No matter how many gaps are filled, there are still some spaces. Of course.

It is readily apparent that many creationists are woefully ignorant of what science actually teaches on the subject of evolution. Some years ago, I was asked by our local school board to review a text that someone had brought to them for possible inclusion in biology classes. It stated that Darwinism has been scientifically refuted, because, if you cut the tails of ten, twenty, thirty generations of rats, they will still be born with long tails. Naturally! External modifications cannot affect the internal genetic code, where such things are determined. (An idea similar to that in the text existed before Darwin in the thought of Lamarck, that of "the inheritance of acquired characteristics." It is doubtful that there are any biologists holding to that today.) One can tell that the garbled "science" of creationism is both common and extreme when cartoons take up the matter. *The Far Side* by Gary Larson (the "patron cartoonist" of scientists) depicts a man at a blackboard writing an equation that includes a two-foot piece of string, a flashlight and batteries, the square-root of a cat, some other symbols involving mass and your age, some "greater than" and "lesser than" symbols, and a chicken, with the entire thing equaling "the world." The caption: "Creationism Explained."

At an event held a few years ago and during a discussion relating to the fossil record, certain participants indicated that "some scientists believe" the world to have once been inhabited by large, scaly reptiles. For the benefit of those who, in that manner, were being vague about the existence of dinosaurs, University of California Berkeley paleontologist Kevin Padian placed a dinosaur bone on the table and asked, "Do you think we have a museum full of *beliefs*?" In presentations about the prehistoric world, I have often said something similar, holding up a dinosaur foot-bone and affirming, "This is no illusion!"

Now, why is it necessary to say such things? It is because there are some in the creationist movement who believe that such objects really are illusory, that such fossils never existed as living beings! As in any other movement, there is a range of beliefs, but virtually every community has some who have adopted this view. Being confronted with a dinosaur skeleton in the crust of the earth, deep in the sedimentary layers, signifies to most people a great age of millions of years. However, some maintain, instead, that God created the fossilized remains right there *in the strata*—complete with worn teeth, healed fractures in limbs, and arthritic vertebrae—they only *look* like they had been alive. Much like the ancient astrologers, who saw fossil forms to be the result of emanations from the stars or the growth from seeds, this explanation states that God created *Tyrannosaurus rex* as a heap of fossilized bones right there in the ground and that it has never, ever been anywhere else! Some will add that God just put it there to confuse the scientists! (Or was it Satan? The story varies.) Their God is devious, it appears, and why that doesn't bother them is difficult to fathom.

Neither, it seems, does it occur to them that once you start down that road, you can say anything, including the fact that God may have created everything just ten minutes ago and made it to appear as if it had a long history. Why not? Such instantaneous creation could come complete with implanted but illusory memory banks of "the remembrance of things past," complete, also, with fictitious fillings in our teeth and scars from our illusory appendectomies, the birth certificates that only seemed to be about birth, dented cars with worn tires, etc. It's an idea that cannot be refuted, any more than instant dinosaurs in the rock, but what is there to commend it?

Henry M. Morris, longtime chief spokesperson for the creationist movement, has considered the fact that the landscape shows signs of erosion and, in places, of the sort that required huge spans of time. One of his responses is that the landscape was created by God with the *appearance* of age, i.e., instantly created to appear *as if* it had a history of previous existence, but did not. (It is similar to the mental contortions of some of his forerunners about Adam not needing a navel, because the first man was created instantly but might have been given one to be in line with the appearance of all later folk.) Others stated that creation needed to have some superficial appearance of a history, so trees were created with tree-rings already in place. Some creationists appear to have accepted the modern measurement of the speed of light as 186,000 miles per second. However, when it is pointed out that many stars and other celestial objects have been measured to be hundreds of thousands or even millions of light years away and that this implies a creation of great age, the response of others is to say that the light must have been created "on the way," so to speak, in transit! Morris writes in *The Remarkable Birth of Planet Earth*, "The only way we can determine the age of the earth is for God to tell us what it is. And, since he *has* told us, very plainly in the Holy Scriptures, that it is several thousand years in age, and no more, that ought to settle all basic questions of terrestrial chronology." (Of course, the famous chronology of Archbishop Ussher from the seventeenth century is not in the Bible itself; it was merely placed in the margin of some of the King James versions of that era.)

There are several creationist organizations on the scene today, but the main one is that represented by Henry M. Morris, Duane Gish, Ken Ham, and others, at the Institute of Creation Research (ICR) located in El Cajon, California and in Dallas, Texas. They claim to be doing something they call "creation science," and they have sponsored numerous debates wherein they attempt to show that the earth is just a few thousand years old, that evolution did not occur, and that Christianity and evolution are totally incompatible. The following is a portion of the creedal statement, to which all working at the institute must subscribe: "The Bible is the written word of God, and because we believe it to be inspired throughout, all of its assertions are historically and scientifically true . . . To the student of nature, this means that the account of origins in Genesis is a factual representation of simple historical truths." Notice the huge and curious leap from the affirmation that the Bible is the written word of God to—and as Kierkegaard said in quite another context, "the dash should be as long as the earth's orbit"—the conclusion that its assertions are *historically* and *scientifically* true.

Thus, Morris maintains: "The biblical record, accepted in the literal sense, gives the only satisfying account of the origin of all things . . . It is only in the Bible that we can possibly obtain any information about the methods of creation, the order of creation, the duration of creation or any of the other details of creation." Sometimes, when someone says something quite astonishing, there is the urge to stop, slap yourself, and ask, "Is that what he really said?" It is, and that is, apparently, what is meant. Thus, astronomers should shut down the telescopes and physicists must turn off the particle accelerators—for the *only* things that can be known about creation are given literally and straightforwardly in the Bible, and these are true, because "God doesn't lie."

Such an appeal to authority does not require of one a great deal of intellectual aerobics. In c. 1250, Alphonso the Wise of Castile said: "If the Lord Almighty had consulted me before embarking upon creation, I should have recommended something simpler." The creationists do get something a good deal simpler by merely saying that all you need to know about the world is between the covers of one book.

It's all or nothing. Creationists often suggest that if the Bible's so-called scientific and historical teachings cannot be trusted, then neither can one trust its spiritual teachings that are not susceptible to proof. One could not design a more effective method to produce a new generation of atheists or, at the very least, a generation who view the Christian scriptures as now being outmoded and irrelevant, all based on erroneous information.

Such an approach might well be called "The Domino Method of Biblical Interpretation." Touch one item and the whole structure may collapse; therefore, you don't touch any. Instead, you either damn the scientists who raise thorny questions or you try to find events in nature that are descriptive of Bible verses and call what you are doing "creation science," or both. Creation scientists publish in no peer-reviewed journals of science. Their work consists mainly of trying to poke holes in the ideas of the scientific establishment. The result is an attempt to maintain that dinosaurs and people lived together anywhere from 6,000–10,000 years ago, that they were together on the ark, and that the forty-day flood of Noah is what killed off the great reptiles along with almost everything else found in the fossil record. (However, I recently watched the Institute of Creation Research's television program, in which their representative maintains that the natives in Papua New Guinea are still being attacked by pterosaurs!)

∽

There are at least three types of responses to creationists. One is to ignore them, which may give the erroneous impression that those of us who respect science think, in the vein of "different strokes for different folks," that it is permissible to have different *truths* for different folks, as well. When the nature of the cosmos is at stake, it is not.

Another approach is that of directly responding to creationists, using the methods of science itself to refute their more outlandish claims. This is an approach taken by few scientists, inasmuch as the two groups have radically different presuppositions. Creationists begin with their conclusions, based on the concept of an inerrant book, infallible in all it addresses. Scientists start with the scientific method, apply it, and see where it leads. In addition, the work of responding to the creationist claims and attacks would be endless: it is easy simply to affirm something or to put forth an idea, while days, weeks, or months may be consumed in addressing all the factors involved in refuting it. There is, however, a growing body of work, wherein a number of scientists are doing just that.

In debates and presentations, creationists are fond of quoting the second law of thermodynamics, which states that when a system containing a large number of particles is left to itself, it assumes a state with maximum entropy, that is, it becomes as disordered as possible. In a closed system, things "run down" as the temperature decreases over time. It's the "water cannot run uphill" sort of thing. The conclusion drawn by creationists is that evolutionary development can never occur. However, it is the universe *as a whole* that is a closed system. Planet earth is an open system, continually receiving energy input from the sun, so that tulips and turtles, moose and magnolias continue to grow. Yes, that will all run down, too, but not for a long, long, long time: about 5 billion years. After a detailed analysis in *Scientists Confront Creationists*, the engineering professor John Patterson concludes, "Hence, by misrepresenting the second law, whether by ignorance or deliberate deception or both, the creationists are able to convince unwitting audiences that evolution is impossible . . . The creationists' second law arguments can only be taken as a willingness to bear false witness against science itself."

The fossil record of large vertebrate animals has been examined with an eye toward how their remains would have "settled out," had there been a worldwide flood of the sort the creationists maintain. No human remains or artifacts have ever been found with the dinosaurs; creationists claim they were contemporary. Among numerous points, consider fossil elephants. (There are only two living species but many prehistoric ones.) They are found in well-defined terrestrial deposits, i.e., sediments from streams and rivers, instead of marine deposits. Also, why are the bones of elephants and dinosaurs of a similar size never found together? In the scenario of the flood, you would expect them to be mingled. Instead, they are separated by rock layers several thousand vertical feet apart.

Arthur N. Strahler was, for many years, the head of the geology department at Columbia University. He is the author of *Science and Earth History: The Evolution/Creation Controversy*, which is a huge volume of more than 500 large, double-column pages and the equivalent of a book of perhaps 1200 standard pages. In it, he lays out almost every conceivable creationist argument and answers them. He refers to how the Bible scientists attempt to explain the huge volume of water needed to cover the earth to that of the highest mountains. Where did it come from? A pre-existing "water vapor canopy" is invoked, this in spite of the fact that Genesis neither describes nor implies such. Strahler then cites the work of two professors of earth science from St. Cloud State University in Minnesota, Leonard Soroka and Charles Nelson, who calculated that the amount of water necessary to flood Everest is 4.4 billion cubic kilometers. That, in turn, leads them to conclude: "First, the atmospheric pressure would be about 840 times higher than it is now. Second, the atmosphere would be 99.9 percent water vapor and would be impossible for humans and other animals to breathe such an atmosphere." Furthermore, "clouds would have prevented nearly all sunlight from reaching the surface. In short, such an atmosphere would not have allowed terrestrial life as we know it to exist on the surface of the earth." Even more damaging, if that is possible, is what would happen when that entire vapor condensed to rain. Soroka and Nelson calculated that the liberation of the latent heat of vaporization would have raised the atmospheric temperature over the entire earth to something like 6,400 degrees Fahrenheit—it would have set the ocean to boiling and cremated the ark!

~

There is still another response, one, in my judgment, that is even more fruitful, and it is a consideration of the principle of literary form. It is to ask, "What kind of document is the Bible, anyway? What sort of literature is it?" No, God does not lie, but God *can* be misunderstood.

It may be said, of course, that all language falls short of its intent. The theologian Joseph Sittler excelled in the beautiful use of words, yet he knew that "Even in its most ample and precise exercise, language is a verbal groping for sufficiency, a grammar stalking elusive relations, flung loops of sentences tightening around the undulant and evanescent." Thus, Scripture is misunderstood, and seldom in ways more destructive to its meaning and spirit, than if one attempts to read it as a kind of newspaper account, wherein words are taken merely in their flat, literal sense.

"Literally." This word itself is often misused in casual speech. Someone says, when important news broke, that they were "literally glued to the television screen," something that is to be doubted. What kind of glue was used and what part of the anatomy was stuck to the silver tube? I watched an interview of a geologist after one of the California earthquakes. He described the subsoil in a certain area as packed sand and said that when the quake hit, "That soil literally turned to Jell-O!" We might doubt that, also. These people meant to use the word "figuratively." If someone says to you, "Go jump in a lake" and you take him literally, then that is exactly what you do.

The Bible and so many other writings of the Near East and Far East are filled with non-literal language. For a simple example, consider Isaiah 55:12, wherein "the mountains and hills before you shall break forth into singing, and all the trees of forest shall clap their hands." If you look for that to happen "literally," you will wait forever. It is, instead, a poetic way of pointing to a time of great joy on earth. Likewise, when Isaiah speaks of the time when "they shall beat their swords into plowshares and their spears into pruning hooks" (Isa 2:4), it is a poetic expression of the profound hope of humanity for world peace. (In that spirit, and with that passage as its inspiration, is the magnificent bronze statue in front of the United Nations building of the strong man actually pounding a huge sword into a plowshare.)

Involved here is simply the appreciation, shared by most people but severely lacking among creationists, that language is of different types. In addition to simple narration, there is satire, parable, tragedy, comedy, allegory, proverb, riddle, joke, and song, and all of them are in the Bible. They ought not be reduced to the objective sort of language used in the instruction manual for installing the garage door opener, but a wooden literalism attempts to do just that.

Rather, is it not the case that the kind of language employed needs to be appropriate to the subject? By way of analogy, you can splash around on the surface of the ocean in your swimsuit, but if you want to go down fifty fathoms, you need a pressurized suit and oxygen, and you would need a steel-hulled bathysphere, should you want to go down into the deep ocean trenches. In some such manner, one needs to shift ways of speaking when talking about love, meaning, destiny, and God. A language that describes the mere exterior of things, where a word simply means what it says, will not work when applied to interior values and dreams and all the deepest dimensions of life. The lyrics to a love song are often rather corny, making little sense in any literal fashion, and yet they often work. Literalism, applied like a blanket to language, does great violence to its many and various forms.

Years ago, a scientist put forth a satire on the subject that heaven might be hotter than hell. (This was likely at some conference, but it is now impossible to find the origin; there are many versions. The subject would make a good supermarket tabloid headline.) The scenario states that the Book of Revelation describes hell as a lake of brimstone, which, we are informed, is melted sulfur. Sulfur has a melting point of 828 degrees Fahrenheit. Revelation also describes heaven, saying the light there "shall be as seven suns," the light of the sun "sevenfold." Applying the Stephan-Boltzmann equation for solar radiation, one arrives at a temperature in heaven of 972 degrees—Heaven is thus 144 degrees hotter than hell! That being the case, some people may wish to reconsider where they want to go. However, at those temperatures, a mere 144 degrees may not make a hell of a lot of difference!

Literalism works only in limited realms. One of the stories about Picasso is that he was once commissioned to paint a portrait of a man's wife. You know how it turned out: strange angles, blocks and cubes, and showing both sides of the face at once, and so forth. The man didn't like it, saying that it didn't *look* like her. "How *does* she look?" asked Picasso. The man took a photo out of his wallet and showed it. "Is this how she really looks?" pressed the artist. "Yes," he was told. Then, this response: "*Small*, isn't she?"

In addition, in order to use anything rightly, you need to know its *purpose*. Thus, you don't use a meat-grinder as a pencil sharpener or an umbrella as a parachute. The question any reader of the Bible, or, for that matter, any other book, must ask, is, "What is the purpose of the book?" You will not find what you are seeking, if you look in the wrong place. Thus, if you want to know something about French cooking or Chinese pottery, you do not consult a textbook on microorganisms; that is not its purpose. Along those lines, most believers maintain that the purpose of a book such as the Bible is *not* scientific, that it was never intended to tell us "how the heavens go," answering questions of cosmology and natural history and how things all came to be. Its purpose, instead, is *religious*. Religious questions are those of value and meaning. They are issues like What do I believe, What is the meaning of life and death, How do I treat those who are sharing this journey with me, What things will endure, How should I live, What shall I become, and Why am I here, anyway? Those are questions in the realm of ultimate concerns. (No one can live very long without answering such questions in practice, if not in conscious thought. Thus, it may be said that everyone is religious, whether they know it or not and whether or not their answers are adequate. Thus, human beings are "religious bipeds," the beings that ask and seek to answer questions of ultimate concern.)

In the tradition in which I am most involved, the Bible has great authority for Christians not because it fell from heaven—it did not, and neither is it because it gives the correct answers to the questions of cosmology and such—it doesn't, for the writers shared the three-story universe of all the peoples of ancient times. It is, rather, because it speaks to the most important questions of humanity. In the early days of motion pictures, when the western thrillers were first shown in the frontier towns, it is said that cowboys rode in from far and wide to sit in the dingy halls and watch the villains as they moved across the screen to rob the bank and tie the boss's daughter to the railroad tracks. It is said that some of the tipsy cowhands would become so involved in the drama that they pulled their guns and shot at the outlaws on the screen. In that moment, they did not realize that the bad guys were somewhere else.

The biblical writers do not make that mistake. With penetrating accuracy, they zero in on the core problems of the human family, which have to do with the inclinations of the spirit. As pressing as many external problems are, the most serious issues are in the heart and mind of man. In the words of Thoreau, "There are a thousand people hacking away at the branches of evil for every one striking at its root." The Bible deals, then, with *root* sorts of things, things at a deeper level than does either the terminology of science or that of ordinary conversation. To get at this level, it uses *symbolic* language.

There is, of course, historical narrative and the like, wherein words mean just what they say, as in this passage: "Jesus went down and was baptized by John in the river Jordan." However, a different sense applies to his words, "I am the Light of the world," and "I am the Bread of life," or "I am the Vine, you are the branches." The Bible, in fact, is filled with what must be called *picture language.* (In telling of Jesus teaching the crowds, the Gospel of St. Mark says, "He did not speak to them without a parable.") Jesus said, "The kingdom of heaven is like a pearl of great price which a merchant finds and goes and sells all that he has in order to possess it." "The kingdom of heaven is like a net thrown into the sea, which gathers fish of every kind." The kingdom of heaven is like a householder who went out early in the morning to hire laborers for his vineyard." "The kingdom of heaven is like a grain of mustard seed, which a man took and sowed in his field." The kingdom not *is,* but *is like.* The words point beyond themselves, because that of which they speak cannot be described in any literal fashion. This, too, is why John Calvin said that the creeds should be *sung:* to make it clear that they are not definitions of God but have to do with ultimate mystery. The theologian Conrad Heyers writes, "Religion is not concerned with just counting sheep or asking how things operate or trying to get straight the exact chronological order of things. Religious language is concerned with the deep mysteries of existence, the moving spirit of the whole . . . If one wants to know how many chairs are in a room, one can count them. If one wants to know what tables are made of, one can examine them. Yet if one asks, What is the source of the universe? or Whither lies human destiny? the very character and scope of these questions requires a symbolic mode of discourse."

This picture-language stands in marked contrast to the mode of expression in the ancient empires of Greece and Rome, which funneled to the whole of the western world much of our thought patterns and which relied heavily upon definition. For example, you can read page after page of Plato and Aristotle, and you may understand them, because you know the abstract dictionary-type definition of the words (the dictionary is an invention of the West), but you do not get any mental pictures. Therefore, today, we need specialists: artists and poets to do what does not come naturally for most of the rest of us. Thus, how does one describe a person's indecision, his or her desire to escape from the constant dilemmas of freedom and the need to choose? (You understood that sentence because you know the meaning of the words.) T. S. Elliot did it this way:

> I should have been a pair of ragged claws
> Scuttling across the floors of silent seas.

Here, we are closer to the language of religion, where the attempt is to communicate to the whole person, speaking not just to reason but, also, to feelings, emotions, and every sense. To reach the depths, the great poets have always employed *images*, and the Bible is filled with them. Instead of being abstract, it is specific, concrete. It is language focused on the *optical*. It speaks to and through the eye.

Thus, a person of ancient Greece might say, "In unity there is strength." Again, we all know what that means by the definitions. In contrast, a person of the ancient Hebrew culture might say, "Five hyenas killed a lion" and intend very much the same thing. You get the meaning, but you also get a *picture*. In fact, you are unable to *not* get a picture. So, in Scripture, the rather nebulous notions of love, compassion, charity, and altruism are expressed by the story of the Good Samaritan in Saint Luke's gospel: "A man went down from Jerusalem to Jericho and he fell among robbers, who stripped him and beat him, and departed, leaving him half-dead" (Luke 10:29–30). Or, consider the prophet Jeremiah speaking to his peoples' misplaced confidence in alliances of power, which will finally prove insufficient and fail. Instead of voicing that concern in such an abstract manner, for a people living in the desert, he speaks for God and says that "they have forsaken me, the fountain of living waters, and hewed out cisterns for themselves, broken cisterns, that can hold no water" (Isa 2:13).

In our culture, a lecturer might address the topic "The Immutability of Character," by which the speaker means the deeply engrained nature of our adult personalities and the difficulty of basic transformation. (That is abstract language, indeed. It is understandable, again, but no pictures arise in the mind.) Jeremiah said the same thing but said it differently, tersely, vividly: "Can the Ethiopian change his skin or the leopard his spots?" (Jer 13:23). We speak of the influence of heredity and environment upon the next generation, whereas, to say the same thing, the prophet Ezekiel alluded to a proverb, "The fathers have eaten sour grapes, and the children's teeth are set on edge" (Ezek 18:2). A modern Arabic proverb is in that spirit: "If the father be onion and the mother garlic, can the child have sweet perfume?"

Thus, one can take biblical passages *seriously* without taking them *literally*. In fact, in order to get the message intended, one *must* take strong account of non-objective or symbolic language, the kind that has an impoverished history in our own culture but a rich and varied one in that of the Near East, out of which the Bible emerged. People reared in a culture that honors computing, calibrating, and calculating will quite naturally have difficulty in thinking symbolically. (In this connection, it has been noted that the creationist movement contains a disproportionate number of engineers, whose education has been mostly in terms of technology.) The problem for so many of us, so much of the time, is that we are reading the Bible through the glasses of a western culture, seldom aware of the constrictions and distortions imposed in the process.

∾

This brings us back to the question of creation and evolution and the Genesis creation stories. There is evidence that in the early Church they were understood *primarily* with reference to their symbolic meaning and that a literalistic misunderstanding of those Genesis stories did not come until later. St. Augustine, in the fourth century and in the culture of ancient Rome, warned against taking the stories literally and making them ridiculous, causing those on the outside "to laugh the Bible to scorn." The scholar Alan Richardson writes, "Treat the story of the Creation as a literal interpretation of what happened 'in the beginning' and you are landed in every form of absurdity; regard it, on the other hand, as an attempt to express in temporal pictures a truth about something beyond time, and it is at once filled with religious meaning." By their misguided attempts to defend the Bible, the creationists are engaged in folly of the most extreme form, and it leads many people to ridicule and dismiss the book before they even know what it is.

A key to the Genesis creation stories is the fact that the word *Adam* is not a name, such as Tom, Dick, or Harry. It is, instead, the Hebrew word for humanity or humankind. In other words, these are not about "long ago and far away," but *these are stories about us.* The stories concern human nature and the sorts of things that are true of people in every age, whether they rode a donkey in ancient Mesopotamia or whether they fly in a jet plane today. To get the point of the stories, we need to insert ourselves into them.

I have used the term creation *stories*, in the plural. This is intentional, because there are *two*: Genesis 1:1—2:4 and Genesis 2:5 ff. (There might be said to be several more elsewhere in the Bible.) The first begins with the statement, "In the beginning, God created the heavens and the earth." After everything else, humankind is created in two forms, man and woman, this at the very end of the creative process. In the second story, the order is quite different: man is created first, then all the creatures, fish, birds, animals and, at the very last, woman. This contradiction tells one immediately that the stories are not intended to provide a chronology; they are not a newspaper-type description of what happened.

Both stories affirm, as their central points, our total dependence upon our creator. The first account views us as the crown of creation, echoed by the affirmation in the Psalms that we are "created a little lower than the angels and crowned with glory and honor." The second story, the one about the Garden of Eden, views us as having almost everything in common with the other creatures and created, like them, out of the dust of the earth: "Dust you are, to dust you shall return." There is a Jewish tale of a man who kept two pieces of paper in his pocket. When he was depressed and felt worthless, he would take out the one that read, "You are the crown of creation." When he got to feeling arrogant and self-important, he would take out the other paper that read, "You are dust and ashes." Pascal wrote, in similar fashion, that humanity is "both the pride and the refuse of the universe." So, we need, as did the ancient peoples who first recorded them, *both* stories. Both stories are true.

In addition, both are *stories*; that is to say, they are expressive, once again, of that picture-language mode of thought. In such, the main thing *is* the main thing, not the details. They are, in a sense, *myths*, using the term here not for something that is untrue but for that which is very true, so much so that ordinary language cannot express it. (Writers such as C. S. Lewis and Tolkien have used fantasy figures of demons and other creatures because they found that, in dealing with the complexities of human nature, it was a way cut through the flat, inexpressive language of science or of history.)

The creation stories, with all their imagery, have the simple point that the world is not self-sufficient; instead, the world is created. The world is utterly dependent upon God. (This is, surely, a more Greek manner of speaking. While we are at it, we may as well include the philosophers' rendition, that the world is ontologically contingent.) The same point, however, has been made by the poet, E. E. Cummings:

> when god decided to invent
> everything he took one
> breath bigger than a circustent
> and everything began

Thus, the writers of Genesis gave us "truth embodied in a tale." Writing thousands of years ago and in a culture that valued such expression, how else could they have done it?

～

In addition to the factors outlined above, there is another reason for the creationists' hostility to the theory of evolution, this being that the concept has been used to promote agendas that have had horrific consequences. At the end of the nineteenth century and the first half of the twentieth, Darwinism became, in some quarters, *Social* Darwinism.

To the cataclysm of World War II, with its unspeakable suffering, can be attached any number of causative factors, including even philosophy, inasmuch as the writings of Friedrich Nietzsche (1844–1900) were frequently quoted by the Nazis. However, scholars have noted that the issue is complicated by the author's use of character portrayals and dramatic symbolism. Thus, while the Third Reich made racial purity a dogma, there are also passages in Nietzsche's works that, instead, extol the "mixing" of races in order to produce a higher humanity. The main character in the allegorical *Thus Spake Zarathustra* turns to the subject of conflict: "Ye shall love peace as a means to new wars—and the short peace more than the long . . . Ye say that it is the good cause which halloweth even war? I say unto you: it is the good war which halloweth every cause." It is conceivable, as some say, that this may have to do with combating one's own limited self in the effort to become something more; on the other hand, it may be, as it seems to be, a glorification of war. The place accorded women by Zarathustra is less ambiguous: "Man shall be trained for war, and woman for the recreation of the warrior: all else is folly."

It is also conceivable that Nietzsche's concept of the Übermensch or "overman" deals with the idea of individual self-perfection; however, a less convoluted interpretation is that it surely lends itself to the promotion of a master race, one freed from the restraints of a limiting culture. In *The Geneology of Morals*, he writes that it is the very nature of civilization to domesticate the animal nature; he prefers it be let loose, describes such ferocity, and then writes, "It is impossible not to recognize at the core of all these aristocratic races the beast of prey; the magnificent *blond brute*, avidly rampant for spoil and victory" (italics in original). However, Nietzsche also includes the Arabs and the Japanese in the concept. The scholar Walter Kaufmann, in *Nietzsche: Philosopher, Psychologist, Anti-Christ*, says of the author of these controversial writings that "he delights in antithesis to what is current: it is as if he were swimming against the stream for its own sake; and he makes a sport of being provocative." Nietzsche's extreme hostility to Christianity is impossible to overstate; on many other things, his highly complex style virtually guarantees a multitude of interpretations. However, most readers will readily understand how his graphic images could very easily be put in the service of power-hungry aggressors. In the atrocities of World War II, they were.

William L. Shirer lived through a part of the war in Berlin and went on to write one of the definitive histories of the period, the comprehensive 1200-page volume, *The Rise and Fall of the Third Reich*. In it, he says, "I think no one who lived in the Third Reich could have failed to be impressed by Nietzsche's influence on it," relating that "Nazi scribblers never tired of extolling him." He tells of Hitler often visiting the Nietzsche museum in Weimar to pose for photographs of himself gazing in rapture at a bronze bust of the philosopher. Shirer writes:

> Finally there was Nietzsche's prophecy of the coming elite who would rule and world and from whom the superman would spring. In *The Will to Power* he exclaims: "A daring and ruler race

is building itself up . . . The aim should be to prepare a trans-valuation of values for a particularly strong kind of man, most highly gifted in intellect and will. This man and the elite around him will become the 'lords of the earth.'" Such rantings from one of Germany's most original minds must have struck a responsive chord in Hitler's littered mind. At any rate, he appropriated them for his own—not only the thoughts but the philosopher's penchant for grotesque exaggeration, and often his very words. "Lords of the earth" is a familiar expression in *Mein Kampf*. That in the end Hitler considered himself the superman of Nietzsche's prophecy cannot be doubted.

Nietzsche died in 1900 after several years of insanity. Hitler was then a boy of eleven; he would go on to enmesh the world in a war that spanned the entire earth.

Hitler was attracted to occult interpretations of history. He also drew inspiration from the grandiose music of Wagner and made pilgrimages to the house where the composer had lived. Those theatrical operas were filled with demons and dragons, battling gods and heroes, mythical figures, and larger than life Teutonic ancestors, all dealing not just with the splendor of life but also with the nobility of death and destiny. Shirer quotes Hitler himself as saying, often, "Whoever wants to understand National Socialist Germany must know Wagner." Shirer references *Götterdämmerung*, the twilight of the gods, in which Wotan, after all his tribulations, sets Valhalla on fire and perishes within, then concluding: "It is not at all surprising that Hitler tried to emulate Wotan when in 1945 he willed the destruction of Germany so that it might go down in flames with him."

Thus, in retrospect, if both rationalistic philosophy and the emotive force of music and dramatic art could be so employed, it is hardly surprising to find that the new perspectives concerning biology and its perspectives on the evolution of the entire world of living things would also become fodder for those eager for war.

In an episode of the old TV reruns of *All In The Family*, the bigoted Archie Bunker—who was often wrong but never in doubt—pointed his finger at his son-in-law, "Meathead," and said, "I've been makin' my way in the world for a long time, Sonny Boy, and one thing I know: A man better watch out for Number One. It's the survival of the fittes'!" Contrary to popular belief, it was the English writer Herbert Spencer, not Darwin, who coined the phrase "survival of the fittest" in his 1851

Social Statics. There, he attempted to buttress his agenda for society with the authority of the new biology. In reference to the so-called "unfit," he was not subtle but wrote, "The whole effort of nature is to get rid of such, to clear the world of them and to make room for better . . . it is best that they should die." He was talking about human beings.

In Germany, the biologist Ernst Haeckel promoted Darwinism by making Spencer's idea of the survival of the fittest into an evolutionary cliché. He also performed condensations in a more extreme manner: In *Darwin's Century*, Eiseley cites a remark quoted in the *Fortnightly Review* in 1886, wherein Haeckel summarizes everything: "The cell consists of matter, called protoplasm, composed chiefly of carbon with an admixture of hydrogen, nitrogen, and sulfur. These component parts, properly united, produce the soul and body of the animated world, and suitably nourished, become man. With this single argument the mystery of the universe is explained, the Deity annulled and a new era of infinite knowledge ushered in." Since those words, the discovery of the genetic alphabet has hardly supported such a dismissal of life's intricacy. Nevertheless, it was simple to him: the message of biology was that of philosophical naturalism.

Everywhere in nature, Haeckel saw the struggle of neighbor to annihilate neighbor, and he applied the theme to nation-states. Edward J. Larson, in his 2004 work *Evolution: The Remarkable History of a Scientific Theory*, takes note of this face of social Darwinism by quoting Haeckel's 1868 *History of Creation* where he stressed that "the whole history of nations . . . must therefore be explicable by means of *natural selection*. Passion and selfishness—conscious or unconscious—is everywhere the motive force of life." Writes Larson: "This Social Darwinian version of national progress fed German militarism leading up to World War One" and, again, leading up to World War Two: "Haeckel's biology helped unleash the militant nationalism and murderous racism that cultural and social norms usually keep in check." Haeckel's 1899 book, *Riddle of the Universe*, sold more than a half-million copies in the pre-war era, making it a runaway best-seller even by modern standards. His phrase, "politics is applied biology," resonated with many in positions of leadership, including the SS monster, Heinrich Himmler.

Thus, those eagerly anticipating conflict and conquest alluded to Social Darwinists. Drawing the conclusion that man is an animal bound to obey the laws of nature, the struggle observed in the realm of fur, fin, and feather was viewed as innate to the social order, as well. This was not a view adopted with reluctance; instead, it was extolled. The law of the jungle became the lens through which to view a nation's neighbors. Because the fittest survive, German military leaders felt moved to demonstrate their nation's superiority by going to war, a war in which the conquered lower races would be enslaved or eliminated. Social Darwinists noted that hybrids are usually sterile; the conclusion was drawn that marriage outside the race was unnatural; therefore, only the union of Aryans with other pure Aryans could produce more pure Aryans. Anything that might contribute to making the master race less than masterful was to be culled, thus a policy of "racial hygiene" was instituted, whereby many of those considered defective were either sterilized or killed.

The phrase "nature red in tooth and claw" is from a poem by Tennyson, and few would doubt that the description of nature is accurate. It was appropriated and became identified with a paradigm of human society viewed through glasses that were not rosy—but red. Hitler it seems did not actually use quotations of Darwin in his speeches at the huge Nazi rallies in the stadium at Nuremburg. Almost anything can be perverted in the effort to justify hate, racism, greed, and violence, including religion and a garbled notion of "evolution."

Marx and Lenin also appropriated the "fittest" doctrine and applied the struggle for existence to class struggles within nations. Violent revolutions were seen as part of the way the world worked.

In addition, early twentieth-century American industrialists and capitalists, the so-called robber barons, justified cutthroat competition and their exploitation of the immigrant working class with the idea that this was simply natural selection in operation and that millionaires, like them, were being selected because of their intrinsic superiority. When Spencer visited America, Andrew Carnegie met him and was enthralled by what he learned of "survival of the fittest" sociology. Carnegie, the steel industry tycoon and the richest man in the world, quickly adopted such an outlook: "The light came in as a flood, and all was clear. Not only had I got rid of theology and the supernatural, but I found the truth of evolution." Carnegie was the greatest philanthropist of his time; he said that it is a sin to die rich and gave away much of his fortune. However, in terms of making that fortune, he became a Social Darwinist. In the climate of the times, there were numerous others, too, who looked to the so-called truth of evolution to support what they were already doing, and the writings of Darwin, as well as those of his many admirers, were plucked for quotes.

There is no denying that the struggle for existence pervades the natural world. The eighteenth-century Irish satirist, Jonathan Swift, nodded to it in verse:

> So naturalists observe, a flea
> Hath smaller fleas that on him prey;
> And these have smaller still to bite 'em;
> And so proceed, *ad infinitum.*

It was, however, a huge perversion to apply biological evolution to human culture and social structures, something strongly underscored by the primary proponent of the idea of evolution, Thomas Huxley. He wrote *On the Relations of Man to the Lower Animals*, in part, to defend Darwin's evolutionary concepts from those who thought "that the belief in the unity of the origin of man and brutes involves the brutalization and degradation of the former. But is it really so? . . . Is mother love vile because a hen shows it or fidelity base because dogs possess it?" In addition, it was to emphasize that our evolutionary origins do not preclude the highest aspects of our humanity: "At the same time, no one is more strongly convinced than I am of the vastness of the gulf between civilized man and the brutes; or is more certain that whether *from* them or not, he is assuredly not *of* them." Huxley loathed those who would justify man's inhumanity to man with a call to follow nature and by referencing the Darwinian model. Writing in *Evolution and Ethics* in 1893, he maintained that progress in society depends, not upon imitating what he called the cosmic process but in combating it: "In place of ruthless self-assertion, it demands self restraint . . . its influence is directed not so much to the survival of the fittest, as to the fitting of as many as possible to survive. It repudiates the gladiatorial theory of existence . . . The intelligence which has converted the brother of the wolf into the faithful guardian of the flock ought to be able to do something towards curbing the instincts of savagery in civilized men."

Not all creationists are aware of the history of social Darwinism, but some certainly are, and the rest have an intuition that the idea of evolution could be used in a cruel or careless manner. (Their suspicions about science in general are not defused by the naïve and flippant optimism displayed by some evolutionists. Dinosaur researcher Gregory S. Paul said in a 2006 interview, "Why would I fear humanity going extinct as we replace ourselves with hyper-intelligent robots? That's evolution, baby! Looks like folks will be downloading their minds into cyber forms in a few decades. Now, that's real progress." It is extremely doubtful that even a few others would consider that to resemble progress.) The ideas that clustered around the Darwinism of the past are ingredients contributing to the present reaction and overreaction on the part of creationists to the concept of evolution. Given the bloody history of the twentieth century, the reaction may be understandable.

Thus, so-called Darwinism is no simple thing. It truly is the case that in it we meet much more than biology. In the words of Ted Peters and Martinez Hewlett, "Trying to get to the science is like trying to get to one's E-mail for the day. Pop-ups and advertising and junk messages clutter the computer screen, just as Social Darwinism and genetic reductionism and materialistic philosophy clutter the basic Darwinian theory."

∼

Whatever the reasons, creationists are focusing on defending Scripture, which they often interpret in literalistic fashion. Scripture is true, they say, because it was *verbally* inspired; for many of them, this means virtually a dictation of every word. It also means that Scripture is an authority on everything it addresses. Henry Morris, again, "The real truth of the matter is that The Bible is indeed verbally inspired and literally true throughout. Whenever it deals with scientific matters or historical matters of fact, it means exactly what it says and is completely accurate . . . The Bible is a book of science!" Nowhere does the Bible itself claim *this* sort of inspiration, and, of course, science as a rigorous discipline was not around when the Bible was written, but many of the creationists have no hesitation in conflating science and Scripture. What has been conjured up is the concept of the Perfect Book, infallible, without errors of any kind. (Strangely enough, that idea has much more in common with fundamentalist expressions of Islam than with historic Christianity. Islam believes that Arabic is the very language of God, and that the Koran is not merely the Word of God but the very *words* of God. This explains why it is officially unlawful to translate it into other languages;

it also contributes to some of the fanaticism surrounding the book that has surfaced in recent years.)

Are there errors in the Bible? Of course, and of many and various kinds, for fallible human beings were involved in its production. (In televised debates, wherein he extolled "pure reason" and science, the atheist Christopher Hitchens got attention by demanding, "*Is* the Bible the word of God or *isn't* it?" Basically, he accepted only a Yes or No answer, either of which would be disconcerting, much in the manner of being forced to answer the question, "Have you stopped beating your wife?" If you say "Yes" to the question about the Bible being the word of God, Hitchens would point to any error, untruth, or absurdity in the book as totally discrediting all of it. It was to his advantage to utilize the infallible, Perfect Book concept held by fundamentalist creationists, to read everything literally, and then to criticize, in straw man fashion, that simplistic reading. A more complex or nuanced concept of inspiration and communication was largely ignored.)

Christians believe God speaks through the Bible and regard it as an authoritative witness to faith and life, but most do not feel any need to prop it up with a dogma of textual perfection. The Word became flesh, not words. Thus, the Bible's flat-earth cosmology, for instance, is that of ancient times, instead of the universe as shown us by modern science. (Parenthetically, such things as Genesis 1 placing the creation of light before the sun should neither be considered a mistake of a primitive cosmology nor something a creationist should need to contort to fit with modern science. It was almost surely a deliberate construct to make a *theological* point, i.e., to say very clearly to an audience of the time, wherein many people held astrological ideas of the sun, stars, and planets being gods, that such ideas were wrong. God could even create light apart from the sun! It was a way of deflating, demoting, and putting the heavenly bodies in their place as part of the created order.) There are errors of geography, and the Greek grammar of Peter, the fisherman, is rather crude, as you might expect. Martin Luther said that the Bible is the crib in which Christ is laid. He made no claims of perfection for the rude and rustic crib. Imperfections that are more serious exist from times when the people of Israel misunderstood the will of God and went far astray; not everything is portrayed in high and lofty terms, but that is consistent with an honest and accurate assessment of human nature.

Concerning the errors in the Bible, if one wishes to call them that, consider the following scenario. Suppose I am out of town at a meeting and I telephone my wife. In the course of the conversation, she tells me that she loves me, and, also, that last evening she heard a nightingale singing in the back yard. That is interesting to me, because I have never seen one in our area. I check the ornithological sources and discover that the bird is European and that there has never been a record of it in our entire country, so I have to conclude that Rochelle does not have her facts straight about nightingales. But does that mean that neither does she love me? In similar fashion, the majority of Christians regard the Bible less like an encyclopedia of purported facts and more like a love letter, in which dissection and critique of the details are largely beside the point. In it, some things are much more important than are others, and it is those major concerns of the Bible that are the focus for believers and that they find to ring true to life and to be trustworthy.

Thus, dinosaurs are not in the Bible. Why would we expect to find them? They were not really recognized, as such, until the nineteenth century and the term for the group, *Dinosauria*, was not coined until 1841. Thus, the concept of evolution is not in the Bible, a fact that does not mean it isn't true. (It is interesting, however, that the sequence of events in Genesis chapter 1 is roughly the same as the sequence of the development of the earth and living forms in evolutionary thought.) The coherence of the theory of evolution seems, to many of us, to be well described by the editors of *Natural History* magazine, who replied to a creationist call to have evolution excised from its pages: "Sorry, but the Darwinism stays. The depth and breadth of the scientific evidence for evolution, its general plausibility, and its predictive power are all over-whelming . . . If you doubt evolution, you might as well doubt gravity."

◦～◦

Creationists often attempt to criticize the idea of evolution by saying, "It's only a *theory*," by which they mean to imply that it is mere specu-lation. This reveals a further misunderstanding of how science works. Perhaps, in horse races or in politics, a theory is equivalent to specula-tion and may be on shaky ground, but in science a "theory" is the *most* solid construct of all. It is, instead, the term "hypothesis" that is used to convey uncertainty. In science, things progress from observation to hypothesis to experimentation, testing, and verification to, finally, a theory that encompasses and best accounts for all the facts under consideration. The germ theory of disease is one. And, yes, gravity is "just" a theory: Newton's theory of universal gravitation.

In their presentations, creationist speakers rely on the public's poor understanding of science to discredit evolution and science in general. In their forums, debates, and television appearances, creationists often score points with the general public with their demand that scientists *prove* their assertions about cosmology and evolution, as if that could be done in a sound bite. For example, in speaking to young people who are uncertain about many things, Ken Ham's rapid-fire message is this: "Here's the point: Unless you have *all* the evidence, how can you be sure about *anything*? And, so, you've got a real problem. No matter how much you know, there's an infinite amount more *to* know, which means, no matter how much you know, you don't know how much more there *is* to know, anyway, which means no matter *how* much you know, you don't *know* how much you know, which means *you just don't know much at all*!" Ham's answer to such dire uncertainty is that *God* knows everything: "The only way I can be sure about coming to the right conclusions about *anything* in the world is to start with the word of one who knows *everything*!" He's talking about the Bible, which he construes as being true in the literal sense about everything related to creation. Once again, this is the concept of a Perfect Book that has all the answers, and Ham calls people to trust it for true science. Regarding the theory of evolution, his position is that because scientists were not at creation to see it, there is no proof. Somehow, he overlooks the logical extension of this line of thought, which is that one must also doubt the existence of George Washington, Julius Caesar, and Jesus Christ: after all, we were not there to see them. (Would a forensic detective say that a crime is capable of being solved only if there were an eyewitness? In fact, almost all crimes are solved otherwise.)

Moreover, it is an elementary fact that *science never really proves anything*, at least not in the sense of logic or mathematics. What science does do is provide hypotheses that are tested against the evidence and then decisions are made about which ones most nearly fit the observed facts. Science is a method for arriving at the most adequate explanation of physical phenomena. In the face of new evidence, it is always open to revision, something that is the source of its progress. However, creationists create the impression that science *should* absolutely "prove" things, and when it cannot, science is supposedly discredited.

In addition, scientists are challenged to disprove the creationists' claims that life was created quite recently and in forms very much the same as exist today. And, of course, the evolutionary biologists cannot do it. Why not? Because you can *never* prove the negative. For example, can you prove that your neighbor is *not* a space alien? Or, can you prove that another neighbor is *not* a cannibal? (If you "catch him in the act" with *homo sapiens* on the fork, you could demonstrate that he *is*. But, if you don't catch him—and you can't monitor him every minute of every day—he still might be a cannibal: you can't *prove* that he is not.) Further, can you prove that you are not dreaming right now? Therefore, we cannot absolutely, positively prove that the universe was not created just six thousand years ago and merely made to look ancient. However, in spite of falling short of rock-hard 100 percent certainty on such issues, some explanations are clearly of more substance than others. Ian Tattersall, a curator of anthropology at the American Museum of Natural History in New York, when confronted with the idea that an evolutionary construct is deficient because hypotheses are involved, said, "If so, then we might as well throw out *all* of science, for the same is true of all scientific knowledge."

⁓

The creationists' attempts at legislation that creation be taught as an alternative to evolution in the public schools is really an attempt to have their narrow brand of religious dogma taught to a wide and captive audience at public expense. It has repeatedly been struck down by the courts as being in violation of the establishment of religion clause of the Constitution that separates church and state, decisions that have been supported by virtually all the mainline religious denominations. In the rulings, creationism has been seen for what it is: a thinly veiled fundamentalist religion masquerading as science.

This is true, also, regarding the most recent expressions called *intelligent design*, which received much publicity in the last decade. Many who promote this are young-earth creationists, although some will make allowances for long spans of time. What all have in common is that they claim to be doing science by pointing to certain aspects of nature that have what they call "irreducible complexity." This, it is said, demonstrates the existence of an intelligent designer (whom they never call God, since, again, they claim to be doing science, but who else is there?). However, intelligent design is not testable in any manner, and therefore, is not science. It is, instead, an affirmation of faith and one that is appropriate for faith, for you surely have to be a calloused soul not to be awe-struck at the amazing complexity of the world, and anyone who can hold a newborn baby and not feel that life is a miracle has a deficiency of humanity. The Psalms are full of such praise: "O Lord, how wondrous are your works; in wisdom you have made them all!" (Ps 104:24). However, this grows out of a *prior* faith and is an *expression* of it. It is not deduction but doxology. It is simply praise. In tune with that, evolutionary biologist Joan Roughgarden writes, "Intelligent design offers a backdoor route to belief in God. It turns you away from the Bible to look at scientific data. If you don't believe the Bible's miracles, check out the bacterial flagellum. Instead, all of creation is the miracle, not bits and pieces here and there."

God has been invoked to explain not only things tiny and intricate but also phenomena on a grand and global scale. Louis Agassiz explored both Europe and North America and, in the process, discovered the Ice Age. Time after time, he noted grooves and scratches on bedrock. He found huge boulders or "erratics" far from their point of origin, as well as mounds and hillocks made of a jumble of rocks and soil, such as those in Wisconsin and Maine that are similar to those found today in Alaska at the terminals of glaciers. He envisioned not only mountain glaciers, but, in addition, a truly continental glacier composed of an ice sheet more than a mile thick. From a center in the region of Hudson Bay, the ice gradually expanded and pushed southward over the land, engulfing nearly half of North America and shaping many of the landscapes we see around us now. It is something that happened not just once but several times. In scope and scale, such a vision truly does stagger the imagination. Thus, based on hundreds of observations, Agassiz's discovery was a truly monumental one, making him one of the founders of modern geology. Some of his writings on the subject were gathered into his *Geological Sketches*, published in 1875, and it is a classic in the field. In the chapter entitled, "Ice-Period in America," Agassiz writes:

> One naturally asks, What was the use of this great engine set at work ages ago to grind, furrow, and knead over, as it were, the surface of the earth? We have our answer in the fertile soil which

spreads over the temperate regions of the globe. The glacier was God's great plough; and when the ice vanished from the face of the land, it left it prepared for the hand of the husbandman . . . The soil we have now over the temperate zone is a grain-growing soil—one especially adapted to those plants necessary to the higher domestic and social organizations of the human race. Therefore, I think we may believe that God did not shroud the world he had made in snow and ice without a purpose, and that this, like many other operations of his providence, seemingly destructive and chaotic in its first effects, is nevertheless a work of benefice and order.

However, one could equally say that such soil conducive to agriculture was simply the result of the glaciers, which were, in turn, the result of numerous forces acting together on a planetary scale. In this perspective, the Ice Age happened by virtue of natural causes resulting in natural effects, and it was simply fortunate that the soil turned out to be productive for raising the wheat that humans had domesticated, and so forth. Ascribing a specific purpose to the ice sheets themselves, i.e., a design, is something that goes beyond any scientific evidence. I love the phrase "God's great plow," and I think it is a favorite of more than a few geologists. As a poetic statement of faith relating to the ultimate origins of a world that operates by God-given natural law, it is, I think, wonderful, but glaciers do not prove God.

Again, devotees of intelligent design often point to specific occurrences in nature that are so intricate as to be difficult to describe, much less to explain. However, it must be recognized that many of those things which have seemed mystifying in the past have, over time, yielded to scientific explanations. Darwin wrote to his young friend, John Lubbock, "I daresay when thunder and lightning were first found to be due to secondary causes, some regretted to give up the idea that each flash was caused by the direct hand of God." To Asa Gray, the American botanist and devout Christian with whom Darwin carried on a correspondence over many years, he wrote that surely no one should believe "that when a swallow snaps up a gnat that God designed that that particular swallow should snap up that particular gnat at that particular instant." Both knew that simply pointing to God as the answer would shut down inquiry and be the end of science. (So, you would be jumping too quickly to the argument from design if you cited as one of the most striking examples of God's providence that God almost never sends rain to the desert, where it would be wasted, but only to the fertile regions of the earth, where it does the most good!)

The Lutheran theologian Dietrich Bonhoeffer (hanged in April of 1945 by the Nazis for his involvement in the bombing plot to kill Hitler) wrote from his prison cell of the folly of positing a "god of the gaps," for the gaps may soon be filled. That kind of god is too small and is soon edged out of our mental universe: "How wrong it is to use God as a stop-gap for the incompleteness of our knowledge. For the frontiers of knowledge are inevitably being pushed back further and further . . . We should find God in what we know, not in what we don't . . . We must not wait until we're at the end of our tether; God must be found at the center of life."

~

Part of what bothers many people about the idea of evolution is that nature appears to be a theatre of the happenstance. It was with good reason that one of the world's great poets, W. H. Auden, wrote the following:

> I do not personally believe there is such a thing as a "random" event. "Unpredictable" is a factual description; "random" contains, without having the honesty to admit it, a philosophical bias typical of persons who have forgotten how to pray . . . I must now state my own bias and say that I do not believe in Chance; I believe in Providence and Miracles. If photosynthesis was invented by chance, then I can only say it was a damned lucky chance for us. If, biologically speaking, it is a "statistical improbability" that I should be walking the earth instead of a million other people, I can only think of it as a miracle which I must do my best to deserve.

The concept of randomness is, indeed, quite often wrongly applied. Creationists often compare the *un*likihood of evolution to a tornado going through a junkyard and, fantastically, producing a 747 jumbo jet. That is hardly an apt comparison, for evolution doesn't just happen; it happens in stages. Whether in physical or in biological evolution, there is always something prior, out of which the present grows. There was always a past that shaped any current event, and, in the process, narrowed the field for any possible event in the future. Nothing is completely random in the sense of being completely arbitrary.

In spite of this, many cannot help viewing with some discomfort the idea that things they thought were specifically designed may be, instead, the result of random variation. This is understandable, especially if one has the idea that everything should arrive in its place according to predetermined goals. However, what if the future is open and the goal *itself* is variation and its consequent diversity? We do live in a universe of unimaginable possibilities. Any road taken soon branches off to others and those, in turn, to still others. Consider the intricate game of chess. It has been calculated that if every man, woman, and child in the world were to spend every hour of every day playing chess at the impossible rate of one game a minute, it would still take billions of years to cover all the variations on just the first ten moves! There are thirty-two chess pieces and sixty-four spaces on the board. In just the first ten moves by each of the two players in a game, the number of variations turns out to be 169,518,892,100,544,000,000,000,000,000. As Casey Stengel, onetime manager of the New York Yankees, used to say about all sorts of things, "You can look it up."

Arthur Peacocke is a scientist who held academic posts in physical biochemistry for more than twenty-five years at Birmingham and Oxford universities. In addition, he is a systematic theologian who is Dean of Clare College at Cambridge and an ordained priest in the Church of England. In *Paths from Science to God*, he suggests, "Instead of being daunted by the role of chance in genetic mutations as being the manifestation of irrationality in the universe, it would be more consistent with the observations to assert that the full gamut of the potentialities of living matter could be explored only through the agency of the rapid and frequent randomization which is possible at the molecular level of DNA." In *Theology for a Scientific Age*, he maintains that "it has become increasingly apparent that it is chance operating within a law-like framework that is the basis of the inherent creativity of the natural order . . . It is the combination of the two which makes possible an ordered universe capable of developing within itself new modes of existence. *The interplay of chance and law is creative.*" (italics in original) I take it he is saying that if you load the dice with ironclad laws, you get predictable results, but you don't get *all* results, i.e., you don't get, eventually, every possible combination. What we see in the natural world is living things filling and adapted to virtually every conceivable niche. Thus, ironically, you could not *design* a superior, more efficient method for achieving diversity than that of random variation. The unattractive alternative is the image of the creator as an obsessive tinkerer who requires direct intervention to make every slight change in every insect's antennae or in every stickleback's stickle. Instead, according to Darwin's contemporary, the Rev. Charles Kingsley, God makes things make themselves, which is a more creative act. Henry Ward Beecher, the famous nineteenth-century New England clergyman, colorfully put it that "Design by wholesale is grander than design by retail."

∽

As one looks at nature, questions are bound to arise. Darwin, who at various times described himself both as a theist and an agnostic, was most bothered by questions like those that involved the larvae of wasps, i.e., why a beneficent God "would have designedly created the Ichneumonidae with the express intention of their feeding within the living body of caterpillars." "On the other hand," he wrote to Asa Gray, the Christian who gave him a sympathetic ear, "I cannot anyhow be contented to view this wonderful universe and especially the nature of man, and to conclude that everything is the result of brute force. I am inclined to look at everything as resulting from designed laws, with the details, whether good or bad, left to the working out of what we may call chance. Not that this *at all* satisfies me." Showing much more humility than some of his later devotees, Darwin concludes, "I feel most deeply that the whole subject is too profound for the human intellect. A dog might as well speculate on the mind of Newton."

Creationism is not going away any time soon, and varied approaches in line with its agenda continue to be tried. Dinosaurs remain hugely popular, so all over the country creationists are now building their own museums to display their rendition of things, i.e., to show, to their satisfaction, at least, that evolution did not happen and that evolution is either a gross mistake or a lie. A new 50,000 square-foot museum in Kentucky cost more than $27 million, and there are others. Some contain dioramas showing dinosaurs on the prairie along with bison; dinosaurs and humans are often depicted as living peacefully together. Dinosaurs (all babies, to save space) are shown boarding Noah's ark only a few thousand years ago. Land is being leased in western states in order to hold workshops over dinosaur bones, so people can come and see for themselves the "evidence" of the great flood of Noah.

Some creationist exhibits portray all dinosaurs as vegetarian, because, in their literalism regarding Genesis, there was no death before the Fall; therefore, it is maintained that even animals that are now carnivores were originally herbivores. Such museums, while demonizing the conclusions of paleontologists who have made the dinosaur discoveries, seek to use those same discoveries to promote "the truth" about the falsity of evolution. Concerning a new museum in Dallas, Dennis Lindsay, who was involved in its founding, told a newspaper reporter from the *Chicago Times*, "Everyone is totally fascinated by dinosaurs. It will be an attraction to have those and share the story that . . . dinosaurs did not live 65 million years ago." G. Thomas Sharpe, founder of Creation Truth Foundation, said, "If we lose Genesis as a legitimate scientific and historic explanation for man, then we lose the validity of Christianity. Period." Again, evolution and a literalistic interpretation of Genesis are seen as opposites and you are told you must choose between them. Many do.

Such efforts to contradict established earth science are widespread. They are, in the judgment of virtually all scientists, so wrongheaded as to represent an attempt to make a virtue out of ignorance. Concerning the plant-eating meat-eaters, geologist David R. Schwimmer says, "The image of a *Tyrannosaurus rex*, or a saber-toothed cat such as *Smilodon fatalis*, gnawing on roots and twigs, should be sufficiently bizarre to reveal to any audience the scientific la-la-land occupied by this curious, American-bred phenomenon called 'Creation Science!'" The sad result may be that a large percentage of our populace will stereotype religion as being backward. Many people may take the literalists at their word and reject any biblical passage as having been superseded by modern science. One thinks of the words in the musical *Porgy and Bess* by George and Ira Gershwin and Dorothy and Du Bose Heyward:

> It ain't necessarily so.
> It ain't necessarily so.
> De t'ings that yo li'ble
> To read in de Bible—
> It ain't necessarily so.

A huge segment of society, knowing that fundamentalism is an intellectual dead-end—ludicrous, in fact—might laugh the Bible to scorn. The creationists are an embarrassment to most religion. Augustine would weep, and I do.

~

In the face of this, however, there are increasing numbers of people with the highest scientific credentials who are speaking out against both a perverted religion and a perverse scientism and affirming the middle ground.

Dale Russell, for many years in Canada at the National Museum of Natural History in Ottawa and now at North Carolina State University, is widely known as one of the truly great and creative thinkers in the realm of paleontology. He is eminently qualified to consider the larger picture of the history of life through time and its philosophical implications. His 2009 book, *Islands in the Cosmos: The Evolution of Life on Land,* surveys the procession of such living things as revealed by the fossil record and describes their environmental contexts. It is a massive scholarly work, documented by some 1500 references to books and articles in scientific journals.

At a very few points, Russell's thoughts edge onto the meaning of it all, as with this statement: "We tread on hallowed ground." In spite of the most comprehensive the analysis of natural processes, he finds that "At a basic level, evolution is not an explanation but a mystery." He alludes to the general trend toward fitness in organisms that is "obtained through the operation of 'laws impressed upon matter' [phrase from Darwin]. The trend . . . appears to point beyond space and time toward a nonmaterial, perfect, and creative Reason." I think we do not misunderstand the scientist, if we equate his term Reason—with a capital R—to that of God, much as physicist Freeman Dyson sometimes used the word Mind. In the Epilogue, Russell concludes, "For me, the presence of a creative Reason fits more compatibly with what is known of our situation in life, is more interdisciplinary, accesses a broader spectrum of knowledge, and is inherently much more interesting."

Thus, after all the scientific descriptions of the details and the mechanisms of evolution: natural selection, genetic variation, and so forth, there persists the underlying question concerning the ultimate source (and goal?) of a universe that has order, an order that unfolds over time with such astonishing variety, newness, and beauty.

Francis Collins is quite explicit about his views. Since 1993, he has been the Director of the National Human Genome Research Institute, where he heads up the multinational team of 2,400 scientists who have mapped the 3.1 billion biochemical letters of the human genetic blueprint. In an interview published in *National Geographic*, Collins says, "The God of the Bible is also the God of the genome . . . He can be worshiped in the cathedral or in the laboratory." Further, "God is most certainly not threatened by science; He made it all possible." Evolution, to Collins, is self-evident, but he's also impressed by the finding of physicists that if the so-called gravitational constant were "off by one part in a hundred million million, then the expansion of the universe after the Big Bang would not have occurred in the fashion that was necessary for life to occur." "When you look at the evidence," he said in a *Time* magazine interview, "it is very difficult to adopt the view that this was just chance." God is, for him, "a rather plausible explanation for what is otherwise an exceedingly improbable event—namely our existence." Collins is also interested in "those answers that science isn't able to provide about the natural world—the questions about why . . . I find many of those answers in the spiritual realm."

That is also the sentiment of some sixty leading scientists, including twenty-four Nobel Prize winners, whose ideas are put forth in the book, *Cosmos, Bios, Theos.* They were all asked to answer the same questions on the relationship between science and religion, evolution, the origin of the universe, of life, and of *Homo sapiens.* Not one of them finds the evolutionary process itself to be problematic. They all look at a deeper level than the details and mechanics of life processes. Many take note of the large questions concerning the origin of life and the origin of everything. William A. Little, professor of physics at Stanford, wrote about the origin of life: "It's hard to believe that all this just happened as a result of the initial conditions. In fact, if that is how it happened, it is all the more remarkable!" Typical is the response of UCLA astronomer and physicist, Stuart Bowyer: "Ultimately, the origin of the universe is, and always will be, a mystery. Science has pressed the level of what can be explained further and further into the early universe, but the mystery is nonetheless there." Arnos Penzias (who, with R. W. Wilson, discovered the background radiation of the big bang) holds that "Astronomy leads us to a unique event, to a universe created out of nothing, one with the very delicate balance needed to provide exactly the conditions required to permit life, and one which has an underlying (one might say 'supernatural') plan. Thus, the observations of modern science seem to lead to the same conclusions as age-old intuitions." Also, Princeton mathematician Edward Nelson: "One of my earliest memories is a feeling of great surprise that there is anything. It still strikes me as amazing. And for me this is the fundamental religious emotion. I believe in, pray to, and worship God."

As of 2011, nearly 13,000 clergy from all across the nation signed a letter composed in opposition to the highly publicized efforts in Dover, PA in 2004 to discredit the teaching of evolution in the public schools. The letter states, in part, that the theory of evolution "is a foundational scientific truth" and that "to reject it is to deliberately embrace scientific ignorance and transmit such ignorance to our children . . . We believe that among God's gifts are human minds capable of critical thought and that the failure to fully employ this gift is a rejection of the will of our Creator." Some 650 congregations observed a so-called Evolution Sunday to help make the point.

S. Dillon Ripley, when Secretary of the Smithsonian Institution, commented in *Smithsonian* magazine concerning letters he received charging that the museum's exhibits depicting evolution were "atheistic, anti-Christian and hostile to Bible teachings." His response: "I do not believe this for a moment. As a Christian, I believe the achievements of science in understanding the evolution of the universe have only magnified our wonder at creation." Wilbur E. Garrett, speaking as Editor of *National Geographic*, writes, "The universe we know today—billions of years old, populated with almost incomprehensibly complex life-forms programmed with astonishingly clever plans for heredity, change, and survival—might inspire . . . in so many people of faith today . . . an even greater respect and devotion for the Creator." The cell biologist Kenneth R. Miller, who testified at the Dover trial, writes in *Finding Darwin's God*, "Understanding evolution and its description of processes that gave us the modern world is an important part of knowing and appreciating God. As a scientist and a Christian, that is exactly what I believe. True knowledge only comes from a combination of faith and reason."

The story of evolution has powerful capacity to look at the tangled bank of living things and to disentangle many of those elements in order to discover what came from where. It answers a great many of the questions but, of course, not all.

Loren Eiseley taught for many years at the University of Pennsylvania, where he was Benjamin Franklin Professor of Anthropology. His subject was Ice Age humanity, and he had the long perspective of one who deals in geologic time (one of his many books is called *The Immense Journey*).

He was at the forefront of his field in science, but he combined that with a rare poetic sense. (This resulted in his being the recipient of thirty-six honorary degrees, these without fanfare; most of his colleagues never knew about them.) Eiseley once described himself this way: "I am a man who has spent much of my life on my knees, though not in prayer." That might be said to be debatable, however, and certain only for a narrow definition of prayer, for his sense of wonder at life is profound and it led him to raise ultimate questions. He wrote, "There is no logical reason for the existence of a snowflake any more than there is for evolution. It is an apparition from that mysterious shadow world beyond nature, that final world which contains—if anything contains—the explanation of men and catfish and green leaves." Consider this passage from his essay, "The Secret of Life:"

> I do not think, if someone finally twists the key successfully in the tiniest and most humble house of life, that many of these questions will be answered, or that the dark forces which create lights in the deep sea and living batteries in the waters of tropical swamps, or the dread cycles of parasites, or the most noble workings of the human brain, will be much if at all revealed. Rather, I would say that if "dead" matter has reared up this curious landscape of fiddling crickets, song sparrows, and wondering men, then it must be plain to even the most devoted materialist that the matter of which he speaks contains amazing, if not dreadful powers, and may not impossibly be, as Hardy has suggested, "but one mask of many worn by the Great Face behind."

The challenge and the opportunity of our times is to investigate this astounding universe of both living and inanimate things, and this in the conviction that truth found in one realm will not *ultimately* conflict with truth found in another and by different means. So viewed, the "two books" of science and religion are capable of truly enriching and enhancing one another.

With regard to evolution, the spirit of Louis Leakey may be commended to all. Leakey was born in 1903, the son of missionary parents in East Africa. He was the first white baby born in that entire region, and the natives came from far and wide to spit on him—in that culture, a sign of respect. As a young man, Leakey was part of the crew in Tanzania that dug up the skeleton of the giant sauropod *Brachiosaurus,* which stands in the Humboldt Museum in Berlin. It is the largest mounted dinosaur skeleton in the world. He went on to become a paleontologist on the trail of early man, and, with his wife, Mary, searched Africa's Oldovai Gorge in the Rift Valley for some twenty-five years until they found a creature that pushed our human ancestry back an additional million years from what was known at the time. In a television interview late in his life, he was asked why he spent his life in that way, for most of that time ignored by the rest of the scientific community, and he answered: "You may call it curiosity. But call it a *major* curiosity—*I want to know who I am.*"

That is the inescapable question, the one with more ramifications than any other. Part of the answer is found in the realization that, as the stream of time flows onward, all of life is involved in an even larger process in which the entire universe itself is constantly developing, unfolding, and evolving. It is the longest, most intricate, and most expansive story the human mind has yet produced.

11

Take Care

We have built our nest in the tree of life; now we must save the tree.

Richard Cartwright Austin

Never doubt that a small group of thoughtful, committed citizens can change the world; indeed, it's the only thing that ever has.

Margaret Mead

NEAR THE END OF the last Ice Age, Europe was home to a vast array of large mammals, including woolly mammoth and rhinoceros. There were also horses, reindeer, and large straight-horned bison, as well as a kind of giant deer with antlers of a thirteen-foot spread, most of them moving in immense herds. Following the plant-eaters were numerous carnivores: great bears, lions, and saber-toothed cats, hyenas, and leopards. The fossil bones of all of them testify to a diverse fauna that is matched today only by East Africa. And out on the fringe of such processions, dwarfed by the sheer number of large animals in this snow-clad northern Serengeti and intimidated by the dangers of such an environment, were the human ancestors of so many of us.

In our own time, when, in most places, even seeing a wild animal is a rarity, we find it difficult to imagine a time when people lived in small bands in the most severe wilderness, surrounded by mighty herds of hundreds and thousands, but so it was for almost all of human history.

From cliffs overlooking valleys through which animals moved, they watched and waited for the dying or the straggler herbivores that might present an opportunity for a kill with their stone tools. They lived the only way they could, by hunting and gathering, but they were also the hunted. In those days, humanity was a part—and only a small part—of nature, which was, indeed, red with tooth and claw. For tens of thousands of years, those early humans struggled to hang on in a world that was threatening to erase their very presence. As icy winds blew off the glaciers, they huddled in small groups at the entrances to caves, where they built the fires that cooked their meat and, at least some of the time, kept the huge predators at bay.

They also went down into some of those caves and there, in those deep, dark recesses and, for reasons at which we can only guess, produced some of the finest art the world has ever seen. In their fire-lit drawings on cave walls and ceilings, they only rarely pictured themselves; rather, the paintings and carvings are of those powerful animals in whose midst they lived and upon which they were utterly dependent for survival. In the caverns of what is now France and Spain, at Lascaux, Font-de-Gaume, Rouffignac, Niaux, Chauvet, and Altamira, they created images of their quarry, images likely designed to influence those vast and dimly comprehended forces that had to do with the turning of the seasons and the success or failure of the hunt. 20,000 years before Christ, this was the prayer, "Give us this day our daily bread."

The discovery of the art of Altamira is one of the great stories in the annals of prehistory and merits a brief retelling here. In 1879, Marquis Don Marcelino de Sautuola, a Spanish nobleman and amateur archaeologist, was digging for bones and artifacts at the entrance to the cave in the northern part of the country, something he had done several times before. He was accompanied by his young daughter, Maria, who, at some point, wandered off into one of the side chambers with the torch that had been used to give light to her father. The chamber was too low for an adult to walk upright, but just right for the child. The father was accustomed to looking down; she had no such prejudice. Holding the torch over her head, she suddenly saw a herd of bison galloping across the ceiling and cried out, "Toros! Toros!"

The colorful pictures were of numerous bison, as well as deer, horses, and wild boar. Father and daughter spent many days exploring those grandly decorated limestone halls, after which de Sautuola wrote to his friend, Professor Vilanova of the University of Madrid, who visited the cave and was astonished by what he saw. The Madrid newspapers featured the story, creating a sensation. Later that year, King Alphonso XII came to see the wonders for himself, crawling down into some of the most narrow and remote galleries.

The marquis soon set to work on a treatise about the discovery. Earlier, he had befriended a mute and destitute artist who had been stranded in the area, and he now put him to work making sketches for the publication. The next year (1880) brought scholars from all over the world to the International Congress of Anthropology and Prehistoric Archaeology in Lisbon, where Professor Vilanova announced the discovery. The public had been duly impressed; the authorities in the field, however, were not, and greeted all of it with skepticism in the extreme. A prominent artist, who had seen the cave murals, dismissed them on artistic grounds, saying, "Such paintings are simply the expression of a mediocre student of the modern school."

Accusing fingers were pointed at the artist staying with de Sautuola, for the images looked fresh and vivid, almost as if the pigment had been applied a short while ago. In addition, the paintings were met with cynicism born of the presupposition that our ancestors of the remote past surely were not advanced enough to have produced such images. What sort of art could one expect, after all, from savages? Thus, the cave paintings were declared frauds. In vain, the discoverer tried to get the experts in prehistory to listen to him, but he was ignored. He died in 1888 at the age of fifty-seven.

Just fifteen years later, the marvelous cave art was declared to be absolutely genuine, a conclusion forced by the discovery of other such caves, one following another, until it could not be doubted that the magnificent graphics had been produced by artists of tens of millennia ago. In 1940, four French schoolboys wormed their way into a hole that had been exposed by an uprooted tree and found therein the great galleries of Lascaux with their hundreds of spectacular images. Now, the entire world knows of those images and, through the eyes of those ancient painters, can glimpse scenes from the distant past when our ancestors hunted reindeer, long-horned bison, and hairy elephants on ground now covered by the brick and asphalt of the great European cities.

North America, too, had Ice Age faunas. Some of the creatures were quite similar to those in Europe and some were different. By ten thousand years ago, most of the larger Ice Age animals were gone from both continents. Before that, humans had migrated from Asia to North America. Moving at just five or ten miles a year, one generation after another, they could have traveled from Alaska to the tip of South America in only one or two thousand years. Debate still rages concerning whether the great extinctions were caused by natural changes in climate or were the result of increasingly efficient hunting methods employed by our human ancestors both here and in the rest of the world. One thing is certain: the great mammoth and most of its large animal contemporaries are extinct, while human beings survived, have proliferated to billions, and now dominate the entire planet.

$$\approx$$

The concept of *extinction* was a long time in coming. As fossils began to be unearthed of creatures that were unlike those of the present age, the idea surfaced, but it was not readily accepted. Thomas Jefferson, in 1799, wrote a scientific description of what turned out to be a giant ground sloth (now called *Megalonix jeffersoni*) and, as President, kept mastodon bones in the White House. He spoke for most when he wrote, "Such is the economy of nature, that no instance can be produced of her having permitted any one race of her animals to become extinct; of her having formed any link in her great work, so weak as to be broken . . . The movements of nature are in a never-ending circle. The animal species which has once been put into a train of motion is probably still moving in that train." That outlook was behind Jefferson's instructions to Lewis and Clark in advance of the great expedition to keep an eye out for the mastodon and mammoth, which he believed may have survived in the great forests of the West.

We know now that extinction has been the fate of most species, in fact, of perhaps 99 percent of all that have ever lived. The process has been spread throughout geologic time, but there have been two major peaks, two truly massive extinctions. The largest was the first of those, it taking place at the end of the Permian Period some 245 million years ago, when as much as 90 percent of all living things on earth died off. The second and last such major event is the one that marks the end of the Cretaceous Period 65 million years ago, when perhaps 40 percent of life was deleted; this is the one that took the dinosaurs, the marine reptiles, the ammonites, and a whole host of other creatures.

Often, the process leading up to extinction has been a gradual one, ending with a whimper. Sometimes, however, or so many now believe, it has been with a bang. In the eighteenth century, scientists were skeptical of peasants' claims that rocks fell from the sky. We now know they do. In fact, were it not for the weathering agents of the earth's atmosphere and the movement and subduction of the continents in plate tectonics, which over millions of years have obliterated the traces of most impacts, earth's surface would resemble that of the moon, with crater piled upon crater. Still, as the twentieth century dawned, surely there was no evidence that truly major disruptions of life on earth could be traced to anything like that.

In 1920, H. G. Wells published his *Outline of History*, a two-volume work that began with a chapter titled, "The World Before Man." In it, he recounted the disappearance of the dinosaurs and wondered about the cause. In what must rank as an idea far ahead of its time, he wrote, "Some huge dark projectile from outer space may have come hurtling through the planets and deflected or even struck our world and turned the course of evolution in a new direction. Little projectiles are always striking us . . . Most of these meteors are burnt to nothing before they reach the ground, but many have reached and continue to reach the earth. Some in our museums are several yards in diameter. Perhaps, once one was big enough to produce a change such as we have proposed. But this is a lapse into pure speculation. Let us return to the facts."

The facts are, according to a great many scientists, that one *was* big enough: an asteroid six to eight miles in diameter—like a Mt. Everest—hurtling at 60,000 miles per hour, did indeed strike the earth about the time the dinosaurs disappeared. The evidence is found in a submerged crater some 150 miles wide on the coast of the Yucatán Peninsula and in many other places around the globe in the form of a one-inch zone of sediment called "the iridium layer." It contains debris from the asteroid itself as well as the crater material that was blasted into the atmosphere and then settled out over time. It is a dramatic story, one that easily lends itself to publicity, paintings, and special effects in films. It may be correct, and most scientists now believe that it is.

In *Annals of the Former World*, John McPhee describes one of the covers featured on *Geology*, the magazine of the Geological Society of America when the editor was Eldridge Moores. It was, he says, "a painting of a *Triceratops* being eaten alive by a *Tyrannosaurus rex*. In the heavens close above the struggling creatures is the Apollo Object—an asteroid, roughly six miles in diameter—that is believed to have collided with the earth and caused the extinction of the dinosaurs. In the editor's notes on the contents page, Moores referred to the painting as 'the Last Supper.' There were outraged complaints from geologists."

However, that idea may also be wrong. The situation may be more complex than the asteroid scenario. The dinosaurs were already in steep decline when the asteroid hit, and some maintain that they were already gone. There is also evidence of volcanic flows in India on the most massive scale, which would have filled the atmosphere with debris. It could also have been a combination of factors: volcanoes, climate, disease, falling sea levels, or something else entirely, and there are no small numbers of paleontologists who believe that multiple causes operating more gradually are the explanation. In any case, the undeniable fact is that of massive extinctions. For whatever reasons, the dinosaurs disappeared.

There is an unspeakable finality about extinction. That which has taken billions of years to emerge as a unique species is gone and can never be recalled. No power on earth can reconstitute the elements that made up the *Ankylosaurus* or the passenger pigeon.

We tend to think of such extinctions as past events and as applying to a few select animals. Neither assumption stands up to scrutiny. Extinctions are proceeding today and at a pace, according to all that has been learned in recent decades, which will soon produce a reduction of plant and animal types on the scale of those events that took out the dinosaurs. The most optimistic estimates are that something like 27,000 species are going under each year. It is entirely possible that 20 percent of the earth's creatures could be lost in the next thirty years, and half may be either gone or headed for extinction by the end of this century. Ornithologist John Livingston sums it up: "The terrifying trends are readily visible . . . The torpedoed Ark is settling with all hands—varieties, races, populations, species, associations, communities, whole faunas—and almost without a sound." Thus, it may well be that we are living in the very midst of the third major extinction event in the history of life on earth. This time, for certain, the blame cannot be put on a huge rock careening our way from the asteroid belt. This time, there is every indication that a single species—*Homo sapiens*, humanity, we ourselves, humankind—has everything to do with it.

~

Humanity has everything to do with it in two major ways. In the first place, there is the *dramatic increase in our population* over just the last two hundred years. In the 1800s, with a population of 25 million, most Americans viewed the continent as providing an inexhaustible amount of land. Europeans, however, facing population pressures there, warned that such a situation would not last and that many people and little land would lead to great trials. Our trials have begun. Almost every problem we now face, from energy, water, and other resource shortages to pollution and crime can be either traced to or made worse by the population problem. When I was in high school, our nation had 150 million people; now we are more than 300 million.

For the entire world, the figures are dramatic in the extreme. It is believed to have taken from the dawn of human history until about 1830 to reach a population of a billion people living at one time on planet earth. The second billion took only a century, until 1930. Since then, the figure has more than tripled, and the population curve is going almost straight up. In the 1980s, an ad ran in many magazines that showed a table set in a cornfield and it stretched as far as the eye could see. The caption was simple and powerful: "We're expecting a few extra people for dinner tonight." An asterisk directed one to learn just how many those few extra were: the figure was some 220,000. That means that 1.5 million people were being added to the world every week. (This was not just births, but births over deaths, i.e., net increase. It is as if the planet added a city the size of Minneapolis-St. Paul every seven days.) Just a few years ago, I noticed a panel on the side of a bus in Denver that read, "6 billion people—How can we be so dense?" We are now at 7 billion.

In 1789, Thomas Malthus, a Presbyterian minister (and amateur scientist) predicted a great change in the population of the earth, saying that one day there would be too many people for the earth to support. (Darwin used his statistical insights in determining the factors influencing natural selection.) Malthus pointed out that food supplies can possibly be increased by a fixed amount on a regular basis, but populations increase by multiplication. Starting with the number 1 and *adding* the number 2 thirty times gives you just 61. However, *multiplying* by the number 2 thirty times gives you over a billion. This is the way the human population is growing; it is now in the process of doubling in just the course of a human lifetime. In the business of survival, no species can afford to triumph too completely without becoming the victims of its own success. In America, population increase has been running about 1 percent per year. To most people, that does not sound like much. However, if that rate had been in operation worldwide for the last 5,000 years, from the time of Egypt's great pyramids, it would have produced 2.7 billion people for every square foot of land surface on the planet! Of course, nothing remotely like this could happen, but it does point out that such a rate of increase has not been going on for very long in the past and that it cannot continue much longer in the future without ecological collapse. Already, while we worry about dieting, millions of others worry about dying, since the days of food surpluses—if they ever existed—are long over and now are barely a crumb on the table of the world. World hunger is a problem that will be solved one way or another; however, some of those ways involve death and disease on a planetary scale. The truth is that if we saw this kind of population curve in any other species, we would summon every killer chemical or the H-bomb itself to control it. What do we do when we, ourselves, are the problem?

There is a passage in the Old Testament that tells of the prophet Isaiah coming before one of Israel's kings to deliver the bad news that destruction is coming upon the kingdom at the hands of Babylon. However, the warning added that this would happen not quite yet but in the reign of the king's sons. The text says that the king was at first very much disturbed, but when he realized that the calamity was yet some way distant, he said, "The word of the Lord which you have spoken is good. For he thought, 'There will be peace and security in my days.'" (Isa 39:8) It is a picture of the callous, short-sighted, self-absorption to which we are all prone. It's the attitude that says, "What has posterity ever done for me?" If there is even to be a posterity, the time is here to determine the carrying capacity of the earth. We do this routinely with livestock and rangeland; nature does it with all sorts of living things in the struggle for existence. Can the human race be exempt?

One is not an alarmist, if the sky really is falling. In *Either/Or*, the Danish author Søren Kierkegaard tells the parable of a clown who put on his makeup and got all dressed for the performance in a theater when a fire broke out backstage. "The clown came out to inform the public. They thought it was a jest and applauded. He repeated his warning, they shouted even louder. So I think the world will come to an end amid general applause from all the wits who believe that it is a joke."

If we do not take the population problem seriously now, there may not be enough time later to make any difference. Dennis Hayes said that the U.S. is what boxers call a counterpuncher, i.e., what we do best is respond to immediate problems: "Bomb Pearl Harbor and America will pull out all the stops. Launch Sputnik and America will have NASA functioning overnight. What we do *not* do well is anticipate and avoid problems. Unfortunately, many environmental phenomena involve thresholds that, when passed, cause irreversible damage. If we wait until the damage occurs, and then respond, it will be too late." The analogy could also be made of a huge ocean liner cutting through the sea under tremendous power. From the moment the captain says, "Stop!" and the brakes are applied, so to speak, it takes six miles before that action occurs. This is the situation of our crowded world. Unfortunately, our ship is still going full speed ahead and most of our leaders, instead of using the radar we have for things environmental, are perched on the bow probing for icebergs with a ten-foot pole. To turn things around, we must start now.

There are things we cannot control, such as those truly long cycles of the earth (as of late, with global climate change, some of those may not be exempt, either). We are currently in an interglacial stage of the Pleistocene or recent Ice Age. Over the course of the last two million years, the northern ice has advanced and retreated several times, once reaching even as far as St. Louis. It came and went, only to eventually return. Each time, the icecap of Greenland gradually expanded to become a truly continental glacier centered near Hudson Bay, and ice a mile thick inched its way across the land, sliding, pushing, and grinding over the surface, gouging new valleys, and filling others, moving rivers, dumping boulders, gnawing away at mountains. In Central Park in New York City, you can see exposed bedrock with deep grooves and striations made by rocks trapped in the bottom of the glacier as it advanced southward and scraped the region bare. They are silent but not-so-subtle reminders that we are in an in-between time and that the long winter of the ice will come again. The tall buildings of Manhattan will topple before the ice sheet like so many houses of cards and be ground to rubble. If present trends are any clue to the future, however, they will likely have been long deserted, the ribs of crumbling skyscrapers exposed to the sky with the wind whistling through them. They will be empty monuments to a people who learned too late, perhaps, the madness of settling arguments within the human family by force of arms or who learned, too late, that bigger is not always better and whose numbers exceeded the carrying capacity of the earth.

However, there are things we can control, if we only will. Unrestrained population growth, as well as the wars that are made more likely by such growth, are among them. We must start now, for there is only one planet that is home. We only get one experiment.

~

In addition to our sheer numbers, the other way in which our species is implicated in the current extinction cycle is how we have *mistreated the earth* and its web of living things, the biosphere. It has to do with the consequences of our attitudes and our style of life.

A wrong attitude toward nature must imply, somewhere, a wrong attitude toward God, and the result is an inevitable doom. The biblical creation story in Genesis chapter 1 places humankind in a special position of having "dominion over the earth." It is a realistic assessment, one that takes seriously that we have powers unlike that of any other creature to transform the world; there is no doubt about that, is there? The other creation story, the one in chapter 2, more nearly defines *how* the power is to be used: it places man in the role of being a caretaker or steward of that which does not really belong to him. Adam (again, "humanity") is placed in the garden of Eden "to dress, till, and care for the earth." However, human history is the story of unrealized potential and of high ideals distorted and abandoned. That is the meaning of the rest of the story about the garden, the part in chapter 3 that describes the Fall. The lofty intention is unfulfilled and man and woman do what they want, instead of what they ought, and the result is that, instead of harmony, there is alienation, disharmony, and exile from the garden—the garden, which is really the world.

Other images come to mind, also. Thoreau wrote in his journal on March 23, 1856, "I cannot but feel as if I lived in a tamed and, as it were, an emasculated country." The entire entry is a requiem for the eastern cougar and other creatures that had once been abundant in his part of the country: "I think that I have here the entire poem, and then, to my chagrin, I find that it is but an imperfect copy that I possess and have read, and that my ancestors have torn out many of the first pages and grandest passages and mutilated it in many places . . . I wish to know an entire heaven and an entire earth." If he could say that 150 years ago, what must we say now, when mining has literally removed the tops of nearly 500 mountains in Appalachia?

One thinks of the game, which the reader may have also played, consisting of a plastic cylinder full of marbles. The stack is supported at the bottom by a network of slender sticks put in every which way. People take turns pulling out a stick, one per turn, until someone pulls the one that triggers the precariously balanced pile of marbles to fall helter-skelter over the table, and that person loses. However, every small support pulled out before then played just as large a part in the collapse, as the load shifted and tottered. There are many variations on the game, but the point is the same: we have already pulled out many of the supports for rich and diverse life on earth.

Abraham Heschel said, "The world will not perish for want of information, but only for want of appreciation." It is difficult to find much appreciation in what has been transpiring in recent decades. The great African elephants were nearly poached to death a couple of decades ago just for their tusks for the illegal ivory trade, while each six- or seven-ton carcass was left to rot in the sun. When Theodore Roosevelt went on safari in 1910, it is estimated there may have been a million black rhinoceros on the continent. In Zimbabwe, in the middle of the last century, there were 20,000 rhinos; twenty years later, there were only 300, the rest killed for their "valuable" horns used in making traditional medicines in China and dagger handles in the Middle East. A huge and wonderful creature that has been evolving for 40 million years was in danger of being erased from the garden in a single lifetime. Progress against poaching has been made recently, and numbers have begun to build slightly, but shrinking habitat has been added to the threats.

In so many ways, the entire planet is now under siege. Alan Paton's novel about South Africa, *Cry, the Beloved Country*, opens with the description of a lovely valley; the cry of one of the birds of the veld, the titihoya, sounds over the grass-covered hills. The rich soil is its secret: "Stand unshod upon it, for the ground is holy, being even as it came from the Creator. Keep it, guard it, care for it, for it keeps men, guards men, cares for men. Destroy it, and man is destroyed." Then, there is the description of another area, where the hills stand red, desolate, and bare: "Stand shod upon it, for it is course and sharp, and the stones cut under the feet. It is not kept, guarded, or cared for; it no longer keeps men, guards men, cares for men. The titihoya does not cry here any more." Topsoil from America's Great Plains, the breadbasket of the world, is now being dumped in the Gulf of Mexico at the Mississippi delta not by the foot but by the fathom; it is being lost from our best agricultural land at a rate that exceeds many times over the rate at which nature can rebuild it.

The great forests of Europe, through which Caesar's legions could march for months without coming to the end of them, are almost all gone. On any given day, satellite photographs show more than two thousand fires burning in the Amazon. Each year, more than eight thousand square miles of rain forest goes under the bulldozer and the torch, which is an area equal in size to the size of the state of New Jersey. Much of this is due to illegal logging and mining, as well as to clearing space to farm thin topsoil that will soon erode, produce flooding, and leave behind a wasteland. In Ecuador and Peru, 90 percent of the old growth forests are gone, as they are on the West Coast of the U.S. Attempts were made by the administration of George W. Bush to allow logging even the great redwood trees in California in the Sequoia National Monument. Unable to distinguish between needs and greeds, treasures of the natural world are being sacrificed for short-term gain, and they are irreplaceable. The celebrated biologist E. O. Wilson wrote in *The Diversity of Life*, "The richest ecosystems build slowly, over millions of years . . . A panda or a sequoia represents a magnitude of evolution that comes along only rarely. It takes a stroke of luck and a long period of probing, experimentation, and failure. Such a creation is part of deep history, and the planet does not have the means, nor we the time to see it repeated."

There is not a corner of the earth where human influence is not felt. I can remember when the French oceanologist, Jacques Cousteau, was making some of the first deep-sea descents in a bathysphere. The thick steel capsule settled on the floor of one of the mid-ocean trenches, where he had reached a depth greater than anyone had ever ventured before. What sights would there be, down there, thousands of feet beneath the surface, in that realm where no light had ever penetrated? Cousteau pressed his face against the thick glass window and turned on the floodlights to view things never before glimpsed by any human being—and the first thing that met his eyes was a spread-out newspaper!

Now, the seas are filled with litter. How many shipping containers have gone overboard between Japan and the West Coast? An immense island of plastics is circulating in the Atlantic. The largest creatures on the planet, the great whales, are once again being hunted and killed by several nations, this under the flimsiest pretext of research. The vast oceans have been radically altered by over fishing in the extreme. Nets many miles long sweep up anything and everything in their path, and there are hundreds of trawlers pulling such nets. Up to half the marine life caught is discarded, most of it dead. Nearly 80 million sharks are caught each year; with most of them, just the fins are cut off for shark fin soup, and the struggling creature is tossed overboard, still living, to a slow death. Weighted dragnets have been designed to scrape across vibrant coral reefs to get at even the small fish that inhabit them and, in the process, leave wreckage behind. Boris Worm, a biologist at Dalhousie University in Halifax, Canada, has studied global catch data covering the last fifty years. He and thirteen other researchers have come to stunning conclusions that are summarized in an article titled "Oceans of Nothing." Concerning cod and tuna, once our most abundant food source from the sea, 90 percent are gone; they have been fished nearly out of existence. Scientists are now beginning to talk, even, about the *death* of the oceans, once considered so boundless and fertile, and many say such a description could apply in less than fifty years.

In the 1960s and 1970s, when we first began to learn about the increasing pollution of the environment, reactions were mixed. Many felt threatened by any findings that might mean a change in the way we related to and used the world around us. In the Nixon administration, the chief law enforcement officer of the land, the Attorney General, proclaimed, "The conservation movement is a breeding ground for Communists and other subversives. We intend to clean them out, even if it means rounding up every bird-watcher in the country!" Millions of others reacted sanely. The younger generation, especially, became concerned; however, in spite of good intentions, it was all too short-lived. A young man went to a fortune-teller, who looked deep into her crystal ball and said, "You will be poor and unhappy until you are about forty years old." "And then what will happen?" asked the man, with some eagerness. Answer: "Then, you'll get used to it."

Something like that has been happening with our attitudes toward the contamination of earth, air, and water. Lead is found in most drinking supplies, and bottled water, so popular now, is no cleaner than most tap water. The heavy metal mercury, a neurotoxin, is in waters all across the United States, and it is now deemed unsafe to eat fish from many of our rivers and lakes. Smokestacks send it into the atmosphere and it precipitates out of the sky in acid rain. Mercury is now so prevalent in the environment that the political push is on to designate it as an ubiquitous substance, i.e., to call the unnatural natural. When a crime becomes common, is the answer to legalize it? What happens to a nation's spirit when it becomes more important to maintain the upward path of the economic graph than to safeguard public health?

Perhaps the very word environment has become too nearly an abstract term, a bit too clinical and detached, disguising the fact that when we say the environment is being poisoned, we are really talking about *home*. We are talking about *us*.

Thus, many alien substances are joining the strontium-90 and iodine-131 already in our bones from nuclear testing many decades ago. Fertilizers and pesticides are used to drive crop yields to the maximum but end up in our water and, ultimately, in us. Many thousands of chemicals did not even exist a few years ago; they are substances to which the human body, over the long course of its evolution, has not had sufficient time to adapt. No one who gets cancer feels that this is natural, do they? Dioxins are in the food chain (Agent Orange, of which nearly 20 million gallons were used as a defoliant in the Vietnam War, is one). DDT is so virulent a pesticide that in very short order it put our national symbol, the bald eagle, on the road to extinction by contaminating the fish on which it feeds and causing thinning of the bird's eggshells. (In 1962, Rachel Carson's book *Silent Spring* raised warning flags concerning the situation and may be said to have initiated the modern environmental movement.) The chemical was banned in this country decades ago, as were PCBs, but the body of almost any adult tested in America today will still have the substances. The National Geographic Society recently sponsored a comprehensive analysis of the toxic and unnatural substances in the body of a typical person and, to that end, tested one individual for 320 chemicals: most of them were found.

Industry seeks to introduce something like 1,700 chemicals each year, and more than 82,000 chemicals are now in use in the U.S.; only a quarter of them have ever been tested for toxicity. "Life is better through chemistry" was the slogan of one company a few years ago, and our lives are made better by new compounds like those that produce nonstick frying pans and serve as flame retardants in furniture and those that make plastic more flexible for all sorts of products, but those substances are now inside all of us. In Minnesota and Wisconsin, frogs and other amphibians, which may be functioning like the coal-miner's canary to detect something deadly, are showing up with previously unknown mutations: missing or extra legs. "Something in the water."

Add to all this the fact of climate change, global warming, caused or increased by the human activity of putting greenhouse gases into the atmosphere. In a smoke-filled room, the added ingredient is obvious, but in some of our large cities, just breathing the outside air is the equivalent of inhaling forty cigarettes a day. The planet is not boundless; it is only some eight thousand miles in diameter and, on that scale, too, there must be limits to what we can exhale into that extremely thin canopy of air that sustains life. The glaciers in Glacier National Park are melting rapidly and "The Snows of Kilimanjaro" on the other side of the world may be gone in as little as twenty years. In 2006, data from two satellites using gravity-sensing technology determined that the Antarctic icecap is losing approximately thirty-six cubic miles of ice each year in a trend that shows no sign of slowing down.

At the 1992 Earth Summit in Rio de Janeiro, a twelve-year-old child named Severn Suzuki asked to speak. The speech, which she wrote herself, was the last one on the agenda before the hundreds of delegates would depart. Spoken from the heart, it greatly moved the audience. This is part of what she said: "I'm only a child, and I don't have all the solutions, but I want you to realize, neither do you. You don't know how to fix the holes in the ozone layer. You don't know how to bring the salmon back up a dead stream. You don't know how to bring back an animal now extinct. And you can't bring back a forest where there is now a desert. If you don't know how to fix it, please stop breaking it."

Can we stop breaking it? The source of much of the brokenness is a lifestyle of ever-expanding conspicuous consumption, from which nothing is safe, including the Arctic National Wildlife Refuge. Fully 95 percent of the North Slope of Alaska has already been opened for oil leases to fuel a self-indulgent mode of existence that has become addictive and that we cannot imagine changing: "Just a little longer, just a little more." (A visitor from another planet, as he/she/it cruised in a flying saucer over many of our nations, could easily conclude that the purpose of life is to produce and consume automobiles.) So, we sing about the

"purple mountains' majesty" and claim to love it, but all the evidence indicates that we love commodities more. In the words of Emerson's poem,

> Things are in the saddle,
> And ride mankind.

By certain measures, our standard of living has been the highest in
the world, but these products have by-products. The remarks of Robert
F. Kennedy in 1968, when he highlighted the ugly underbelly of progress
but also pointed beyond, are even more appropriate today:

> Too much and for too long, we seem to have surrendered person-
> al excellence and community values in the mere accumulation
> of material things. Our Gross National Product . . . counts air
> pollution and cigarette advertising, and ambulances to clear our
> highways of carnage. It counts special locks for our doors and the
> jails for people who break them. It counts the destruction of the
> redwood and the loss of our natural wonder in chaotic sprawl. It
> counts napalm and counts nuclear warheads and armored cars
> for the police to fight the riots in our cities. It counts Whitman's
> rifle and Speck's knife, and the television programs which glo-
> rify violence in order to sell goods to our children. Yet the gross
> national product does not allow for the health of our children,
> the quality of their education or the joy of their play. It does not
> include the beauty of our poetry or the strength of our marriages,
> the intelligence of our public debate or the integrity of our public
> officials. It measures neither our wit nor our courage, neither our
> wisdom nor our learning, neither our compassion nor our devo-
> tion to our country. It measures everything, in short, except that
> which makes life worthwhile. And it can tell us everything about
> America except why we are proud that we are Americans.

Thus, beyond basic survival, the issue is the kind of society we are
creating. The issue is not only whether it is sustainable—it is not—but
whether there is anything like enough of the real world to serve the deepest needs of the human spirit, which, after all, came into being in the
wilderness. Separated increasingly from the natural world, artificiality
is the hallmark of modern life. Bread has long been known as the basic,
the staple, the simple food. Now, it is usually a prepackaged item, and
a prayer for daily bread includes, parenthetically, the long list of ingredients of such substances as "butylated hydroxyanisole (anti-oxidant)."

It must be merely as token substitutes that we have attached wildlife totems to professional baseball teams—Marlins, Orioles, Blue Jays,

Cardinals, Diamondbacks, Cubs, Tigers, and Rays—and to pro football teams—Bears, Bengals, Rams, Cardinals, Dolphins, Falcons, Eagles, Ravens, Seahawks, Panthers, Jaguars, and Lions. The real references of most of those symbols are seldom seen, because modern consumerism has an appetite that denies almost nothing to the self and thus cannot allow space for the rest of God's creatures. We confine some of them in parks, these as small as possible and these, increasingly, for the purpose of what Edward Abbey called "industrial tourism," catering to "the indolent millions born on wheels and suckled on gasoline." Wildlife has been turned into another commercial image and consumer product.

George Schaller, who did the classic studies on lions and snow leopards and who has sought to protect all kinds of creatures the world over, recently said, "It is tremendously worrisome that we don't talk about nature anymore. We talk about natural resources as if everything had a price tag. You can't buy spiritual values at a shopping mall. The things that uplift the spirit—an old growth forest, a clear river, the flight of a golden eagle, the howl of a wolf, space and quiet without motors—are intangibles."

We also "harvest" many animals, since we have eliminated most of their natural predators and no longer have room for both them and us. A measure of that is now a necessity, but not all of it. Driving on the interstate highway in eastern North Dakota, thousands of people each day observe a building, on the side of which is a large painted sign, maintained for many years, that reads: "Hunting, Fishing & Trapping: Protect What's Right." I grew up fishing and hunting: it was pervasive as a way of life. (Our Democratic governor here in Montana, Brian Schweitzer, was asked how many guns he had. He answered, "It's none of your business, and not as many as I would like!") I have several rifles and shotguns myself, and while it is less appealing to me as time goes by, I hunted for decades. As a farm boy, I grew up trapping, too, for mink, weasel, and muskrat. Although we could always use the money it brought, I think a large part of the interest was that of learning the mysterious ways of those wild animals, something that can be done in another manner. We are no longer in the position of our Ice Age ancestors who needed fur to survive the winters; we now have substitutes for those pelts to adorn the clothes of high fashion. Now, I agree with the sentiments of John Muir, who, in describing his own boyhood, said of the muskrat, "Millions of the gentle, industrious, beaver-like creatures are shot and trapped and speared every season for their skins, worth a dime or so—like shooting boys and girls for their garments."

John Mitchell lived in Connecticut, where there no longer exists wildlife of the sort that there is farther west. In the 1970s, he interviewed an "old timer" here in Montana about the way this state, too, was changing. He brought up the subject of grizzly bears, and the old fellow was proud to say that he had "killed his fair share." Asked what a fair share might be, he said, "As many as you can get!" When told that not everyone, by any means, would agree with that, he responded, "Why, hell, you know, jus' same as me, the grizz ain't good fur nothin'. Jus' sleeps all winter and eats people all summer." Then, says Mitchell, they talked about the landscape the old fellow had frequented: the Big Belt Mountains and the Tobacco Root country near Bozeman. "Yes, it was a great land once; you could know that without seeing it, from the way the old timer spoke of it with affection. The mountains were full of bear. And wolves, too. And more game than a man could shake a stick at. But that, of course, was a while back." Mitchell asked what had happened and related that the old timer, who had killed as much of everything as he could, looked him square in the eye and said, "Dunno."

All too many millions right now, also, "dunno." Why is it rare to view the rest of nature as existing not merely for our benefit? Why is it rare to look with reverence and respect toward the rest of nature, to all those uncountable creatures of astonishing ability and form, with which we are meant to share our existence? Why is it common, instead, to view animals as having few or no rights, seeing them as existing just to be petted, spoiled, or killed for meat or shoe leather, without any reason for being of their own? Plutarch, the historian of ancient Rome, wrote, "Boys may throw sticks at frogs in sport, but the frogs do not die in sport but in earnest."

~

In contrast, Albert Schweitzer told of how as a small child, even before he began to go to school, he found it incomprehensible that, during evening prayers, people would pray only for people. He began to add a prayer he had composed for all creatures: "Protect and bless all things that have breath; guard them from all evil and let them sleep in peace." Decades later, in the African bush, while he was watching a herd of hippos, there flashed across his mind, "unforeseen and unsought, the phrase, Reverence for Life." It defined the rest of his days, as he worked until the end of his long life as a missionary doctor to the native peoples of the Congo in a jungle setting then largely unchanged since the dawn of human history on that same continent.

Charles Lindbergh had a similar experience in Africa: "Lying under an acacia tree with the sounds of the dawn around me . . . I became aware of the basic miracle of life . . . forms evolved by several million centuries of selection and environment . . . I realized that if I had to choose, I would rather have birds than airplanes." The natural world, after all, was here before the unnatural one we have contrived.

In the Hebrew Scriptures, the Book of Job is not only about the problem of suffering, for which it is often cited; it is also about the marvelous operation of the world beyond human control or understanding. In chapter 38, God speaks out of the whirlwind about the cycles of the heavens, the constellations, the weather, and all cosmic forces, asking Job, "Where were you when I laid the foundation of the earth? Tell me, if you have understanding . . . Can you bind the chains of the Pleiades or loose the cords of Orion?" The end of that chapter and all of the next goes on to celebrate the instincts of wild creatures: "Can you hunt the prey for the lion or satisfy the appetite of the young lions when they crouch in their dens or lie in wait in their covert. Who provides for the raven its prey, when its young ones cry to God?" It describes the calving of the mountain goat, the strength of the wild ass, and the speed of the ostrich: "When she rouses herself to flee, she laughs at the horse and his rider." God inquires of Job, "Is it by your wisdom that the hawk soars . . . Is it at your command that the eagle mounts up and makes his nest on high?" In chapter 41, all thirty-four verses comprise one long ode to the crocodile: "Can you draw out Leviathan with a fishhook? . . . Who can penetrate his double coat of mail? Who can open the doors of his face? Round about his teeth is terror. His back is made of rows of shields, shut up closely as with a seal . . . Clubs are counted as stubble; he laughs at the rattle of javelins . . . He makes the deep boil like a pot . . . Behind him he leaves a shining wake." The effect of it all upon Job, who had claimed to know something, is "Behold, I am of small account; what shall I answer? I lay my hand on my mouth . . . I have uttered what I did not understand, things too wonderful for me."

What scientists call the *biosphere* and what theologians call the *creation* is the same thing. The view of the ecological sciences of one world, with all creatures sustained by a single breath and using it in harmony, has much in common with the biblical vision that includes wholeness as both a present reality and a future hope. Thus, Psalm 148 sings about the sun, moon, and shining stars. It speaks of "sea monsters and all deeps, fire and hail, snow and frost and stormy wind." It points to "mountains and hills, fruit trees and all cedars, beasts and all cattle, creeping things and flying birds," as well as people, "princes and rulers, young men and maidens together, old men and children." Of and to all of them, the writer says, "Let them praise the name of the Lord." And they do—just by being. Can it all continue? Will *we* let them?

Jacob Bronowski's book, *The Ascent of Man*, describes the rise of civilization and the development of science. Near the end is a statement that is both succinct and profoundly true: "We are nature's unique experiment to make the rational intelligence prove itself sounder than the reflex." I am certain that, in the spirit of Job, he agreed that the need is not only for more brains, since intelligence can serve all kinds of masters, both good and evil, but, also, for right dealing and kindness of heart. John Randolph, American politician of the early nineteenth century, assessed another's facile mind but very flawed character with this image: "So brilliant, yet so corrupt, which, like a rotten mackerel by moonlight, both shines and stinks!"

In the midst of the present ecological crisis, all too often is heard the naïve confidence that human ingenuity is the key—"Science to the rescue! Technology will find a way"—this in spite of the fact that a case could be made that it is precisely those things that have produced the current crisis. (Orville and Wilbur Wright thought their invention of the airplane would make war obsolete, because, thereafter, no army could move without being observed from above. We know how quickly the plane was turned, instead, into the most devastating of weapons.) Pinning our hopes on mere technological competence is to live out the legend of Sinbad the sailor, who anchored his boat on what he thought was an island but found it to be, instead, a great beast of the sea that went charging off with him, boat and all, across the tossing ocean. Trusted stabilities fail and drag us with them in turmoil. We need intelligence and competence in the realm of science, now more than ever, but the need is, also, for much more than those.

Charles Darwin cast not only an analytical but also an empathetic eye toward animals—evidenced in many ways but also by his reference to them as "our fellow brethren in pain, disease, suffering, and famine, our slaves in the most laborious works, our companions in amusements." He had the insight that the ties to the living community of things are intricate, indeed, and in *On the Origin of Species* explored the subject in a section titled "Complex Relations of All Animals and Plants to Each Other in the Struggle for Existence." One example was his discovery that bumblebees, because of their long tongues, are the only insects that can effectively pollinate the deep red clover flowers, showing that the success of the plant in England was due to the prevalence of bumblebees there, something not known before that time. In addition, he said, "The number of bumble-bees in any district depends in great measure upon the number of field mice, which destroy their combs and nests . . . Now the number of mice is largely dependent, as everyone knows, on the number of cats." He then cited the fact, provided by another, that there are more bumblebee nests in the vicinity of towns and villages than in the open country, because towns contain a large number of cats, and the cats prey upon the field mice, keeping their numbers down. The result is more clover. He writes, "Hence, it is quite credible that the presence of a feline animal in large numbers in a district might determine, through the intervention first of mice and then of bees, the frequency of certain flowers in a district!"

A German scientist extended the argument. Red clover, he said, was the main food of British cattle, which, in turn, provided "bully beef" to feed the British navy. England was the ruling sea power of that day and credit for its being a world power was thus due to its cats, which kept the mice down, which allowed the bees to live to pollinate the clover to feed the beef to feed the navy.

The great Thomas Huxley, with more tongue in cheek, suggested, because so-called spinsters were the ones most likely to keep cats, that Britannia's ruling the waves might logically—and ecologically—be traced right back to the cat-loving tendencies of the elderly female population.

One could go further, but this particular tale has to end somewhere. In nature itself, however, it never does. This story of cat and clover, while interesting and humorous, points, in all seriousness, to the insight that hardly any fact exists by itself and that there is a web of connectedness that is the substance of what we today call ecology and that cause and effect truly do tie together every element of the natural world.

In his 1967 book, *Beyond the Observatory*, the astronomer Harlow Shapley illustrated the intertwined nature of things by pointing to argon, an inert gas that makes up about 1 percent of the atmosphere. To say that it is inert means that it does not combine with other elements to make new molecules. An atom of argon stays as it is and as it was. Shapley calculated that each breath we take contains, along with mostly oxygen and nitrogen, about 30,000,000,000,000,000,000 or 3×10 to the 19th power of such argon atoms. Exhaled in our next breath, those atoms will be diffused all over the neighborhood in a few hours and scattered by the winds all over the country in a week. By the end of a year, they are evenly distributed over the entire planet to be breathed and re-breathed by all living things. So it has always been. Thus, says Shapley, "Your next breath will contain more than 400,000 of the argon atoms that Gandhi breathed in his long life. Argon atoms are here from the conversations at the Last Supper, from the arguments of the diplomats at Yalta, and from recitations of the classic poets. We have argon from the sighs and pledges of ancient lovers, from the battle cries of Waterloo . . . Our next breaths, yours and mine, will sample the snorts, sighs, bellows, shrieks, cheers, and spoken prayers of the prehistoric and historic past." No doubt, we also share the last breath of the last dinosaur of 65 million years ago.

Nature, the world, life, everything: it is all intermeshed in countless ways, most of which are beyond our comprehension. It is likely that every square mile of the earth's surface contains a bit from every other square mile because of the mixing action of wind and water. At every level, the planet teems with life; in a small handful of soil exist ten billion bacteria that make the soil both a living and a life-giving thing. It all means that what the native people of our land knew from the beginning is true: that what we do to the world, we do to ourselves. In the words of Black Elk, medicine man of the Sioux, "Is not the sky a father and the earth a mother, and are not all living things with feet or wings or roots their children?" It's one wide family. Thus, we cannot care, even out of mere self-interest, just for ourselves: we must care for the whole. It is in and by the whole that we live and move and have our being.

George Catlin was the Philadelphia attorney and self-taught artist who, after seeing a delegation of Indians "from the wilds of the Far West," resolved that "nothing short of the loss of my life will prevent me from visiting their country and becoming their historian." In 1832, he began making his remarkable pictorial record of the life of the Mandan and other plains Indians living along the course of the upper Missouri River. His experiences led to his great desire to protect the tribes' way of life and the prairie wildlife and resulted in his giving voice to the first plea to establish a national park. It is found in his 1841 *Letters and Notes,* where he also records a flight of imagination inspired by a small pocket map of North America. After gazing upon it for a time, as he tells it, he was soon viewing the world as from above: "I was lifted up upon an imaginary pair of wings . . . from whence I could behold beneath me the Pacific and the Atlantic Oceans—the great cities of the East and the mighty rivers. I could see the blue chain of the great lakes at the North, the Rocky Mountains, and beneath them and near their base, the vast and almost boundless plains of grass, which were speckled with the bands of grazing buffaloes!" Catlin's vision of one wide world—"continent after continent passed under my eye"—was rare in his time and was little heeded. It awaited a still more astonishing perspective.

In 1948, the British astrophysicist Fred Hoyle alluded to that view in saying, "Once a photograph of the earth, taken from outside, is available—once the sheer isolation of the earth becomes plain—a new idea as powerful as any in history will be let loose." Powerful, indeed, is that picture we have now all seen of our tiny and marble-like green, white, and blue sphere afloat on the immense black ocean of space. Clear is the message, again, that the earth is a single thing. All that we know as detail and phenomena, disjointed items and isolated events, are really parts of one organic and all-too-fragile whole.

Now, we know it, but, again, is knowledge enough? Will it change how we behave and how we order our priorities? Archibald MacLeish wrote the lead editorial of the *New York Times* for Monday, July 21st of 1969 (The date is significant for being the day after the first moon landing). It reads, "For all his resplendent glory as he steps forth on another planet, man is still a pathetic creature, able to master outer space and yet unable to control his inner self; able to conquer new worlds yet unable to live in peace on this one; able to create miracles of science and yet unable to properly house and clothe and feed all his fellow men; able eventually to colonize an alien and hostile environment and yet increasingly unable to come to terms with the nurturing environment that is his home."

Such contradictions haunt the space program still. Coming to terms with our planetary environment and developing an all-embracing care and stewardship of the earth will mean living a simpler life. America is only 4 percent of the world's population. If the rest of the world were to adopt our standard of virtually unrestrained consumerism, four additional planet earths would be needed to fuel it. A reassessment of our values to determine what sorts of things matter most will mean that we must get along without many things that now are regarded as essential.

Scaling back our expectations and living more simply so that others may simply live: this will not be easy, since the root problem lies in human nature, and that has been the same over long millennia. Tradition has it a group of Greek philosophers were debating how to most concisely describe the human species, distinguishing it from all others. They arrived at the definition that man was "the featherless biped." Yes, that is true. Diogenes, upon hearing of it, got a plucked chicken and threw it over a wall into their midst. There was a featherless biped, but it was clearly not a human being, illustrating, of course, that the descriptive characters we choose must be more nearly at the core of the subject. Those of Dostoyevsky surely were. In *Notes from Underground*, he defined man as "the *ungrateful* biped"—a disturbing assessment not easily dismissed.

The selfish disposition has been deeply ingrained throughout human history. Leonardo da Vinci looked around at the society of his time and recorded his evaluation in his notebook: "How many people . . . practice no virtue whatsoever; all that remains after them is a full latrine." That me-first syndrome is all-too-well entrenched in our own time, common enough that almost every movie and best-selling novel is about it. The difference from the past is that, now, we control tools and technologies that have greatly magnified the impact of that self-centeredness. An unaltered mind-set, the "black hole" that would deny nothing to the self, means that millions desire and strive for luxuries, which, in former ages, were the province of royalty. Such pursuit, of course, will not buy happiness, and the collective price of it all is an environment that is becoming less and less hospitable to life.

It is not extreme to affirm that if we continue to wage war against our landlord, our lease will soon expire, for, as Sir Francis Bacon, one of the founders of the scientific method as we know it, cautioned in 1620, "Nature is only subdued by submission," i.e., nature, to be commanded, must be obeyed. Standing amid the mountains of waste and garbage generated by our society, one cannot but think that all kinds of creatures would take no notice of our passing, for they led much more contented lives before we appeared on the scene. It is a telling fact that, were we to disappear, it is very likely that the cockroach would miss us most. How long before the earth will shrug and cast off a species that has over-reached? That situation is not inevitable, but avoiding it will undoubtedly mean living more nearly in harmony with the way the planet works, living mindful of the fact that the earth's resources are not without limit. It will mean a simpler kind of existence.

That, however, may be a gift in disguise, for the great teachers of the ages have always told us that abundant life is not based on material things and that one does not live by bread alone. There is an old fable of the king who, for all his wealth and power, was ill at ease and unhappy in the extreme. A prophet told him that he could find the peace he craved if he could just wear the shirt of a contented man. His aides searched the kingdom high and low, and they finally found a contented man—but he had no shirt. There is, also, the Aboriginal saying, now a bumper sticker, that reads, "The more you know, the less you need." The sorts of things that really count are not things at all.

Nearly a century ago, Edgar Lee Masters published *Spoon River Anthology*, which is a fanciful piece of literature set in the 1800s in a cemetery in the little town of Spoon River in west-central Illinois. One by one, in a paragraph each, the 214 characters rise up and speak. Each one gives a summation of his or her life, and there are many who, for all their accomplishments and accumulations, are dissatisfied and bitter. One of the characters, however, is Fiddler Jones, who is of a different spirit. His farm and assets—and life, in the eyes of others—never amounted to much, but he says:

> The earth keeps some vibration going
> There in your heart, and that is you.
> And if people find you can fiddle,
> Why fiddle you must, for all your life.
> . . . How could I till my forty acres,
> Not to speak of getting more,
> With a medley of horns, bassoons and piccolos
> Stirred in my brain by crows and robins
> And the creak of a wind-mill—only these?
> And I never started to plow in all my life
> That someone did not stop in the road
> And take me away to a dance or a picnic.
> I ended up with forty acres;

I ended up with a broken fiddle—
And a broken laugh, and a thousand memories
—and not a single regret.

∼

A full life has many ingredients, most of which are, indeed, intangibles. One aspect, and a large one, is a sense of kinship with the crows and the robins and all the other manifestations of life in the wider world. How is that acquired? On the influence of the home in which a person is raised, President Truman's Secretary of State, Dean Acheson, dipped into his gag file and said, "All that I know I learned at my mother's knee and other low joints." In a former age, people were confronted with nature in a more intimate manner. The processes of raising gardens and live-stock reinforced their dependence on the earth, and there was usually a nearby woods or vacant lot in which kids played. Now, most children are wired to and entranced by some form of electronic media for an average of forty-five hours a week, which is more time than they spend in school, a fact that may be one of the greatest long-term threats to conservation. The question is whether it is possible for the coming generation, intensely involved with the artificial, to develop an ethic toward the natural world, when they have such minimal exposure to it. Will Rogers said, "Everybody is ignorant, just on different subjects." Some subjects, however, are more crucial than others are, and it is increasingly clear that the world can no longer afford very many people who have little understanding and appreciation of our roots in the natural order.

For, we evolved from the wild, from the world of rocks and plants and water and the myriad of creatures who shared our space. Its sound was our music. Our deepest values of dignity, beauty, and harmony we first gained from vast world around us. Nature is in our nature; we are part—and only a part—of the vast pulse of life on earth.

And is it not altogether magnificent? André Gide, in his autobiography, tells that as a young boy he reared a caterpillar and was keeping its cocoon in a box on his desk, "like a mummy in a sarcophagus." One day, while his tutor was correcting his arithmetic, Gide glanced at the box: "What did I see! Wings! Great green and pink wings beginning to stir and quiver." He turned to his tutor and said, "If only I had known that while you were explaining those deadly sums, one of the mysteries of life, so great a one, so long expected, was going on at my elbow! A metamorphosis! A resurrection like Lazarus!" The tutor responded to this with a tone of disappointment and disapproval: "Don't you know that the chrysalis is simply the envelope of the butterfly and that every butterfly you have ever seen has come out of it? Why, it's perfectly natural." Gide then concluded, "Yes, indeed, I knew my natural history as well, perhaps better, than he. But because it was natural, could he not see that it is also marvelous?"

So many things are like that, in fact, perhaps everything: absolute wonders to which we have become jaded, if not oblivious. The highly acclaimed geneticist and educator from Canada, David Suzuki, writes, "Every child who has marveled at the growth of a plant from a seed, observed the transformation of a frog's egg into a tadpole, or witnessed the emergence of a butterfly from its cocoon understands in the most profound way that life is a miracle. Science cannot penetrate life's deepest mystery; music and poetry attempt to express it; every mother and father feels it to the core."

It is that sort of emotion, finally, that will put us *in* motion to do everything we can to save as many branches on the tree of life as possible. Intelligence will not suffice. Mere self-interest is incapable. Neither will assessment and calculation, risk-management, and cost-analysis do it, although we need those. The hinge on which it will turn is an apprehension of the miraculous character of existence. Genuine care of the earth will be motivated, mostly, by astonishment at the sheer giftedness of life, by the *wonder* of it all.

And that is, essentially, a religious sentiment. The poet Gerard Manley Hopkins wrote of the unending variety of nature:

> Glory be to God for dappled things—
> For skies of couple-color as a brindled cow;
> For rose-moles all in stipple upon trout that swim;
> Fresh-firecoal chestnut falls; finches wings . . .

He wrote of God's presence in nature showing through to the eyes of faith: "The world," he said, "is charged with the grandeur of God," and, in spite of the negative imprint of humanity, it is remarkably resilient:

> Generations have trod, have trod, have trod;
> And all is seared with trade; bleared, smeared
> with toil;

And wears man's smudge and shares man's smell;
the soil
Is bare now, nor can foot feel, being shod.

And for all this, nature is never spent;
There lives the dearest freshness deep down things;
And though the last lights off the black West went
Oh, morning, at the brown brink eastward springs—
Because the Holy Ghost over the bent
World broods with warm breast and with ah! bright
wings!

Such a sense that nature is inscrutably wonderful imparts its sacred character to us and engenders in us the idea that the care of the earth is, therefore, a moral and sacred trust. It is something that has a power to move and motivate us like nothing else. It is also something that is often overlooked.

I have often been disillusioned by the failure of many religious groups to focus on the central message of certain biblical stories that have the capacity to communicate that truth in profound ways. For example, in the ancient story of Noah's ark, many meanings are sought, except the one that may be the most central. In teaching this story to children, which must be carefully done, we often unwittingly turn it into a story about "what happened," when it is really a story about what *happens.* (As such, it is another grand parable that speaks most deeply to adults.) In addition, in the process of avoiding literalism's folly of mounting those ludicrous expeditions to Mt Ararat to find remnants of a large wooden craft, the story is all-too-often turned into another parable of personal salvation only.

It is much more. There is more than one point (e.g., that there is such a thing as sin and that it has consequences are two such points, something to which the newspapers, also, bear witness every day), but the central affirmation, again in story form and picture-language, is that *God cares for absolutely everything.* It is that God delights in diversity and, therefore, wants to save *every* creature, not just the captain of the ship. Nothing is without value and all the rest on board are not there just for the provision of the crew but have their own reason for being. Thus, the story is, really, the first Endangered Species Act. Two by two, large and little, from the obvious to the obscure, from baboons to beetles, all kinds of animals from the entire earth are called into the lifeboat. God would have no sort of creature perish, for "God so loved *the world*" (in the Greek, the word is *kosmos*). As the children's song has it, and there so appropriately, "All God's critters got a place in the choir."

Thus, before we can be about saving the world, we have to believe the world is worth saving. This truly is a matter of outlook or vision, another instance where the well-worn cliché must be inverted to state, "We'll *see* it when we *believe* it." Thus, before we can save the tiger, there needs to be a mystique about the tiger, and this is something that comes not from anything that we ourselves can impart to it; it comes from the realization that everything is gift. It's the sense that, while nothing *need* be, everything, nevertheless, *is*, and, as such, is not only fragile but *holy*.

Teilhard de Chardin, priest and paleontologist both, while in the Gobi Desert and without the elements with which to say Mass, made the whole world his altar: "Over every living thing which is to spring up, to grow, to flower, to ripen during this day, say again the words, This is my Body. And over every death-force which waits in readiness to corrode, to wither, to cut down, speak again your commanding words which express the supreme mystery of faith: This is my Blood."

Lately, there has been a growing consensus about this sort of thing, which is crucial to the world's rehabilitation and renewal, and it is reflected in a statement contained in The Union of Concerned Scientists' document, *Preserving and Cherishing the Earth: An Appeal for Joint Commitment in Science and Religion*. It reads, in part, "As scientists, many of us have had experiences of awe and reverence before the universe. We understand that what is regarded as sacred is more likely to be treated with care and respect. Our planetary home should be so regarded. Efforts to safeguard and cherish the environment need to be infused with a vision of the sacred."

In addition, all of this is about a cause big enough so that absolutely everyone, however much they may disagree on some things, can put aside those differences to work for the well-being of all life on earth. In Melville's *Moby Dick*, after another kind of lifesaving operation, Queequeg reflects, "It's a mutual joint-stock world, in all meridians. We cannibals must help these Christians." Surely, there can be no larger cause than saving life on earth. With stakes as high as this, poets and technicians, business people, scientists, musicians, farmers and philosophers, atheists and agnostics, theists, deists, and pantheists can surely all come together so that our existence—and that of all the life-systems on the planet—will not be diminished but enhanced.

In addition, as the most advanced beings on the planet, and as those wielding the most power, for us to act not as its plunderers but as guardians is simply the *right* thing to do. Early in Melville's great work, there is a description of the lantern that hung in Captain Ahab's cabin aboard the *Pequod*. Whichever way the ship heaved and tossed in the rolling sea, the lantern hung down exactly in a line to the center of the earth. Our conscience is meant to be such a line, and does it not speak to us of a deeper ethic than that which applies to human societies alone? Does it not speak to the fundamental worth of all the varied forms of life? Near the end of the epic is this affirmation: "And some certain significance lurks in all things, else all things are little worth, and the round world itself but an empty cipher, except to sell by the cartload, as they do the hills about Boston, to fill up some morass in the Milky Way." If anything matters, doesn't it all matter?

Such realizations are steadily growing in the communities of both science and religion. A few years ago, that same Union of Concerned Scientists that issued the Appeal for Joint Commitment also produced a film about both scientific and religious perspectives on the environment entitled, *Keeping the Earth*. It opened with spectacular photography of diverse wild creatures from all over the world, this underlain with those words from Genesis chapter 1:

> In the beginning, God created the heavens and the earth . . . And God said, "Let the waters bring forth swarms of living creatures, and let birds fly across the firmament of the heavens." So God created great sea monsters and every living creature that moves, with which the waters swarm, according to their kinds, and every winged bird according to its kind. And God saw that it was good. And God blessed them, saying, "Be fruitful and multiply and fill the waters in the seas, and let the birds multiply on the earth" . . . And God said, "Let the earth bring forth living creatures according to their kinds: cattle and creeping things and beasts of the earth according to their kinds." And it was so . . . And God saw everything that he had made, and behold, it was very good.

In the film, E. O. Wilson was interviewed and said, "I like to say that it really doesn't matter how you view the origin of the creation, you come to the same conclusion: diversity of life is a gift. It is something that is bequeathed to us and it's something that we bequeath back down to our descendants . . . If our descendants come to realize that in a couple of generations we have destroyed a large part of creation . . . they are going to consider us a ship of fools, in terms of what matters most to them." Theologians from several traditions were interviewed, all affirming the sacred character of creation as that which motivates us to care and all affirming how greatly we *need* to care.

Graphically illustrating the aspect of sacredness and/or giftedness, the film included a procession of varied animals into the great stone cathedral of Saint John the Divine in New York City. Every year since 1984, the congregation has held a Feast of Saint Francis and Blessing of the Animals in order to affirm human relatedness to all creation and to accent our responsibility toward it. So the huge two-ton bronze doors swung open, and down the center aisle, almost as long as two football fields, came an elephant, a camel, a llama, and a chimpanzee. Carried in procession were an owl and a tarantula, an opossum, a parrot, a python, and numerous other creatures, symbolic of "all things wise and wonderful, all things great and small." There they were, in the *nave* of the cathedral (that very word for the central space comes from the same root as our word "navy" and means ship or boat—or *ark*). There they were, moving to music and reminding everyone that nature, too, has a song. It is not excessive to say that perhaps most of the four thousand worshippers, there in a huge and human-centered metropolis, experienced something profound: a deepening or a broadening of the idea of reconciliation to include the entire natural world. Paul Gorman, director of the National Religious Partnership for the Environment, says that it was a symbolic "challenge for churches and synagogues to open their doors more nearly to Life itself . . . What's out *there* belongs in *here*, inside our congregations—inside our *hearts*."

We are the dominant species, poised—whether we like it or not—in the pivotal role of determining so much of what happens to all the rest. Thus, it is our hearts that will decide whether our planetary home will be bleak or grand: not our intellects, not our technology, not our megatons of raw power, but our moral sense and our spirit of gratitude, compassion, and care. Can we truly extend these, beyond just humanity, to embrace all those wondrous creatures of the natural world? And what kind of people are we, if we don't?

～

We can sometimes be skeptical of the outcome, because of the recent pressures and threats to the natural world and humanity's insufficient response. We human beings engage in all kinds of self-destructive behavior, thinking the consequences, however well documented, will not happen to us. Warnings about the destruction or degradation of the entire planet meet a similar sense of denial. Nevertheless, we must hope, but doing so with the realization that this sentiment is of two kinds. If one simply hopes for nice weather for a picnic, then hope has no influence whatsoever on what happens. On the other hand, concerning many of the most important things, hope is a transformative force, for only if we hope are we moved to act in order to bring the hope to fruition. Thus, we must hope, and, out of that hope, we must act.

And there's no time to lose. Right now, on my desk are two seeds. One is a grain of wheat from last year's harvest in the Great Plains. Were it to be put in the ground, it would germinate, sprout, and grow to produce more. Were all of its descendants to be planted, then, over the course of many seasons, it would be enough to feed the world. The other is a fossil seed of some 60 million years ago. If it were to be placed in the earth, nothing would happen. Its time has passed. But not ours. As we consider our role as caretakers of the garden, the time is late, but there is still time.

Much of what needs to be done involves major readjustments to how entire nations and societies behave, but cities and towns and neighborhoods all have a large role, and there are numerous actions and small gestures that are within the province and the capability of every single one of us.

In his essay "The Star Thrower," Loren Eiseley describes a coastline following a huge storm. Moving among the debris at the water's edge is a solitary individual, picking up starfish and casting them back into the surf. Eiseley is impelled to join in the effort to save the struggling creatures by returning them to the sea. As he works, his mind travels far beyond: "I picked and flung another star. Perhaps far outward on the rim of space a genuine star was similarly seized and flung. I could feel the movement in my body. It was like sowing—the sowing of life on an infinitely gigantic scale . . . I flung and flung again, while all about us roared the insatiable waters of death . . . For a moment, we cast on an infinite beach together beside an unknown hurler of suns." I can imagine that a passerby might have told Eiseley that such actions were futile, if not ridiculous, for—considering the thousands of miles of shoreline and millions of starfish—they could not possibly make a difference. I can imagine, too, that the thrower would have replied, as he hurled another over the breakers, "It makes a difference to *this* one."

In the care of the earth, it all adds up. What we do matters. And, as usual, everything hinges on vision. So may it be that sight is blended with insight.

Let us *see*.

***

Bibliography

Sources are listed according to the chapters in which they were referenced. As is customary in this method, if an identical source occurs in more than one chapter, the listing is confined to the earliest usage.

PART I. OUR CONTEXT IN NATURE

1. Into the Badlands

Conrad, Joseph. *Heart of Darkness and The Secret Sharer*. New York: New American Library of World Literature, 1957.

Eiseley, Loren. *The Unexpected Universe*. New York: Harcourt, Brace & World, 1969.

Lewis, Meriwether, and William Clark. *The Journals of the Lewis and Clark Expedition, Vol. 8, June 10-September 26, 1806*. Lincoln: University of Nebraska Press, 1993.

Parsons, Keith M. *Drawing Out Leviathan: Dinosaurs and the Science Wars*. Indianapolis: Indiana University Press, 2001.

2. Fossils: Stories in Stone

Browne, Janet. *Charles Darwin: The Power of Place*. Princeton, NJ: Princeton University Press, 2002.

———. *Charles Darwin: Voyaging*. Princeton, NJ: Princeton University Press, 1995.

Jepsen, Glen L. "Riddles of the Terrible Lizards." *American Scientist* 52 (1964): 227–46.

Marcus Aurelius. "Meditations." In *Marcus Aurelius and His Times: The Transition From Paganism to Christianity*. Roslyn, NY: Walter J. Black, 1945.

Muir, John. *My First Summer in the Sierra*. Boston: Houghton Mifflin, 1911.

Ovid. *Ovid: The Metamorphoses Book XV*. Translated by A. S. Kline, 2000. Online: http://www.poetryintranslation.com/PITBR/Latin/metamorph15.htm.

Schultz, Frances E. "Future Tech: Shutterbug Contributors Get Out The Crystal Ball." *Shutterbug*, December 2007: 136.

Simpson, George Gaylord. *Life of the Past: An Introduction to Paleontology*. New Haven, CT: Yale University Press, 1968.

Viens, Rob. "Geology of the Pacific Northwest." Online: http://scidiv.bellevuecollege.edu/rv/208/.

Bibliography

3. Deep Time

Augustine. "The Confessions." In *Basic Writings of Saint Augustine*. Vol 1. Edited by William J. Oates. New York: Random House, 1948.

Boorstin, Daniel J. *The Discoverers: A History of Man's Search to Know His World and Himself.* New York: Random House, 1983.

Durant, Will. *The Life of Greece*. New York: Simon and Schuster, 1939.

Dyson, Freeman. *Infinite in All Directions*. New York: Harper & Row, 1989.

Isaacson, Walter. *Einstein*. New York: Simon and Schuster, 2007.

Jastrow, Robert. *God and the Astronomers*. New York: Norton, 1978.

Kurtén, Björn. *The Innocent Assassins: Biological Essays on Life in the Present and Distant Past*. New York: Columbia University Press, 1991.

Matthiessen, Peter. *The Tree Where Man Was Born*. New York: Penguin, 1995.

Moore, Ruth. *The Earth We Live On: The Story of Geological Discovery*. New York: Knopf, 1956.

Russell, Bertrand. *Power: A New Social Analysis*. New York: Norton, 1969.

Thoreau, Henry David. "Walden." In *Walden and Other Writings of Henry David Thoreau*. Edited by Brooks Atkinson. New York: Random House, 1950.

Wells, H. G. "The Grisly Folk." In *H. G. Wells: Short Stories*. New York: Penguin, 1979.

Whitman, Walt. *Leaves of Grass*. Norwalk, CT: Easton, 1977.

4. If These Bones Could Speak

Asara, John M., Mary H. Schweitzer, Lisa M. Freimark, Matthew Phillips, and Lewis C. Cantley. "Protein Sequences from Mastodon and Tyrannosaurus rex Revealed by Mass Spectrometry." *Science*, April 13, 2007: 280–85.

Bakker, Robert T. *The Dinosaur Heresies*. New York: William Morrow, 1986.

———. "Dinosaur Renaissance." *Scientific American*, April 1975: 78.

Cicero. *De Natura Decorum*. Translated by H. Rockham. London: William Heinemenn, 1951.

Colbert, Edwin H. *Dinosaurs: Their Discovery and Their World*. New York: Dutton, 1961.

Erickson, Gregory M. "Breathing Life into Tyrannosaurus rex." *Scientific American*, September 1999: 42–49.

Erickson, Gregory M. and Kenneth H. Olson. "Bite Marks Attributable to Tyrannosaurus rex: Preliminary Description and Implications." *Journal of Vertebrate Paleontology* 16:1 (March 1996): 175-78.

Erickson, Gregory M., Samuel D. Van Kirk, Jinntung Su, Marc E. Levenston, William E. Caler, and Dennis R. Carter. "Bite-force estimation for Tyrannosaurus rex from tooth-marked bone." *Nature* 382 (August 22, 1996): 706-08.

Horner, Jack. *Dinosaurs under the Big Sky*. Missoula, MT: Mountain Press, 2001.

Horner, Jack, and Edwin Dobb. *Dinosaur Lives: Unearthing the Evolutonary Saga*. New York: Harper Collins, 1997.

Horner, John R., and James Gorman. *Digging Dinosaurs: The Search that Unraveled the Mystery of Baby Dinosaurs*. New York: Harper Perennial, 1995.

Horner, John R., and Don Lessem. *The Complete T. rex*. New York: Simon and Schuster, 1993.

Horner, John R., and David B. Weishampel. "Dinosaur Eggs: The Inside Story." *Natural History*, December 1989: 61–67.

Larson, Gary. *The Prehistory of the Far Side: A 10th Anniversary Exhibit.* New York: Andrews and McMeel, 1990.

Norell, Mark A., Eugene S. Gaffney, and Lowell Dingus. *Discovering Dinosaurs in the American Museum of Natural History.* New York: Knopf, 1995.

Ostrom, John H. *Osteology of Deinonychus antirrhopus, an Unusual Theropod from the Lower Creaceous of Montana.* Bulletin 30, Yale University, Peabody Museum of Natural History, 1969.

Sanders, Scott Russell. "Tokens of Mystery." In *Finding Home: Writing On Nature and Culture From Orion Magazine,* edited by Peter Sauer. Boston: Beacon, 1992.

Scannella, John B. and John R. Horner. "Torosaurus Marsh, 1891, Is Triceratops Marsh, 1889 (Ceratopsidae: Chasmosaurinae): Syonomy Through Ontogeny." *Journal of Vertebrate Paleontology* 30, no. 4 (July 2010): 1157–68.

Schweitzer, Mary H., Jennifer L. Wittmayer, and John R. Horner. "Gender-Specific Reproductive Tissue in Ratites and Tyrannosaurus rex." *Science,* June 3, 2005): 1456–60.

Schweitzer, Mary H., Jennifer L. Wittmeyer, John R. Horner, and Jan K. Toporski. "Soft-Tissue Vessels and Cellular Preservation in Tyrannosaurus rex." *Science,* March 25, 2005: 1952–55.

Sternberg, Charles H. *The Life of a Fossil Hunter.* Indianapolis: Indiana University Press, 1990.

Ward, Peter D. *The Call of Distant Mammoths: Why the Ice Age Mammals Disappeared.* New York: Copernicus, 1997.

5. To Be a Naturalist: On Seeing

Auden, W. H. "New Year Letter." In *Collected Poems.* New York: Vintage, 1991.

Austin, Richard Cartwright. *Baptized into Wilderness: A Christian Perspective on John Muir.* Atlanta: John Knox, 1987.

Bartlett, John, ed. *Familiar Quotations.* 13th edition. Boston: Little, Brown, 1955.

Bateman, Robert. *Bird Watcher's Digest.* Sept./Oct. 1993: 40.

Bierce, Ambrose. *The Devil's Dictionary.* New York: Oxford University Press, 1999.

Bradbury, Ray. *Fahrenheit 451.* New York: Random House, 1991.

Browning, Elizabeth Barrett. "Aurora Leigh." In *The Poetical Works of Elizabeth Barrett Browning,* edited by Harriet Waters Preston. Boston: Houghton Mifflin, 1974.

Cummings, E. E. *100 Selected Poems.* New York: Grove Press, 1954.

Dillard, Annie. *Pilgrim at Tinker Creek.* New York: Bantam, 1979.

Eiseley, Loren. *Darwin and the Mysterious Mr. X.* New York: Harcourt Brace Jovanovich, 1979.

Eliot, George. *Middlemarch.* New York: Barnes & Noble, 2003.

Emerson, Ralph Waldo. "Art." In *The Selected Writings of Ralph Waldo Emerson,* edited by Brooks Atkinson. New York: Random House, 1968.

Krutch, Joseph Wood. "On Being an Amateur Naturalist." In *The Best Nature Writing of Joseph Wood Krutch.* New York: William Morrow, 1969.

Leveson, David. *A Sense of the Earth.* New York: The Natural History Press, 1971.

Lewis, Sinclair. *Babbitt.* New York: New American Library, 1964.

Lopez, Barry. "The American Geographies." In *Finding Home: Writing on Nature and Culture from Orion Magazine,* edited by Peter Sauer. Boston: Beacon, 1992.

Melville, Herman. *Moby Dick.* Norwalk, CT: Easton, 1977.

Bibliography

Mueller, Lisel. "Monet Refuses the Operation." In *Second Language*. Baton Rouge: Louisiana State University Press, 1986.

Muir, John. "The Range of Light." In *The Wilderness Reader*, edited by Frank Bergon. New York: New American Library, 1980.

Shakespeare, William. *King Henry IV, Part One*. In *William Shakespeare: The Histories*. New York: Heritage, 1958.

Wells, H.G. *The World of William Clissold: A Novel at a New Angle*. New York: George H. Doran, 1926.

6. Things Change

Baylor, Byrd, and Peter Parnall. *If You Are a Hunter of Fossils*. New York: Macmillian, 1980.

Holmes, Oliver Wendell. "The Chambered Nautilus." In *The Harvard Classics: Tennyson to Whitman*, edited by Charles W. Eliot. Danbury, CT: Grollier, 1910.

Kurtén, Björn, and Elaine Anderson. *Pleistocene Mammals of North America*. New York: Columbia University Press, 1980.

Tennyson, Alfred Lord. *In Memorium*. Vol. 1 in *The Complete Works of Alfred Lord Tennyson*, edited by Charles Howard Johnson. New York: Frederick A. Stokes, 1891.

7. The Big Picture

Abell, George. *Exploration of the Universe*. 2nd edition. New York: Holt, Rinehart and Winston, 1969.

Baker, Robert. "The Aliens Among Us: Hypnotic Regression Revisited." In *The Outer Edge: Classic Investigations of the Paranormal*, edited by Joe Nickell and Barry Karr. Amherst, NY: Committee for the Scientific Investigation of Claims of the Paranormal, 1996.

Belkora, Leila. *Minding the Heavens: The Story of Our Discovery of the Milky Way*. London: Institute of Physics, 2003.

Berendzen, Richard, ed. *Life Beyond Earth & the Mind of Man*. Washington, DC: National Aeronautics and Space Administration, 1973.

Proctor, Richard A. *Myths and Marvels of Astronomy*. New York: Putnam, 1877.

Sagan, Carl. *The Cosmic Connection: An Extraterrestrial Perspective*. New York: Dell, 1973.

Santayana, G. "Dr. Fuller, Plotinus, and the Nature of Evil." *Journal of Philosophy, Psychology and Scientific Methods* 10, no. 22 (Oct 1913): 559.

Universe. Directed by Roman Kroitor and Colin Low. National Film Board of Canada, 1960.

Wiley, John P. "Waiting for the Phone to Ring." *Natural History*, August/September 1972: 72–73.

PART II. ISSUES AND IMPLICATIONS
8. Nature Is . . .

Bhagavad-Gita. Translated by Swami Prabhavananda and Christopher Isherwood. New York: Barnes & Noble, 1995.

Beston, Henry. *The Outermost House: A Year of Life on the Great Beach of Cape Cod.* New York: Ballantine, 1976.

Buechner, Frederick. *Listening to Your Life.* San Francisco: Harper Collins, 1992.

Farrer, Frederic William. "December 3." In *Springs in the Valley*, edited by Mrs. Charles E. Cowman. Los Angeles: Cowman Publications, 1950.

Greene, Graham. *The Power and the Glory.* New York: Viking, 1965.

Hart, John. *The Spirit of the Earth: A Theology of the Land.* New York: Paulist Press, 1984.

Hobbes, Thomas. *Leviathan.* In *Great Books of the Western World: Machiavelli/Hobbes*, edited by Robert Maynard Hutchins, Vol. 23. Chicago: William Benton, 1952.

Kuhn, Thomas S. *The Structure of Scientific Revolutions.* 2nd edition. Chicago: University of Chicago Press, 1970.

Leopold, Aldo. *A Sand County Almanac.* New York: Oxford University Press, 1966.

McGrath, Alister. *The Twilight of Atheism: The Rise and Fall of Disbelief in the Modern World.* New York: Doubleday, 2006.

Moorman, Margaret. "Leo Steinberg and the Sexuality of Christ." *Art News*, March 1985: 79.

Neihardt, John G. *Black Elk Speaks: Being the Life Story of a Holy Man of the Oglala Sioux.* Lincoln: University of Nebraska Press, 1961.

Nietzsche, Friedrich. *Thus Spake Zarathustra.* Translated by Thomas Common. In *The Philosophy of Nietzsche.* New York: Random House, 1954.

Owens, Virginia Stem. "Faith, Perception, and the New Physics." In *The New Religious Humanists: A Reader*, edited by Gregory Wolfe. New York: Free Press, 1997.

Paine, Thomas. *The Age of Reason: Being an Investigation of True and Fabulous Theology.* New York: Wiley, 1942.

Pascal, Blaise. *Pensées.* In *Pensées/Provincial Letters*, translated by W. F. Trotter. New York: Random House, 1941.

Plato. *Phaedo.* In *The Works of Plato: Four Volumes Complete in One*, translated by B. Jowett. New York: Tudor, n.d.

Plato. *The Republic.* In *The Works of Plato: Four Volumes Complete in One*, translated by B. Jowett. New York: Tudor, n.d.

Ritvo, Harriet. *The Platypus and the Mermaid and Other Figments of the Classifying Imagination.* Cambridge, MA: Harvard University Press, 1997.

Spinoza, Benedict. *The Ethics.* In *The Chief Works of Spinoza.* Vol. 2, translated by Robert Harvey Monro Elwes. New York: Dover, 1951.

Time. "Peru: The New Conquest." March 12, 1965.

Turner, Frederick. *Beyond Geography: The Western Spirit Against the Wilderness.* New Brunswick, NJ: Rutgers University Press, 1992.

9. *The Two Books: Science and Religion*

Aquinas, Thomas. *Summa Theologica*, In *Basic Writings of Saint Thomas Aquinas*, edited by Anton Charles Pegis, Vol. 1. New York: Random House, 1945.

Auden, W. H. "Shorts II." In *Collected Poems: Auden*, edited by Edward Mendelson. New York: Vintage, 1991.

Brooke, John Hedley. *Science and Religion: Some Historical Perspectives.* Cambridge: Cambridge University Press, 1995.

Chesterton, G. K. *Orthodoxy.* San Francisco: Ignatius, 1995.

Copleston, Frederick Charles. *Aquinas.* Baltimore, MD: Penquin, 1961.

Cornell, Eric. "What Was God Thinking? Science Can't Tell." *Time*, November 14, 2005: 100.

Dickens, Charles. *Hard Times*. New York: Pocket Books, 2007.

Dodson, Peter. "Faith of a Paleontologist." In *Paleontolological Society Papers, Vol. 5. The Evolution-Creation Controversy II: Perspectives on Science, Religion, and Geological Education*, edited by Walter L. Manger. Pittsburgh, PA: New Image, 1999.

Dubos, René. *So Human an Animal*. New York: Scribner, 1968.

Dyson, Freeman. *Disturbing the Universe*. New York: Harper & Row, 1979.

Eddington, Arthur. *Space, Time and Gravitation: An Outline of the General Relativity Theory*. New York: Harper, 1959.

———. *The Philosophy of Physical Science*. Ann Arbor: University of Michigan Press, 1958.

Eiseley, Loren. *Darwin's Century: Evolution and the Men Who Discovered It*. Garden City, NY: Doubleday, 1961.

Emerson, Ralph Waldo. "The Over-Soul." In *The Selected Writings of Ralph Waldo Emerson*, edited by Brooks Atkinson. New York: Random House, 1968.

Evolution Resources. National Academy of Sciences and Institute of Medicine, 2008. Online: http://www.nationalacademies.org/evolution/Compatibility.html.

Ferris, Timothy. *The Mind's Sky: Human Intelligence in a Cosmic Context*. New York: Bantam, 1992.

Feynman, Richard P. *The Meaning of It All: Thoughts of a Citizen Scientist*. Reading, MA: Addison-Wesley, 1998.

Foss, Sam Walter. *Songs of the Average Man*. Boston: Lothrop, Lee & Shephard, 1907.

Gingerich, Owen. "More Than Machines." In *Finding God at Harvard*, edited by Kelly Monroe. Grand Rapids, MI: Zondervan, 1996.

Goodall, Jane. *Reason for Hope: A Spiritual Journey*. New York: Warner, 1999.

Gould, Stephen Jay. *Darwin's Revolution in Thought*. 1992. http://www.stephenjaygould.org/multimedia.html.

———. *Rocks of Ages: Science and Religion in the Fullness of Life*. New York: Ballantine, 1999.

Heschel, Abraham Joshua. *God in Search of Man: A Philosophy of Judaism*. New York: Farrar, Straus and Giroux, 1978.

Hoffer, Eric. *Between the Devil and the Dragon: The Best Essays and Aphorisms of Eric Hoffer*. New York: Harper & Row, 1982.

Hume, David. "An Inquiry Concerning Human Understanding." In *The English Philosophers from Bacon to Mill*, edited by Edwin A. Burtt. New York: Random House, 1939.

James, William. *The Varieties of Religious Experience: A Study in Human Nature*. New York: Longman's, Green, 1902.

Khayyam, Omar. *The Rubaiyat of Omar Khayyam*. Translated by Edward FitzGerald. Roslyn, NY: William J. Black, 1942.

Lewis, C. S. *Miracles: A Preliminary Investigation*. New York: Macmillan, 1947.

Lewontin, Richard C. "Billions and Billions of Demons." *New York Review of Books*, January 9, 1997.

Lipmann, Walter. *A Preface to Morals*. New York: Time, 1964.

Longfellow, Henry Wadsworth. "A Psalm of Life." In *The Complete Poetical Works of Longfellow*. Boston: Houghton Mifflin, 1975.

Masefield, John. "Sea-Fever." In *Salt-Water Poems and Ballads*. New York: Macmillan, 1913.

Mead, Frank S., ed. *The Encyclopedia of Religious Quotations*. New York: Fleming H. Ravel, 1965.

Menninger, Karl, M.D. *Whatever Became of Sin?* New York: Hawthorn, 1973.

Myers, Philip Van Ness. *Mediaeval and Modern History*. Boston: Ginn, 1905.

Newton, Isaac. *Mathematical Principles of Natural Philosophy*. In *Great Books of the Western World: Newton/Huygens*, edited by Robert Maynard Hutchins, Vol. 34. Chicago: William Benton, 1952.

Norell, Mark, and Mick Ellison. *Unearthing the Dragon: the Great Feathered Dinosaur Discovery*. New York: PI Press, 2005.

Sandburg, Carl. *Complete Poems of Carl Sandburg*. New York: Harcourt, Brace & World, 1950.

Scott, Eugenie C. *Evolution vs. Creationism: An Introduction*. Berkeley: University of California Press, 2004.

Shakespeare, William. *Cymbeline*. In *The Complete Works of William Shakespeare*. Roslyn, NY: Walter J. Black, 1937.

Stace, W. T. "Man Against Darkness." *Atlantic Monthly*, September 1948: 53–58.

Steinbeck, John. *Travels With Charley: In Search of America*. New York: Bantam, 1963.

Tillich, Paul. *Systematic Theology*. Vol. 1. Chicago: University of Chicago Press, 1951.

Tolstoy, Leo. *The Death of Ivan Ilych*. In *The Death of Ivan Ilych and other Stories*, by Leo Tolstoy. New York: New American Library, 1961.

Torrance, Thomas. *Einstein and God*. Princeton, NJ: Center of Theological Inquiry, 1997.

van Gogh, Vincent. "van Gogh's Letters." Translated by Mrs. Johanna van Gogh-Bonger, edited by Robert Harrison, number 418. WebExhibits. Online: http://webexhibits. org/vangogh/letter/15/418.htm.

Weisskopf, Victor. *The Joy of Insight: Passions of a Physicist*. New York: Basic, 1991.

Whitehead, Alfred North. *Science and the Modern World*. New York: Free Press, 1967.

Wilson, E. O. *On Human Nature*. Cambridge, MA: Harvard University Press, 1978.

Wordsworth, William. "Lines." In *Poems of Wordsworth*. Vol. 1. New York: Co-operative Publication Society, n.d.

10. Creation, Evolution, and Creationism

Agassiz, Louis. *Geological Sketches*. Boston: James R. Osgood, 1876.

Anderson, Lisa. "Museum Exhibits a Creationist Viewpoint." *The Chicago Tribune*, August 27, 2005.

Auden, W. H. "Concerning the Unpredictable." *The New Yorker*, February 21, 1970: 121.

Augustine. *The Literal Meaning of Genesis*. Vol. 1. Translated by J. H. Taylor. New York: Paulist Press, 1982.

Beecher, Henry Ward. *Evolution and Religion*. Boston: Pilgrim Press, 1885.

Bonhoeffer, Dietrich. *Letters and Papers From Prison*. Edited by Eberhard Bethge. Translated by Reginald H. Fuller. New York: Macmillan, 1962.

Carnegie, Andrew. *The Autobiography of Andrew Carnegie*. New York: Houghton Mifflin, 1920.

Chadwick, Douglas. "Evolution Right Before Their Eyes." *The New York Times Book Review*, May 22, 1994.

Cray, Dan. "God vs. Science." *Time*, November 13, 2006: 52.

Curley, Vince J. J. "Interview: Gregory S. Paul." *Prehistoric Times*, December/January 2006: 46.

Darwin, Charles. *On the Origin of Species by Means of Natural Selection*. 6th ed. Norwalk, CT: Easton, 1976.

Natural History. "Letters.", November 2002: 15.

Eiseley, Loren. *The Immense Journey*. New York: Random House, 1957.

Eliot, T. S. "The Lovesong of J. Alfred Prufrock." In *The Complete Poems and Plays 1909–1950*. New York: Harcourt, Brace & World, 1952.

Garrett, Wilbur E. "Editorial." *National Geographic*, November 1985: 559.

Gershwin, Ira. *The Complete Lyrics of Ira Gershwin*. New York: Knopf, 1993.

Ham, Ken. "The Relevance of Creation." Cassette tape. El Cajon, CA: Institute of Creation Research, n.d.

Heyers, Conrad. *The Meaning of Creation: Genesis and Modern Science*. Atlanta: John Knox, 1984.

Horgan, John. "Francis Collins: The Scientist as Believer." *National Geographic*, February 2007: 33–34.

Huxley, Thomas H. "Evolution and Ethics." In *Evolution and Ethics/Science and Morals*. Amherst, NY: Prometheus, 2004.

———. "On the Relations of Man to the Lower Animals." In *Gateway to the Great Books*, edited by Robert Maynard Hutchins, Vol. 8. Chicago: William Benton, 1963.

Kaufmann, Walter. *Nietzsche: Philosopher, Psychologist, Anti-Christ*. Cleveland, OH: World Publishing, 1961.

Larson, Edward J. *Evolution: The Remarkable History of a Scientific Theory*. New York: Random House, 2004.

Larson, Gary. *The Valley of the Far Side*. Kanas City: Andrews, McMeel & Parker, 1985.

Margenau, Henry, and Roy Abraham Varghese, eds. *Cosmos, Bios, Theos: Scientists Reflect on Science, God, and the Origins of the Universe, Life and Homo Sapiens*. LaSalle, IL: Open Court, 1992.

Miller, Kenneth R. *Finding Darwin's God: A Scientist's Search for Common Ground Between God and Evolution*. New York: Harper Collins, 2002.

Milner, Richard. "Darwin in Court." *Natural History*, June 2007.

Morris, Henry M. *The Remarkable Birth of Planet Earth*. Minneapolis, MN: Dimension, 1972.

Nietzsche, Friedrich. *The Geneology of Morals*. Translated by Horace B. Samuel. In *The Philosophy of Nietzsche*. New York: Random House, 1954.

Numbers, Ronald L. *The Creationists*. New York: Knopf, 1992.

Patterson, John. "Thermodynamics and Evolution." In *Scientists Confront Creationism*, edited by Laurie R. Godfrey. New York: W. W. Norton, 1983.

Peacocke, Arthur. *Paths From Science to God: The End of All Our Exploring*. New York: Oneworld, 2001.

———. *Theology for a Scientific Age: Being and Becoming—Natural, Divine, and Human*. Minneapolis, MN: Fortress, 1993.

Peters, Ted, and Martinez Hewlett. *Evolution from Creation to New Creation*. Nashville, TN: Abingdon, 2003.

Pierce, Kenneth M. "Putting Darwin Back in the Dock." *Time*, March 16, 1981.

Richardson, Alan. *A Preface to Bible Study*. Philadelphia: Westminster, 1944.

Ripley, S. Dillon. "Editorial." *Smithsonian*, March 1978: 8.

Roughgarden, Joan. *Evolution and Christian Faith: Reflections of an Evolutionary Biologist.* Washington, DC: Island, 2006.

Russell, Dale. *Islands in the Cosmos: The Evolution of Life on Land.* Bloomington & Indianapolis, Indiana University Press, 2009.

Schwimmer, David R. "Creation Science Logic and Rhetoric and Some Responses." In *The Paleontological Society Papers. The Evolution-Creation Controversy II: Perspectives on Science, Religion, and Geological Education.* Vol. 5, edited by Walter L. Manger. Pittsburg, PA: New Image, 1999.

Shirer, William L. *The Rise and Fall of the Third Riech.* New York: Simon and Schuster, 1960.

Simpson, George Gaylord. *The Meaning of Evolution: A Study of the History of Life and of Its Significance for Man.* New Haven, CT: Yale University Press, 1950.

Sittler, Joseph. *Essays on Nature and Grace.* Philadelphia: Fortress, 1972.

Spencer, Herbert. *Social Statics: The Conditions Essential to Human Happiness Specified, and the First of them Developed.* New York: D. Appleton, 1864.

Strahler, Arthur N. *Science and Earth History: The Evolution/Creation Controversy.* Buffalo, NY: Prometheus, 1987.

Tattersall, Ian. "Science Versus Religion? No Contest." *Natural History,* April 2002: 100.

Teilhard de Chardin, Pierre. *Hymn of the Universe.* Translated by Simon Bartholomew. New York: Harper & Row, 1965.

———. *The Phenomenon of Man.* Translated by Bernard Wall. New York: Harper & Row, 1965.

Weiner, Jonathan. *The Beak of the Finch: A Story of Evolution in Our Time.* New York: Vintage, 1995.

Zimmerman, Michael. *The Clergy Letter Project.* May 22, 2011. Online: http://blue. butler.edu/~mzimmerman/Christian_Clergy/ChrClergyLtr.h.

11. Take Care

Abbey, Edward. *Desert Solitaire.* New York: Ballantine, 1968.

Bacon, Francis. *Novum Organum.* In *Great Books of the Western World: Fancis Bacon,* edited by Robert Maynard Hutchins, Vol. 30. Chicago: William Benton, 1952.

Brownowski, Jacob. *The Ascent of Man.* Boston: Little, Brown, 1973.

Campbell, Robert. "The Intersection of Two Great Rivers Helps Sustain the Earth's Vital Biosphere." *Smithsonian,* September 1977.

Catlin, George. "Buffalo Country." In *The Wilderness Reader,* edited by Frank Bergon. New York: New American Library, 1980.

Dostoyevsky, Fyodor. *Notes From Underground / Poor People / The Friend of the Family: Three Short Novels.* Translated by Constance Garnett. New York: Dell, 1960.

Duncan, David Ewing. "Pollution Within." *National Geographic,* October 2006: 116–43.

Emerson, Ralph Waldo. "Ode." In *The Oxford Book of American Verse,* edited by F. O. Mathiessen. New York: Oxford University Press, 1950.

Forum on Religion and Ecology at Yale. January 1990. Online: http://fore.research.yale. edu/publications/statements/preserve.html.

Gide, Andre. *If It Die: An Autobiography.* New York: Vintage, 2001.

Greene, John C. *The Death of Adam: Evolution and its Impact on Western Thought.* New York: New American Library of World Literature, 1959.

Hayes, Dennis. "Earth Day 1990: The Threshold of the Green Decade." *Natural History*, April 1990.

Hopkins, Gerard Manley. "God's Grandeur." In *Poems and Prose*. New York: Knopf, 1995.

————. "Pied Beauty." In *Poems and Prose*. New York: Knopf, 1995.

Keeping the Earth: Religious and Scientific Perspectives on the Environment. VHS. Produced by New Wrinkle, Inc. for the Union of Concerned Scientists, 1996.

Kennedy, Robert F. "Remarks of Robert F. Kennedy at the University of Kansas, March 18, 1968." *John F. Kennedy Presidential Library and Museum*. March 18, 1968. Online: http://www.jfklibrary.org/Research/Ready-Reference/RFK-Speeches/Remarks-of-Robert-F-Kennedy-at-the-University-of-Kansas-March-18-1968.aspx.

Kierkegaard, Søren. *Either/Or*. Translated by David F. Swenson and Lillian Marvin Swenson. Vol. 1. Garden City, NY: Anchor, 1959.

Lindburgh, Charles A. "Is Civilization Progress?" *Reader's Digest*, July 1964.

Livingston, John A. *The Fallacy of Wildlife Conservation*. Toronto: McClelland and Stewart, 1982.

MacLeish, Archibald. "Voyage to the Moon." *The New York Times*, July 21, 1969.

Masters, Edgar Lee. *Spoon River Anthology*. New York: Macmillan, 1970.

McPhee, John. *Annals of the Former World*. New York: Farrar, Straus and Giroux, 1998.

Mitchell, John G. "Why We Need Our Monsters." *National Wildlife*, April/May, 1978.

Muir, John. *The Story of My Boyhood and Youth*. Madison: University of Wisconsin Press, 1965.

Paton, Alan. *Cry, the Beloved Country*. New York: Scribner, 1948.

Pfeiffer, John. *The Creative Explosion: An Inquiry into the Origins of Art and Religion*. New York: Harper & Row, 1982.

Randolf, John. Quotation in *The Great Thoughts*, edited by George Seldes. New York: Ballantine, 1985.

Rienow, Robert, and Leona Train Rienow. *Moment in the Sun: A Report on the Deteriorating Quality of the American Environment*. New York: Ballantine, 1967.

Rogers, Will, and Joseph H. Carter. *Never Met a Man I Didn't Like*. New York: Harper, 1991.

Schaller, George. "Voices." *National Geographic*, October 2006: 41.

Schweitzer, Albert. *The Light Within Us*. New York: Philosophical Library, 1959.

Shapley, Harlow. *Beyond the Observatory*. New York: Scribner, 1967.

Suzuki, David. *The Sacred Balance: Rediscovering Our Place in Nature*. Vancouver, BC: GreyStone, 2002.

Thoreau, Henry David. *The Heart of Thoreau's Journals*. Edited by Odell Shepard. Mineola, NY: Dover, 1961.

Wells, H.G. *The Outline of History: Being a Plain History of Life and Mankind*. Vol 1. New York: Garden City, 1956.

White, Michael. *Leonardo: The First Scientist*. London: Time Warner, 2000.

Wilson, E. O. *The Diversity of Life*. Cambridge, MA: Belknap, 1992.

Worm, Boris. "Oceans of Nothing." *Time*, November 13, 2006: 57.

Zinsser, William. "A Fantasy For Earth Day." *Life*, April 24, 1970: 43.